Grains from Grass

Grains from Grass

Aging, Gender, and Famine in Rural Africa

Lisa Cliggett

Cornell University Press
Ithaca and London

First published 2005 by Cornell University Press
First printing, Cornell Paperbacks, 2005

Printed in the United States of America

Design by Scott Levine

Library of Congress Cataloging-in-Publication Data

Cliggett, Lisa, 1965–
    Grains from grass : aging, gender, and famine in rural
Africa / Lisa Cliggett.
        p. cm.
    Includes bibliographical references and index.
    ISBN-13: 978-0-8014-4366-4 (cloth : alk. paper)
    ISBN-10: 0-8014-4366-0 (cloth : alk. paper)
    ISBN-13: 978-0-8014-7283-1 (pbk. : paper)
    ISBN-10: 0-8014-7283-0 (pbk. : paper)
    1. Tonga (Zambesi people)—Zambia—Gwembe District—
Social conditions.   2. Tonga (Zambesi people)—Social
networks—Zambia—Gwembe District.   3. Rural elderly—
Zambia—Gwembe District.   4. Sex role—Zambia—Gwembe
District.   5. Food supply—Zambia—Gwembe District.   6.
Ethnology—Zambia—Gwembe District.   7. Gwembe District
(Zambia)—Rural conditions.   I. Title.
    DT3058.T65C55 2005
    306.85'2'096894—dc22

                                                            2005016052

Cornell University Press strives to use environmentally responsible suppliers and materials to the fullest extent possible in the publishing of its books. Such materials include vegetable-based, low-VOC inks and acid-free papers that are recycled, totally chlorine-free, or partly composed of nonwood fibers. For further information, visit our website at www.cornellpress.cornell.edu.

Cloth printing   10   9   8   7   6   5   4   3   2   1
Paperback printing   10   9   8   7   6   5   4   3   2

Contents

Maps

Preface

This book tells how women and men in one region of rural Africa have become vulnerable to material insecurity in gendered ways, and how they use gendered strategies to secure their well-being as they age. Living with scarcity forces everyone to develop survival strategies that make use of what they have at hand. In extreme circumstances, the only resources at people's disposal are the social support networks that allow those with less to get something from those who have a bit more.

Strategies to manage material insecurity are no different from other institutions; they have a core base in social relationships. When one family's maize crop fails, they will turn to a family related through kinship for assistance. When the rains fail in one region, people may travel in search of relatives living in areas where rain fell and harvests succeeded. When uncertainty plays a regular role in people's livelihoods, broad social networks help to lessen the blow of crises such as failed harvests, job loss, and chronic illness.

This book takes the social basis of survival strategies as its focus—something often captured in our popular knowledge of Africa—but it also argues for a deeper understanding of the social systems that facilitate people's ability to survive in the midst of material insecurity. The first lesson in deepening our understanding comes from recognizing "difference": different groups of people have different exposure to scarcity; different groups have experienced history differently, resulting in different social positions in the contemporary landscape; and different groups employ different strategies for survival. By giving attention to the many levels of difference, particularly in a continent that often suffers from media gener- alizations, we recognize the complexity of people's lives, and consequently move away from stereotypes and misleading generalizations.

In this book, I explore different age groups and the life cycle process itself. I also explore the history of one region in rural Zambia, the Gwembe Valley—well known for the longitudinal research of anthropol- ogists Elizabeth Colson and Thayer Scudder—and how development- induced change, particularly in agriculture since the 1950s, has resulted in different access to resources for women and men over their lifetimes. And finally, I explore the different ways women and men negotiate with their relatives and neighbors for assistance and support as they age.

The lenses through which we consider difference and vulnerability are "age," "aging," "women," and "men," but the bigger picture is family and kinship. The Gwembe Tonga have a matrilineal descent system that de- fines proper family, kin, resource ownership and transmission, and a host of other cultural features. So, while focusing on specific features of Gwembe social life, we also learn about the workings of a matrilineal kin- ship system. Ultimately, by concentrating on elderly women and men, we examine what it means to be family. What obligations do different family members have to particular relatives? What rights does an old person have over particular offspring and descendents? When resources are scarce, which family members find themselves excluded from social support net- works? And importantly, why do some people find themselves excluded and others not? By delving into details of daily life for the oldest people in a community, and the differences within that group (elderly women as op- posed to elderly men), we emerge on the other side of those explorations with a nuanced understanding of family, kinship, and survival amid scarcity.

I wrote this book for those who have interests in kinship and family, economy and ecology, aging cross-culturally, and people of Africa. In my teaching over the past decade, I have struggled to find ethnographies that address the classic anthropological topic of social organization in lively and useful ways, and without dense analyses of theoretical arguments and obscure disciplinary jargon. While theory is critical to framing our re- search questions and analyzing our data, explaining our theory should not alienate our readers, as it often can, particularly if they are not experts in our field. In this book I sought to reduce the complexity of my theoretical framework by illustrating ideas with examples, and refraining from the jargon of the anthropological discipline. Instead, I wrote with the goal of explaining classic anthropological themes (social organization, descent systems, economy, ecology, life cycle), with useful, and accessible, theoretical nuggets, illustrated through description and examples, to an audience of interested readers, but not experts in the field.

In pondering the style and audience of this book, I also faced the challenge of how to weave the thread that runs through the fabric of the book. In the process of analyzing my data, I needed to make sense of what I had witnessed as products of moments in time. I had to reconcile particular events with what I saw occurring over the full time-frame of research in the Gwembe from the 1950s until the present, that is, historical change. Deciding how to tell a story—whether to emphasize snapshot descriptions through time, or emphasize the explanations for the shifting social landscape—could be called the interpretive dilemma of authorship. In the same way that our practices in the field in the day-to-day collecting of information emerge directly from our ideas and theories (i.e., the theory-driven method I discuss in chap. 2), the written products of our research emerge directly from the interpretive framework we chose to employ.

In the case of the Gwembe elderly, the interpretive dilemma includes deciding how to handle specific features of people's lives, particularly issues of (1) access to land resources and ownership of cattle and (2) shifting matrilineal kinship dynamics. Should these issues be presented as examples of a particular circumstance that compels awareness of the elderly poor and the comparative understanding of the elderly around the world? Or should the shifts and fluctuations in lived experience be explored analytically as a larger example of historical change, beyond the elderly or Gwembe Tonga specifically?

To ground this abstract pondering, let me take the example of the role of cattle in Gwembe life, a theme that is revisited in more detail in chapter 3. Before the 1950s, cattle were not central to Gwembe people's subsistence or economic systems, marriage and kinship, or prestige systems. Yet in less than thirty years, cattle have taken on primary importance in Tonga lives in all those aspects of daily life. In telling the story of the role cattle play in people's lives, I can describe the importance of cattle now and in the past, and emphasize the way people have adapted to and triggered some of the changes. But a different interpretive frame could have me exploring the larger trajectory of this historical change, and what it stands for in reference to changes in monetary and value systems and societal change more broadly.

Although compelled by the challenge of making sense of historical change at a broader theoretical level, in the story I tell here I have nevertheless emphasized the first interpretive frame. That is, I capture and describe events and issues at moments in time, and document how they have changed through time, but not with the overall goal of explaining substantial societal-level change. My choice in this emphasis emerges for two particular reasons. First, with my goal of making this book resonate with students, fostering a deep appreciation for the lives of the elderly in the Gwembe was central. Building a story around thick description and specific events makes accessing the lives of the "subjects" somewhat easier for readers.

Second, there is value in laying out descriptions and documenting events as they stand, without encapsulating them immediately in a large system for overall interpretation. Sometimes building a base of descriptive knowledge fosters a later and more nuanced step toward broader interpretation. With that in mind, in the first four chapters of the book I capture descriptive nuggets of Gwembe people's lives. These chapters provide the background for appreciating the way change enters the lives of the Gwembe people. The last half of the book also injects a deeper description of the way institutions and systems have changed over the fifty years that Gwembe Tonga society has been followed.

Because I intend this book to be used in classrooms, as well as to provide knowledge about social organization in Africa more generally, I include discussions of different contexts in which social organization plays out. Following my introductory discussions, I address different arenas of social life, such as economic systems, residential arrangements, ritual life, and the phenomenon of migration, and the way social systems in these arenas have changed over time. In order to understand the lives of elderly women and men, we need to explore the broad context of daily life in their communities. Consequently, my discussions of livelihoods and economy, the spiritual world, and the migrant context include description and consideration of the relatives and neighbors of the elderly in question, not just the elderly in abstraction. That is, I describe the lives of the young, the middle-aged, and the elderly in order to understand what it means to age in this social context.

In chapter 1 I introduce the research topic of elderly populations in non-Western societies. I discuss the ideas that informed my focus on support systems for the elderly in rural Africa and briefly summarize my argument about gender differences in old people's strategies for mobilizing support. In the context of matrilineal Gwembe Tonga lives, gender differences in control and ability to manipulate resources, whether material, social, or supernatural, permeate people's experiences and become a primary source of securing fundamental support as women and men age.

Chapter 2 addresses the fieldwork experience, including a discussion of my field sites, methodologies, the people with whom I conducted research, and the ways my research design, and indeed theory, shaped those processes. I tell the story of my first descent into the Gwembe Valley, and other stories about living in rural Zambia for extended periods of time, interspersed with how I came to the topic of intergenerational support systems, this particular field site, and this project, as well as the kinds of questions I asked and the data I collected. I argue that personal interests, theoretical models, data collection methods, and lived experience inform each other; they do not exist separately or in a linear path of intellectual development.

In chapter 3 I give the historical and contemporary background of Zambia and the Gwembe Valley, and the ways both the nation and the region experience vulnerability. Although I discuss the theoretical model of material vulnerability as laid out by Watts and Buhl (1993), I explore that framework through examples of different kinds of vulnerability and vulnerability at different levels, not in an abstract intellectual manner. At the end of chapter 3 I provide the historical background of how senior women and men have diverged in their access to important resources, specifically land and cattle, and how women in particular have become marginalized from material resources, consequently experiencing greater risk to their well-being than do men of the same age.

In chapters 4–6 I explore the nature of women's and men's relationships to relatives and neighbors. By focusing on different aspects of village life, I uncover variations in gender dynamics as they relate to access to resources, residential arrangements, and ritual activities. Chapter 4 presents a broad discussion of village economy and livelihoods. In order to understand the context in which old people live their lives, we need a firm grounding in the way that all people in these communities make their living. In this chapter we begin to see the kinds of differences that exist in the material lives of women and men, and the ways that these differences might play out through the life cycle.

Chapter 5 examines village domestic units and men's and women's preferences for residential arrangements. The residential setting is the primary location where resource distribution takes place—that is, where people get their food, clothing, shelter, and other material resources. Exploring the differences in women's and men's residential arrangements reveals components of their different strategies in negotiating relationships with relatives and neighbors. In this chapter I also highlight the variety of support and nonsupport that old women and men experience as a result of their residential context.

Chapter 6 addresses the roles of the elderly in ritual and supernatural activities, again highlighting the differences between women's and men's activity. Although Christianity has a solid place in village life, this chapter focuses on the system of ancestor belief, and rituals associated with those beliefs, because old people's roles are so pronounced in this system. As illustrated in earlier chapters, here again gender differences in control and abilities to manipulate resources, in this case supernatural, play important roles in how elders gain support from relatives and neighbors.

In chapter 7 I consider how the migration of young adults affects the lives of the elderly in their village homes. In this chapter I take the stance that relationships over distance and time are indicative of fundamental attitudes toward support for the elderly. Distance puts stress on social relationships, and consequently, behavior in these situations can reveal the limits of kinship ties. In addition to looking at how migration affects the elderly, we look at the lives of migrants and the uncertainty of making a living outside of the familiar social world of the village. We glean information about how migrants may begin to anticipate their own aging process, and the important strategies, particularly "remitting" gifts, that they must use to maintain social networks that will benefit them in their old age.

In the conclusion I briefly summarize the themes of each chapter, with a goal of stepping beyond details to see the bigger picture—the complexity of family and kinship, the complexity of concepts such as vulnerability and scarcity, and the creativity of people living in very difficult circumstances. I ask questions such as What do we learn by looking for difference within broad labels such as Africa, family, and elderly? with a goal of instilling the need to break from stereotypes and generalizations, in order to gain more reality-based knowledge.

Like the people of the Gwembe Valley, I rely on a broad social network to get through my days. This book is no exception. My fieldwork over the past decade was supported financially by Fulbright, the National Science Foundation, the Overseas Development Administration (United Kingdom), the Mellon Foundation, the Social Sciences Research Council, and grants from Indiana University and the University of Kentucky.

In Zambia there are many people to thank. I am deeply indebted to the people of Sinafala and Mazulu villages, and migrants throughout Southern and Central provinces, whose names have been changed in this book to maintain anonymity. They tolerated my presence and persistent questions with goodwill and patience. I especially thank the old women of Sinafala, who provided me with some of my most happy field experiences. Without my primary research assistant, Drivas Chikuni, my research and this book would not have been possible; he alerted me to the subtleties of village life, and has been my ears and eyes over the past decade. Kaciente, Malia, Benedetta, and Serida Chifumpu continue to offer their homes and hearths to me and welcome me as a family member, for which I will be eternally indebted. Other research assistants over the years to whom I offer thanks include Nicolas Makafi, Jailos Mazambani, Bernard Siakanomba, Emmi Mazulu, Joseph Kayuna, Richard Chimiimba, Speedio Hachekuyu, and David Michelo. Special thanks must go to Maggie Sibwela, who died in 1999: she acted as guide during our first meeting and then became a treasured friend who shared her delicious food, insight, and dance steps with me as I passed through Chipepo on my travels to and from the valley. I miss her friendship and her personal style, which always made me smile.

Throughout Southern Province, a network of people made my long journeys to field sites easier. The Catholic Sisters at Fumbo Mission welcomed and calmed me with their generosity and cool drinks. Father Wafer eagerly shared with me his vast knowledge of Tonga language and culture. While tracking down migrants in frontier regions, Bert and Chimunya Witcamp and Grezyna Zoucha offered stimulating coffee and conversation. Tom and Thea Savory gave me a refuge where I processed data and my village experiences. I benefited from Tom's thoughts on Zambia's economy and from Thea's medical knowledge, but most of all from their kindness and friendship.

The Institute for Social and Economic Research (previously the Institute for African Studies, IAS) at the University of Zambia facilitated research clearance from the government of Zambia, for which I am deeply indebted. Ilse Mwanza, the former research affiliation officer at the IAS, was an energetic and thought-provoking supporter of my research and always had the best tea party in town. Dr. Mubiana Macwan'gi shared her thoughts on the elderly in Zambia and encouraged my research from the start. Dr. Bennett Siamwiza has been a valuable colleague over the years, offering thoughtful intellectual exchange as well as a Gwembe person's reflections on my work. Many other researchers I met through the IAS have had a beneficial impact on my work. In particular, Virginia Bond, Solveig Freudenthal, and Lyn Schumaker inspire me with their insight and commitment to their work. My conversations with the people at Harvest Help and HODI, especially Anthony Hovey, Chileshe Chilangwa, and Terry Mukuka, provoked my thoughts on social change and rural development in Zambia. Thanks to James Copestake, who facilitated my continuing investigations into migration. I am grateful to the Agricultural Offices in Monze and Mkushi districts, and numerous others throughout Zambia who must go unnamed, who have assisted with many aspects of my work over the past decade.

In the United States my intellectual lineage can be traced most directly to Richard Wilk, who, first as an adviser and now as a friend and colleague, continues to inspire my development of ideas on global economy, ecology, and family, and the meaning of life. Also at Indiana University, George Alter, Gracia Clark, and Emilio Moran influenced the development of this project from its inception. Anne Pyburn as mentor, colleague, and friend has encouraged me and shared important insights on women's experience of academia, which have been extremely helpful in my professional development.

Elizabeth Colson and Thayer Scudder read drafts of this book and offered detailed and valuable comments, for which I am extremely grateful. I am indebted to them for inviting me to join the Gwembe Tonga Research Project, for sharing with me their vast knowledge of the Gwembe Valley and Zambia, and for their patient reading and commenting on my work. Deb Crooks, Sandra Kryst, and Karen Tice read earlier drafts of this book and offered valuable feedback, guidance, and encouragement, for which I offer sincere thanks. I am also grateful for conversations and feedback related to this book from Kate Crehan, James Ferguson, Jane Guyer, Henrietta Moore, Pauline Peters, and Karen Tranberg-Hansen. My editors, Ange Romeo-Hall at Cornell University Press and Kathryn Gohl especially, have helped to craft this book and made it much better than I could have done on my own.

Over the years other colleagues have played important roles in my scholarly development; in particular I offer thanks to Nora Haenn, Jeff

Cohen, Michele and Ziggy Rivkin-Fish, Sangeetha Madavan, Nancy Luke, and Liz Faier for our valuable conversations. My students, especially at the University of Kentucky, and the International Honors Program Global Ecology study abroad year, have forced me to think of ways to explain and describe Gwembe people's lives that are accurate but also translate into the classroom; for the creative challenge my students pose, I am very grateful.

Although I call many colleagues friends, I am lucky to have friends beyond the academy as well, who remind me that our lives should be bigger than our livelihoods. I offer a lifetime of thanks to Martha Mendoza, Jennie Weise, and Christine Champe for a lifetime of friendship. To Mickey Needham I owe more than just a thank you; she has provided a home when I'm homeless and been a friend-almost-sister, editor, and puppy co-parent. I owe Joey Breckel gratitude for his patience, generosity, and humor through thick and thin. Thanks also to Sal and Yukon.

Finally, I thank my family for their love and support. I attribute my interest in anthropology to the family vacations we took when I was a child and my parents' willingness to explore other cultures. My brother and sister-in-law, and their children, Will and Wyatt, have given me wonderful moments of rest and joy. My grandfather, Fred Haug, died the spring of 1993, when he was ninety-nine years old, before I began my long-term fieldwork in Zambia. I wish I could tell him some of the stories that are in this book. I can imagine him sitting back in his chair saying, "Yep, I guess people know how to get by."

LISA CLIGGETT

Lexington, Kentucky

Grains from Grass

1. Aging in the Non-Western World

Children care for their mothers because those people have suffered a lot to make us grow. A long time ago when there was hunger, a mother used to walk to the plateau to find grains . . . and you were on her back. . . . she couldn't throw you away because you were her baby . . . you were nine months in her womb. She cared for me when I was young . . . I have to care for her when she's old.

Maxwell, March 1995

In July 1995 Muchembele, a sixty-five-year-old mother of five, died of star-vation. Or at least that's what her neighbors told me. By the time Muchembele was in her fifties, her husband, Siabama, had married a sec-ond, and much younger, wife. The village neighbors told me that while Muchembele went house to house pleading for food during May, June, and July, her husband and co-wife were in the fields eating their harvest. At Muchembele's funeral, relatives from the region came to honor her, and in the process they made songs telling the story of her death and blaming her husband and co-wife for neglecting her. No one made songs about her neglect by the neighbors, or by her own children for that matter, despite the fact that they too had not offered sufficient food to sustain her during that hunger year.

This story is not what we typically expect to hear about life in rural Africa, where people supposedly care for and respect the elderly. When North Americans and Europeans think of family in places such as Africa— places where people "live close to their environment" and where life is more "simple"—we invoke notions of altruistic social groups whose mem-bers live by a higher moral code than we do in the West. In the West we often have a sense that individualism rules, and we like to believe that a place exists where moral life is still strong—where elders are respected and

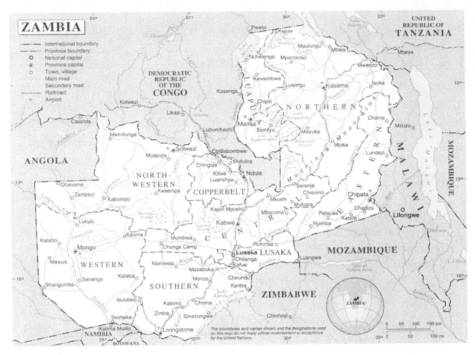

Fig. 1.1. Zambia political boundaries, including provinces. Map no. 3731 Rev. 4, January 2004, courtesy UN Cartographic Section.

cared for—because we see those modes of behavior slipping out of our own lives, in the same way that homemade pies, porch swings, and the corner soda fountain have all slipped away.

But this Shangri-la may exist only in our dreams. In Africa, a place imagined to be so many things that it is not, the systems of cooperation, altruism, and assistance are as varied as the more than 1,800 languages spoken on the African continent (Heine and Nurse 2000). Sometimes support systems exist for reasons other than clear-cut moral obligations or a sense of what is "right." On a continent intertwined with a global economy that has treated it, and continues to treat it, as a region of global sacrifice, people fashion a livelihood by using far more complicated means than simple altruistic support. Indeed, most people living in Africa, including the elderly, have developed highly subtle and creative ways of making a living. These creative livelihoods, in fact, often depend heavily on webs of social networks, but the glue that holds these networks together is not moral duty or altruistic sentiments; the glue is necessity in the face of limited choices.

This book tells the story of how some elderly people in rural Zambia manage to continue receiving support from their relatives, despite the dire circumstances of most Zambians during this era of socioeconomic upheaval and rapid environmental change. This book also tells of how some elderly people, like Muchembele, have not managed to harness enough support and resources to survive. In all of these stories, gender plays a central role. Because of the particular historical circumstances of Zambia's Southern Province and the political economy of the Gwembe Tonga people who live there, women and men have different access to important resources such as land and cattle, and also have developed gender-specific styles in their relationships with relatives and neighbors—all things that fundamentally influence their ability to survive into old age.

Through exploring the lives of rural elderly in Africa, this book also intersects with current discussions about vulnerable populations around the world, environmental change, and socioeconomic strategies of local people living in a highly complex global system that links villagers living in clay-brick thatched-roof houses to a suburban-raised American woman teaching about those African lives at a southern U.S. university. All of these components—scholarly discussions, policy concerns, and the lived experience of the researcher and the researched—tie together in building the lens through which we understand lifestyles that do not live up to our hopes of moralistic, altruistic communities.

About three months after settling in Sinafala village, my primary home for my first year and a half of residence in the Gwembe Valley, I walked through a maize field that appeared abandoned. My research assistant, Drivas, told me that the field's owner had not planted any maize in that field the previous year because the rains never came, and the farmer didn't want to waste his seed. Now, on this field that had not seen a plow in almost three years, wild grasses grew almost waist high. Off in the center of the field, about fifty yards from the path where Drivas and I walked, an old woman, crooked with arthritis and years of hard agricultural labor, reached her frail hands out to an individual stalk of grass. With one trembling hand, she grasped the stalk at the base of the one-inch tasseled head. With the other hand, she delicately harvested the grains on the tassel by sliding her fingers upward to the top and collecting the individual seeds in the palm of her hand. Releasing her grasp on the stalk, she opened her folded *chitenge*—a woman's waist cloth worn over a dress or skirt—from where she had tucked it into her skirt waist, poured the grains from her palm into the "pocket" of the cloth, and retucked the ends back into the waistline.

She then reached for the next stalk of grass, about two inches from the one she had just harvested. I watched this process for about three minutes—during which time she harvested about three stalks of grass. As I watched, I asked Drivas what she was doing. Despite seeing her action, I didn't understand the overall purpose. Drivas explained that she was collecting grains from grass because she had no maize to eat that day. He also told me that most people don't collect grass grains because the work is too difficult. He said, "only old women do that work." It would take her at least three hours to collect enough grass grains to make a small bowl of porridge, that she alone would eat in one sitting.

Little did I know how unusual it is to witness anyone harvesting grass seeds to make porridge. In all my time spent in the valley, and elsewhere in rural Zambia, I have never again seen someone harvesting grass, although old women spoke of that activity as evidence of the severity of a hunger year. Older women often told me "there was no food this year. We starved . . . we even collected grains from grass just to fill our stomachs." These statements have been offered consistently over the past decade, as the rains have failed more than they have fallen and people increasingly resort to their repertoire of survival strategies during droughts.

All of southern Africa has experienced severe droughts in the last three decades. Zambia's Gwembe Valley, part of the middle Zambezi River valley, including a Zambian northern slope and a Zimbabwean southern slope, is particularly prone to environmental crises such as droughts, flooding, and invasions of pests. In the mid-1990s, including some periods when I was a resident, Zambia suffered some of the most severe droughts on record, with Gwembe experiencing some of the most extreme rain deficiencies. In March 2003, severe flooding occurred, after months of no rain. Zambians expect the rainy season to be well under way by late December, and an extreme downpour after months of complete dryness can result in devastating erosion. During the floods in March 2003 (in which twelve inches of rain fell in three days in some areas), Gwembe fields were literally washed away, with one of my Gwembe friends e-mailing me that "those fields will never be planted again" (Nrindu 2003). A *New York Times* article reported that "more than 10,000 people are homeless as flooding swept away homes, roads, and maize crops in the hunger-stricken Gwembe district south of the capital, Lusaka" (Reuters 2003). The news brief gave dramatic figures, perhaps exaggerated—how we capture homelessness in a region where people often sleep in their fields during the rainy season to protect their crops from birds is one issue such a news feature does not explore—but the sentiment rang true.

In the rural communities of this escarpment valley, where droughts and floods make it virtually impossible to speak of "normal conditions," daily life often consists of simply gathering enough wild foods from the bush to make a meal for the day. When rains fall with more ideal regularity and timing, people grow and harvest their own grain and vegetables for the staple diet of cereal porridge (*nsima*) and sauce (*chissu*), and sell some crops for cash that they can then use to purchase blankets, clothing, and other supplies.

In addition to the unpredictability and extremity of the environment, macroeconomic factors, including development-induced relocation when the Zambezi River was dammed in 1958 to create Lake Kariba, and national economic and political changes have also contributed to difficult living conditions in the Gwembe. The forced relocation of close to 60,000 Gwembe Tonga people in 1958 has had profound reverberations on people's lives ever since. Although the upheaval of establishing new homes, new agricultural fields, new systems for accessing water, new spiritual practices, and integrating into new state-organized market and political systems initially occurred in what seems like a distant past, and at least three generations ago, most facets of current Gwembe life can be traced to changes induced by that relocation.

We are able to trace these changes, and examine the details of Gwembe lives since the 1950s because, remarkably, two anthropologists set about documenting those lives, and the impact that damming the Zambezi River had on the Gwembe, *before* the creation of Kariba Dam. Elizabeth Colson and Thayer Scudder, knowing that the majority of Gwembe Tonga people would be relocated due to the building of Kariba Dam and the flooding of the middle Zambezi Valley, began what was initially a straightforward "before and after" study of a society's experience of a large-scale development effort; subsequently it became one of the longest-running systematic anthropological studies of a society anywhere in the world. In their groundbreaking books *Social Organization of the Gwembe Tonga* (Colson 1960), *The Ecology of the Gwembe Tonga* (Scudder 1962), and *Social Consequences of Resettlement* (Colson 1971), Colson and Scudder document, first, the complexity, resilience, and logic of a mixed subsistence-based population that practiced floodplain horticulture as well as the gathering and hunting of wild foods. In these monographs the authors reveal systems of kinship, identity, political order, and spiritual life that stand as excellent models of the ethnographic tradition. Beyond documenting in great detail Gwembe Tonga lives, both before and after the forced relocation, Colson and Scudder uncovered for the first time in a systematic anthropological tradition the extreme costs that local people pay as a result of seemingly well-meaning development endeavors. The Colson and Scudder findings have informed not only policy in Zambia regarding rural populations and development, but policy across the African continent and around the world regarding forced resettlement and social costs of development; most fundamentally, their work has triggered understanding of continuity and change in small-scale societies more generally.

One of the most startling features of current Gwembe life is the extreme poverty and ecological degradation that most people in the valley cope with on a daily basis. In an "ethnographic-present" gaze, a visitor might assume that these conditions have always existed, and indeed, many well-meaning NGOs working in the Gwembe Valley now operate from a view that the region is inherently poor, inherently undeveloped, and that the people are simply incapable of improving their situation. But looking back to the works of Colson and Scudder, we learn that in past decades, luxuries such as steel-frame beds, bicycles, and radios were accessible through a combination of labor migration and agricultural production. People's lives were filled with a variety of activities, including accumulating resources for investment in bank accounts and in children's education. Parents visited their well-employed children working in cities and towns. Some Gwembe people even traveled internationally for education, workshops, and on occasion, holidays. These days, if visitors look closely inside people's homes, they will see old photos of family members wearing stylish dress clothes for church or a night on the town. Sometimes visitors will see old vinyl LPs decorating the walls of current clay-brick homes. Stereos, LPs, and electricity were some of the luxuries town-dwelling people could enjoy—back when their options for employment were more varied, whether they were highly educated or not, and people believed they could achieve their aspirations simply with hard work.

These days, however, hard work yields barely enough to survive, whether in towns or villages. As Colson and Scudder painfully document in their work of the 1980s and 1990s, "development" does not occur in an always upward, linear trajectory. People who used to sleep on steel-frame beds and foam mattresses in the Gwembe now find a night's sleep on beds made of tree branches, lashed together with sinewy strands of tree bark, and a lumpy mattress of piled-up threadbare clothing and fabrics. River-side gardens that used to produce two or three harvests a year are deep below the lake's surface, and those who plant gardens along the lakeshore get to play the guessing game of when the lake level will rise, flooding their crop just before harvest, or when it will drop, drying out the germinating dry-season maize. Extensive rainy-season fields that yielded surplus food and cash crops in the early days after relocation have become dusty land-scapes that, with an adequate rainy season, still produce a portion of a family's annual food needs (but not quite all). If the rains fail, fall too early or too late, come all at once, or just not come at the key moments in seed ger-mination and growth, harvests in the Gwembe can be nonexistent.

Under these conditions, issues of how families control and distribute re-sources become brutally vivid, as the story of Muchembele suggests. With limited resources, people are forced to make difficult decisions about who in their families and communities gets what, and when they might get it.

The Lens of Individual Agency within the Extended Family

At the core of this book is a consideration of how families living in difficult conditions throughout the world work together to ensure their survival both as family units and as individuals. Exploring these issues includes tak-ing apart our notions of family and applying a critical eye in an effort to understand how individuals act both with and against social structures, such as family. Studies of household economy have helped to unearth the complexity of family and domestic life. Drawing on the ideas of individual agency and household economy, I use the elderly as a central focus for ex-amining the bonds of kinship. When the elderly are predominantly depen-dent and not productive in their household participation (domestic chores, food preparation, agricultural activity, and so forth), they are usually forced to rely on altruistic tendencies of relatives and community for their support. But how they mobilize and inspire their family and neighbors, and how those people respond, points to each person's capacity as an indi-vidual agent. The norms, rules, and morals that each player draws on rep-resent a society's structure—or the playing field on which the players act.

Cultural norms in African societies usually remind people to care for their extended family. In fact, during a 1976 speech outlining national poli-cies, former president Kenneth Kaunda told the people of Zambia that "it is a privilege, nay, a sacred and noble duty to look after the aged" (Kaunda

1976). With this statement of morality and policy, Kaunda was able to justify the closing and ban on old-age homes that some churches and aid groups had begun to establish.

Given that unconditional support for the elderly may be an idealized norm, actual behavior can reveal the intersection of beliefs and practice. In times of plenty and abundance, adhering to cultural norms by providing sufficient support to a materially unproductive member of a household should be easy, as evidenced by rooms overflowing with brightly colored toys for young children in many upper-middle-class American homes. But when faced with conditions of scarcity, behavior may conflict with norms; people are forced to make choices when they have few resources. Newspapers in the United States often tell stories about low-income parents having to choose between the purchase of medicine for chronic illness or food to feed two children. In these cases, food usually wins out over medicine, putting the immediate need for nourishment ahead of the long-term cost of poor health.

In Zambia, and in most of the developing world, people's choices are usually more basic than one between medicine and food. Instead choices often center on much more painful dilemmas: what kind of food? how much food? and in some cases, who will get more or less food? People who live with scarcity also have complex techniques for getting access to as much food as possible, and preventing too many people from eating their limited resources.

I often wondered at the dilapidated state of many grain storage bins during my 1994–95 Gwembe Valley residence—one of the very bad drought years. These round storage bins, built on a raised frame about two feet off the ground, with red clay plaster walls and a thatched roof, somehow looked drunk to me—disheveled thatch, poking in all directions like a head of uncombed hair; supporting beams of the roof exposed like a window frame with no glass; the whole roof structure barely attached to its body, dangling off one edge of the round wall—a drunken figure stumbling through a family's homestead. These disintegrating grain bins looked as if they had been abandoned years before and were simply being kept around because no one wanted to expend the energy to fully dismantle them. Finally, one of my close confidants in the homestead where I lived explained to me, somewhat ashamed, that in fact the bins had been refurbished, including a new roof, just two years before. However, if they did not rebuild the grain bin, then it would appear that the family had no food at all, and consequently extended family and neighbors would not

interesting

come asking for a plate of corn meal. Elizabeth Colson also described how more tightly defined "nuclear" families will eat their meals indoors during hunger times, as opposed to the normal practice of eating outside next to the cooking fires, in an effort to hide that a family is, in fact, eating, and thus avoid unexpected visitors and extraneous relatives appearing at mealtime (Colson 1979).

Clearly Gwembe Tonga people, and any other people around the world living in extreme environments and economic upheaval, are used to coping with recurrent hunger and other challenges to survival. They mobilize broad networks of kin and other social links, use substitutes for many needs, and limit their consumption, both in daily life and ritual activities, to the bare essentials for survival (Colson 1971, 1979). People try to maximize their production while limiting their consumption, as these stories suggest. During the relatively good years of the early 1970s, Gwembe people were consuming more town-bought products and luxuries, and migrants to town were closely linked to relatives in the village through kinship, religion, and business (Colson and Scudder 1975). Sharing profits from business ventures and good harvests was common. More recently, cooperative businesses linking town and village residents have failed, as individuals strapped for money appropriate capital from the enterprises for their own individual needs. In this case, social alliances and networks condense in an attempt to limit the number of people drawing on shared resources. In both the past and the present, the Tonga demonstrate resiliency in their social systems. During the recent years of drought and hunger, some families have encouraged members to move to new locations in an effort to limit consumption and expenditures in the household, and withstand the current stress.

Under conditions of scarcity, focusing on the position of the elderly within the extended family is like placing a magnifying lens over the basic structures of village survival. Relationships to the elderly, a group symbolizing cultural ideals of respect and kinship bonds, can be a measure of how tight those kinship bonds are. Such a focus reveals the foundations of family and distills the bare essentials of society.

What Is Old?

Sitting on small wooden stools in the shade of Musamba's tiny rondoval (a round-walled, wattle-and-dab, thatched living structure), Drivas and I chatted with Musamba about how she manages to live alone in this small house, with no children or grandchildren to help with household chores. Musamba was about seventy-two years old when we had this conversation, and despite her age and spindly stature, she told us she was able to draw a little bit of water once a day from the bore hole about a fifteen-minute walk away. She got her corn meal for porridge by asking various neighboring relatives for a small plate of "meali meal" now and then. She collected wild greens for a sauce from the small damp depressions, *dhambo*, near her home, or while walking back from the bore hole, and periodically a neighboring child (often a "great-niece") would bring back some "rape leaves" (chard) from her mother's garden near the lake so that Musamba could have a "nice sauce." But when I told Musamba that I was impressed with her ability to still cook for herself and draw water, she stopped me in mid-sentence with a violent gesture of her arms outstretched, palms up, and the all-purpose statement "Aaah!" After that meaningful exclamation she continued, "I'm an old woman, I don't have strength—I can't even pound my own grain now." And she proceeded to bow her head, palms of her hands then rubbing the grizzled wiry grey hair. "You see? I'm grey. I'm an old woman!"

The literature on cross-cultural gerontology emphasizes the variety of characteristics that signify "old" (Myerhoff and Simic 1978; Sokolovsky 1990; Albert and Cattell 1994; Ferreira 2000; Makoni and Stroeken 2002; Tengan 2002). Decreasing physical strength and health are important factors in cultural constructions of old age, as are changing reproductive abilities and the number of generations following a person. In the Gwembe communities in which I worked, prerequisites for old age in women were divorce or widowhood and having grandchildren. Women were also expected to be beyond childbearing. And people frequently offered descriptions similar to Musamba's exclamation, including grey hair and lack of strength for domestic tasks like carrying heavy loads, pounding grain (in the case of women), or building houses (for men).

Women, however, were much more likely than men to tell me they were old. Older women would list in great detail all the reasons they were old, often with exaggerated physical expressions. One woman, with arms outstretched like Musamba, showed me the weak muscles that she said had no strength even for cooking and told me that she is old simply because she sits at home with no food. Although aging connotes lack of strength, old women do command some respect from their community. They play key roles in ritual activities, and they are consulted for their kinship and

Fig. 1.2. A group of Gwembe women socializing during a funeral. In the background one of the funeral drums (*budima* drums) hangs on the wall of a grain bin with a collapsing roof.

cultural knowledge. An old woman's identity as a mother also places her in a position of respect and appreciation; she has "given life to her children, fed them from her breast and carried them on her back." On the basis of what she has given or sacrificed in raising children, an elderly woman can make demands for support in her old age. Women often told me simply, "I am old, that's why my children should help me."

Men were very different in their willingness to discuss their own aging. Only one man in the villages where I worked told me that he was an old man, *mudaala*. Jackson explained his situation to me while we sat in the shade of his "stick house" in his nephew's yard. Jackson's nephew had built the house but had not yet completed it by "plastering" the walls with the locally available red clay; consequently the strong winter winds, which contribute to respiratory and eye problems, blew right through the walls. Jackson told me that he was old because he no longer had wives and all of his friends of the same generation had died. He also complained about illness, which made work difficult.

The only other senior man in the village, who also had no wife, was a leper. He told me, "It's not that I'm an old man; it's just this sickness that makes me old." Other men in the villages whom I accidentally called *mu-*

Fig. 1.3. A senior man resting in the shade of his grain bin with a group of grandchildren.

daala looked offended and proceeded to tell me stories of their strength and importance in the community. One man who frequently fell asleep on his chair in the shade of his homestead tree told me he was still a man, *mwalumi* (literally, a married man), because he still had two wives and many children. But his children also told me that he no longer plows or builds houses because he is growing weak.

From these discussions I learned that men in the Gwembe do not want to be called *mudaala.* Nor should they be considered old by the community or by outsiders, unless they have no wives and are truly incapacitated by ill health. The life stage of *mudaala* is undesirable because it means a man has lost his power physically and socially within the family and community. As opposed to women, men want to say "my children should help me because I am their father," not because they are old and helpless. To be a father implies strength and power, and consequently, influence over other people. It is also worth mentioning that senior men are more likely to control resources needed by young adults, an issue that plays out in greater detail in the following chapters.

Being old in the Gwembe Valley, then, is not determined by age or any other particular objective measure. Old age is a package of characteristics,

and perhaps choices. Senior Gwembe women appear to choose, and artic-
ulate, an old-age identity more readily than men do.

Population Aging and Vulnerability: Why Look at Old Age in the Third World?

Although the local, insider, or emic perspective does not adhere to some
kind of clearly measurable and objective definition of old age, nevertheless
literature coming from demography and population studies has identified
aging and old age as topics for investigation in the developing world. Part
of the reason for this attention has to do with ideas of changing population
structures. In Western nations where fertility has declined, that is, where
women are having fewer children, there is increasing discussion of the
aging population that will result. When fewer children are born, the existing adult population represents a bigger proportion of the total population. Over time, a society will have a higher percentage of adults, particularly elderly adults, because fewer children are moving through the
population. The biggest concern in these discussions is how to support a
higher proportion of elderly people, who presumably, as they are debili-
tated by age, are increasingly dependent on the younger population. In
Western societies with infrastructure to support elderly populations, such
as the social security system in the United States or Europe, concern focuses on how to channel sufficient income from younger generations into
the system. When a society experiences population aging, the social security system experiences an increasing imbalance between the withdrawals
of the elderly and the deposits of the young working generations.

Non-Western countries, where governmental structures to support the
elderly generally do not exist, most often depend on extended family to
care for the old. Until recently, population aging in most of these countries
was not an issue because fertility rates remained high, and various illnesses
and health problems led to higher adult mortality rates, so there were always more children proportionally than there were adults, and consequently there were enough younger people to care for the aged. Over the
past thirty years, however, population control campaigns have had success
in many regions where previously high fertility rates were the norm.
China, with its "one child" policy, and other Asian nations, particularly
Taiwan, have seen a fairly rapid decline in population growth. As demog-

raphers like to say, these countries have experienced the "fertility transition"—that is, people have begun to have significantly fewer children. Consequently, these nations needed to begin addressing the question of old-age support because their population structure was changing and over time they could expect to face a heavy burden of dependent elderly people looking for support from fewer and fewer young family members.

The HIV/AIDS pandemic has also impacted the place of the elderly in African families. The illness primarily kills young to middle-aged adults, exactly the population expected to care for aging relatives. In a tragic reversal of family support systems, Africa's aging population has become increasingly responsible for supporting grandchildren, while the parents of those children succumb to a disease with few options for cure (*Economist* 2002; Kamwengo 2002; Nyambedhaa, Wandibbaa, and Aagaard-Hansenb 2003; Frank 2004).

The attention to aging that population studies initiated—from concerns about changes in the fertility and mortality rates to the urgent issue of the impact of HIV/AIDS on population structures—has resulted in other disciplines exploring questions of aging, growing old, and cross-cultural experiences of the life course. Only during the past three decades has aging in a cross-cultural context become a recognized subdiscipline within anthropology.[1] Before this time, the political and status positions of elders, and particularly the men who held such public roles, had been the primary concern of most studies of aging in Africa (Gluckman 1955, 1962; Fortes and Evans-Pritchard 1964; Traore 1985; Glascock 1986). Parallel with increasing attention to aging cross-culturally, feminist perspectives and attention to individuals within their social groupings have led to awareness of the role of women in the African aging process (Kamwengo 2002; Shostak 1983; Udvardy and Cattell 1992). Exploring the role of women in the household and throughout the life course is now an increasingly popular area of study in anthropology and African studies (Reynolds 1991; Apt 1997; Crehan 1997; Hakansson and LeVine 1997; Mikell 1997; Clark 1999; James 1999; Spring 2000; Stone and Stone 2000; Cattell 2002; Cliggett 2003b).

The extended family or lineage has historically had primary responsibility for supporting needy elderly in Africa (Apt 1997; Tengan 2002), and as mentioned earlier, popular stereotypes maintain that elders are respected and cared for in their old age because of their social position and their link to the ancestors. Tied to these ideas are the demographic theories that see high fertility in developing nations as a strategy to guarantee old-age security (Caldwell 1982). However, modernization (e.g., rural–urban migration, change in family composition, education, wage economy) is often believed to change traditional family values and to result in decreased family support for the aged (Meillassoux 1981; Smith, Wallerstein, and Evers 1984). There is debate about the role of modernization in altering traditional values and the status of the elderly. In Zambia, officers from the Ministry of Social Welfare and Development often told me that it was the increasing desire for money that drew children away from their families, leaving elderly parents alone and marginalized in rural areas. However, research from across the African continent demonstrates that the interaction of a variety of power relations, individual choices, cultural practices, and structural changes can dissolve or maintain and empower positions of the elderly (Udvardy and Cattell 1992; Kilbride and Kilbride 1997; Ferreira 2000; Makoni and Stroeken 2002; Kamwengo 2004).

An unexplored theme in understanding the experience of aging cross-culturally is the ways in which the elderly themselves influence the kind of support they receive. In the Gwembe Valley, where living with scarcity forces people to be proactive in harnessing the resources they need to survive, the elderly are active participants in negotiating and manipulating their social worlds to ensure their day-to-day existence. Although support for the elderly may be a moral ideal, more realistically it is a flexible cultural norm operating within a context of individual and group factors. In this framework, all participants in the social setting play fundamental roles in getting what they need out of social interactions. If an old woman is to get enough food during a period of drought, she must actively seek that support in a range of culturally appropriate ways or risk having nothing and perhaps starving to death, as it is believed Muchembele did. However, as the story of Muchembele shows, simply asking neighbors for food will not guarantee sufficient nourishment to sustain oneself during a drought year. During my time working with Gwembe Tonga people, I have come to see the more subtle ways that women and men negotiate their needs on a daily basis, and throughout their lives, in a socioecological context that means no one can have as much as they want, and rarely as much as they need.

Another facet of aging cross-culturally that deserves exploration is the way in which the elderly experience more risk to their well-being than other groups do. Drawing on the past decade's discussions of vulnerability to famine and food scarcity, and vulnerable populations, we can look at the historical circumstances that have created the population of the vulnerable elderly living in rural Africa. Much of rural Africa could be described as vulnerable to the vagaries of global economic transformation, environmental fluctuations, and political upheaval (e.g., Watts 1983; Vaughan 1987; Watts and Bohle 1993; Blaikie et al. 1994; Scoones 1994; Coutsoudis et al. 2000). Within such a broad claim, we can look more closely at which groups of people have more exposure to these triggers and which groups will suffer the most severe consequences of these events. Pastoral herders in East Africa who have been forced by land privatization into increasingly marginal grazing zones suffer more from climatic fluctuations than do herders in Niger who have more extensive land rights that allow them to move more easily across the landscape, making use of the ecological variation that keeps their herds alive (Scoones 1994; Greenough 2003). Unmarried, low-income women living in Uganda's urban centers have greater risk of exposure to HIV/AIDS infection than do educated women with some kind of formal-sector employment (Wallman and Bantebya-Kyomuhendo 1996). These are examples of the social topography of the African continent, which point to the importance of difference and the need to look more closely at specific groups of people.

When we look beyond the surface stereotypes of violence, poverty, disease, and ecological devastation, we see that some people can withstand economic, ecological, and social crises better than others, and that some people lack the range of resources that could facilitate their ability to cope through periods of crisis. Watts and Buhl's (1993) "vulnerability framework" identifies three key factors (entitlement, empowerment, and political economy relations) that play important roles in the creation of famine among particular groups of people. The interrelations of the three factors can lead to distinct groups of people experiencing different levels of vulnerability to their material well-being. This framework proves especially useful for understanding the situation of older women and men in the Gwembe Valley. Although elderly people in general tend to experience more risk to their food security because of physical limitations that prevent them from producing their own food, in the Gwembe the history of agricultural change and the increase in cattle ownership have lead to very different resource access for older women and men. As a result of these changes, we need to consider elderly women and men as distinct groups of people with different economic vulnerability in terms of their entitlement to food and material resources, empowerment to control those resources, and the political economy relations that shape one group's access over that of another. Using a framework of vulnerability that highlights difference in terms of a group's resources and its ability to control those resources forces us to develop a more complex vision of what Africa is. This argument is more fully developed in chapter 3, "The Space and Time of Vulnerability."

The Importance of Social Context: Matrilineal Kinship and Making Sense of Family

To make sense of intergenerational relations in any society, not just Zambia, we must uncover the local ideas of who is family and who is not. By clarifying who is considered family, we clarify who has particular rights, responsibilities, and obligations, and to whom. At their core, this is what kinship systems do—they identify who is family and who is not, and give guidelines for behavior, beliefs, property ownership, identity, and the myriad other facets of interpersonal and interfamilial dynamics. In the West this may seem like a very simple task; our families consist of mothers, fathers, and their parents, our siblings, our parents' siblings and their children, and so on. We could say that our Western kinship system is quite general—we identify as family all people related through our mothers and our fathers. We identify family members as people to whom we have blood *or* marriage relations. Nonfamily, then, are people with whom we have no such relations, through blood or marriage.

Unilineal descent (kinship) systems, on the other hand, are more particular. Unilineal descent traces family through only one parent—either the mother or the father. In the unilineal model, those people who do not belong to the one descent line are not considered family. So in a patrilineal descent system, family identity is traced through a father (and his father, and the offspring of the father's brothers and the father's father's brothers, and so forth). The patrilineal system often seems vaguely familiar to Western observers because frequently in the United States we transmit our last names in a patrilineal path: In the United States someone named Linda Smith often shares that same last name with her father's father, Daniel Smith, and his children, and his male children's children.

Matrilineal kinship, the other unilineal descent system, frequently challenges the understanding of Westerners because it seems so profoundly different from how we identify family and relatives. In the matrilineal system of reckoning family, a child looks to her mother, her mother's brothers and sisters, her mother's mother, and that woman's brothers and sisters as family. A child's father is not part of the child's proper family in the matrilineal system. A child also considers her mother's sisters' children as family but *not* her mother's brothers' children. Why aren't these maternal uncles' children part of a child's matrilineal family? Because a man's children belong to the family of the woman who gave birth to them, not to his family. That man identifies his proper family through his sisters and their children.

This is where the famous anthropological character the "mother's brother" takes on his greatest role—in a matrilineal system in which children rely on him more than their own father to provide the kind of support, protection, and assistance that we in the West expect to gain from our fathers. Importantly, in the ideal matrilineal descent system, the mother's brother also expects to gain the kind of respect, assistance, loyalty, and rights over labor from his sister's children that fathers in the West might expect from their own children.

Given the curiosity of a kinship system that does not acknowledge the father of children as primary family, matriliny has received continued attention from sociologists and anthropologists almost since the birth of these disciplines. Early on, scholars devoted their attention to the origins of matriliny with the assumption that "mother right" was the original "primitive" kinship system, that as cultures evolved, patrilineal descent appeared as a more developed way to reckon family, and that the change to patrilineal descent paralleled developments in economies from subsistence based to more cash and capitalist based (Murdock 1949; Schneider and Gough 1961; Lévi-Strauss 1969; Engels 1972; Schneider 1979). With the coming of critiques of social evolution and a preference for looking at systems as adaptive and appropriate, the emphasis on matriliny as a primitive form of kinship gave way to looking at how the range of kinship systems plays out in different contexts, and how they flex and bend in reference to changing facets of society.

Since those early attempts to unravel the character of matrilineal descent, others have focused less on the origins of such a system and more on the way that identifying family through the mother's line matters in terms of behavior, rights, and identity (Meillassoux 1981; Poewe 1981; Holy 1986; Pritchett 2001). In Zambia's northern regions, Poewe (1981) and Pritchett (2001) have documented two other well-known groups in the heart of Africa's "matrilineal belt" (the east–west swath that girdles the continent at its north–south "waist"). Poewe in particular describes the population in Luapula Province in reference to a very strong adherence to the matrilineal model that delineates distinct patterns of interaction between women and men, something she calls sexual parallelism. By exploring the ways that matriliny influences women's and men's ideology, behavior, and rights or interest over resources, she offers a vision of matrilineal kinship as it plays out distinctly in women's and men's lives. Similarly, Pritchett explores change in Lunda-Ndembu society with attention to the various forms of separation that play important roles in the northwestern region of Zambia, including male–female separation. Speaking of the men and women in Lunda-Ndembu society, Pritchett states, "they have differing residential patterns, differing options for support and assistance, differing relations to their children, and differing bases for planning existential and metaphysical life" (2001, 203).

Indeed, the same can be said for the Tonga of southern Zambia, and for most women and men in strongly matrilineal societies (and some would argue all societies). Throughout this book I explore the ways that women's and men's lives differ and intersect over the life cycle.[2] To understand the variety of action in women's and men's lives, we must accept the matrilineal backbone of Tonga society. Of course, models never capture the variety of reality, and matrilineal kinship, as it is described in the written form, always results in a very perfect abstract model. However, life on the ground, matrilineal or otherwise, is much more messy. Nevertheless, understanding that in Gwembe Tonga society the "normative family" contains only those people traced through mothers gives a starting point for exploring how rights and obligations fall on the young, the middle-aged, and the old.

Gendered Strategies of Support

When we look at how Tonga elders "get by" in the austere living conditions for which the Gwembe Valley is famous, the importance of relationships to children and the differences between men and women in those relationships become clear. Men cling to their identity as powerful individuals in control of their social relationships, even as they age and become unable to perform normal agricultural and domestic tasks. Women make the transition to old age more easily, and perhaps more willingly, for as a widow or divorcee, a woman may work for herself alone for the first time in her life, and ideally be assisted by her adult children.

Differences between men's and women's willingness to recognize their own aging are linked to their styles of manipulation of social relationships. Older women and men use differing strategies to encourage support from their children. Men typically rely on their control of resources, including the labor of their offspring, to draw supporters. Gwembe men historically have had more access to cash-generating activities, including labor migration and cash crop cultivation, giving them a stronger material base from which to establish social relations.

In the Tonga matrilineal kinship system, men do not share the same primary family identity with their children. But through a competing, although less enduring patrilineal tendency, men have rights over their children, particularly their children's labor and the bride wealth paid for daughters. Although men do not share family or "clan" identity with their wives and children, they do have important kinship and domestic roles, and they control important resources held at the "nuclear family" level.

Women do not maintain the same levels and types of control over people and things that men have. Consequently, they have developed tactics for encouraging children and other relatives to come to their assistance. Women's strategies are tied to their identity as mothers who have given life and sacrificed for the benefit of their children. Matrilineal identity also supports a woman's position in negotiating for assistance; clan relatives have obligations to assist one another, to the benefit of a woman skilled in using her identity as a mother and a clan relative.

The Tonga matrilineal clan system, *mukowa*, is challenged by a patrilineal nuclear unit, the *lutundu*, which gives fathers rights to their children. The *lutundu* is not a proper lineage in that members do not have obligations to one another, only to their father and minimally to his father. The *lutundu* plays out most explicitly in men's exploitation of their children. A father demands that sons plow his fields, build houses, and manage his cattle; he also expects a portion of his children's property, whether it be cash, food luxuries, or supplies from town. At my first Christmas in the village, the only people given (indeed, demanding) gifts were fathers. During this holiday (introduced by early missionaries), the community joined together under a huge old tree, which provided the much-needed shade during this peak in the hot season. They launched a multivillage party that included "pop-dance" competitions set to Zairian music played on battery-powered radios. The party resembled a market place: people came with goods for sale; young women sold sweet fritters and buns. While everyone else was expected to pay for their treats, including brothers and sisters, young women gave their fathers gifts of fritters or buns. And when these senior men wanted tea to drink with their delicacy, they went to another daughter and demanded sugar. She gave them what they asked for, but they offered none of their snack in exchange.

Other stories of fathers drawing on their children's labors are more painful, if not for the participants, at least for me, as a witness. During my time working with Gwembe people, I have seen numerous disputes between sons and their fathers, especially over use of agricultural equipment and farming activities. Young adult men who do not own cattle, plows, and other implements rely on their father's equipment to farm their fields. At the same time, fathers rely on their sons' labor to prepare and plow their many fields. When a man believes his son has not performed his duties sufficiently, he may withhold access to his equipment, forcing the son into an undesirable position with few choices. In many of these conflicts, sons end up leaving the village to work in town, or they resettle with matrilineal relatives in frontier farming areas where they can use a cousin's equipment until they manage to establish and head their own farms.

To a large extent, formal rights over children determine men's relationships to their offspring. Women's relationships to children, on the other hand, are based on kinship affiliation and ties linked to the mother–child experience. Cultural ideals of motherhood in the Gwembe Valley emphasize the sacrifices and the energy that mothers invest in raising their children. Mothers are seen as caring, protective, and nurturing. During one of my field trips, one mother came to me asking for money to take her infant son to the clinic for malaria treatment because her husband had refused to give her the needed cash. She offered to work for me or tell me stories in exchange for my help and explained that her husband, even though he was a rich man, didn't care about their son.

Given these differing notions of mother (nurturing, protective) and father (authoritarian, powerful), old women and men do not share the same bargaining power in relation to their children. Old women can make the claim that "I did everything for you, I carried you on my back, I fed you from my breast, so now you can sacrifice for me." Men can only say, "I am powerful, so I will extract your labor, your resources and your loyalty, and as long as I can do that, you will help me." For a woman, becoming physically weak and increasingly dependent on others, that is, aging, encompasses different types of adjustment than for men. Women can use the familiar patterns of social interaction that they have used all their lives to mobilize support. Most men, however, depend primarily on their authority and control to mobilize social links; if they give in to the aging process—increased dependency, weakness, lack of power—they lose their ability to mobilize and control social networks.

Throughout this book, I explore these subtle, and sometimes not so subtle, aspects of the ways that older women and men in the Gwembe Valley negotiate a social world that is critically shaped by resource scarcity, and the equally subtle ways that family and neighbors provide or avoid providing that much-needed support.

This book explores key facets of daily life for elders in one region of rural Africa. Starting with chapter 3, I explore the history of elders' changing access to resources in the Gwembe Valley, as well as their livelihoods, residence patterns, ritual and spiritual life, mobility, and links over distance and time. Each facet can be a context of support or a context of vulnerability for village elders. These stories, however, could easily apply to elders around the world, not just to the senior population of rural Zambia.

In all facets of their lives, elders play roles in building a context of support or vulnerability throughout their life cycle. And some people exist in places and times where vulnerability is more likely. When external structures fail, individual coping capacities can determine whether someone survives or not. With this clarity of vision, we become much better placed to make sense of media portrayals of poverty, starvation, and Africa in general.

This book aims to debunk popular visions of generalized social catastrophe in Africa, on the one hand, and the naïve assumption of the "nobility" of African "families" on the other. Care and support for Africa's elderly population, and indeed the population of elders around the world, are not a given, nor are they a "natural" component of nonindustrialized societies. When families provide care for their senior relatives, it is a choice based on many considerations, including the individual actions of the older person. Recognizing the many levels of decision making inherent in providing support to needy family members makes us much wiser about complexities of family interactions, coping with scarcity, and life in the modern context.

2. Getting Down in the Valley

The ethnographer, like the artist, is engaged in a special kind of vision quest through which a specific interpretation of the human condition, an entire sensibility, is forged. Our medium, our canvas, is "the field," a place both proximate and intimate (because we have lived some part of our lives there) as well as forever distant and unknowably "other" (because our own destinies lie elsewhere). In the act of "writing culture," what emerges is always a highly subjective, partial, and fragmentary—but also deeply felt and personal—record of human lives based on eyewitness and testimony. The act of witnessing is what lends our work its moral . . . character. So-called participant observation has a way of drawing the ethnographer into spaces of human life where she or he might really prefer not to go at all and once there doesn't know how to go about getting out except through writing, which draws others there as well, making them party to the act of witnessing.

Nancy Scheper-Hughes (1992, xii)

"Lisa, Lisa, there's transport! Come quickly." On the evening of my fifth day stranded in the Gwembe District Government Center, or "government boma," of Munyumbwe, located about halfway and thirty miles down the escarpment from the paved road on the plateau above, there was a heavy pounding at my door. Dorothy, the manager of the government guesthouse and my host and language teacher over the past five days, was calling to me urgently. I was just preparing for my bucket bath by kerosene lantern light, having given up on the possibility of transport that day. With the cry of transport, I changed my plans for a bath and dinner immediately. I stuffed my shower things, warm clothes for evening wear, and sleeping bag into the backpack, made sure I had left nothing behind, and, with Dorothy's help carrying the heavy pack, or as Dorothy called it, *katundu* (meaning "big burden of stuff" in the urban language of Nyanja), ran to the bus stop. By the time we got there, out of breath, and my adrenaline surging at the thought of the next leg in my first trip to the valley, and my research site, the darkness of tropical nights had fallen.

In the latitudinal zone of the tropics—twenty-three and a half degrees north (the Tropic of Cancer) and south (the Tropic of Capricorn) of the equator—the twenty-four-hour day is divided almost equally between light and dark. The sun sets between five-thirty and seven o'clock every day of the year, and the sun rises between those same hours in the morning. The closer you are to the equator, the less variability you find. Thus, although it was probably only six o'clock in the evening, and certainly before I had eaten dinner, it already felt like deep dark night to me because I had been in Zambia less than a month and had not yet adjusted to the tropical daylight rhythms.

In the darkness Dorothy negotiated my ride with the driver of what turned out to be a minivan. Within two minutes of my arrival at the bus stop, my backpack disappeared into the depths of the van, and I was shuffled onto the front bench seat—made of a wooden plank—nestled against the driver's arm, with two other adults tucked in after me. As I called my profuse thanks to Dorothy through the window, I noticed that the man next to the passenger door was fiddling with something around the door handle, and then with the upper corner of the door frame and window. But in the darkness I couldn't see clearly, and my mind was distracted with the knowledge that I was again in somewhat unknown circumstances.

As the van started its forward movement, the unknown-ness became somewhat more known. Although seated directly behind the front of what I believed to be the windshield of the van, there was a strong, and cold, wind blowing directly on me, not coming from either side. As my eyes tried to focus in the dark, I reached my hand out to where I believed the glass windshield was attached to the end of the dash board. My hand floated on the wind, and continued beyond the windshield frame—no wonder I felt cold from the wind blowing. There was no windshield. My seat neighbor chuckled a little and offered simply, "no glass," in response to my gesture.

At about that same moment, we passed the end of the level strip of Munyumbwe's main road, bounced over a bouldered section, and began descending. As we bounded, my ears twitched with the clackity noises of loose metal and squeaking joints, sounds that come from a packed toolbox when you shake it. By now, my eyes had adjusted enough that I could see within the front seat area. With each bump, I looked at various joints of the vehicle—the upper left corner where the windshield, door frame, and roof meet—only to see each plane move in independent directions. I couldn't tell for certain, but it looked like they were wired together with something like a twist tie that closes a bread bag, rather than tightly, and permanently, bolted. With the realization that this van was something like a vehicle resurrected from death, I gave myself a little talking to: "Well, you'll probably get to Chipepo, since this van is full of lots of other people who want to go there. So, better just to not think about the sturdiness, and start talking to the people seated next to you." Which is what I did.

Aside from the stress of this first adventure getting to the valley, riding public transportation in other countries has always been one of my favorite "hobbies," especially if I speak the local language with any ability. I love the brief conversations; the spontaneous kindness and generosity of fellow passengers always makes me wonder at the humanity of people around the world. In a place like Zambia, where only a small percentage of the population owns private vehicles, the majority use minivans and pickup trucks, in which they bounce around in the open bed, as their primary mode of transportation. Yet almost all foreigners own or lease vehicles, or their businesses hire drivers for them. Thus, it is fairly uncommon for foreigners—and in Zambia, most foreigners are white so it's obvious that you are a foreigner—to use public transport. And if by chance a foreigner can speak a local language, local people are that much more surprised.

Although I did not yet speak Citonga in any functional way, I had learned the evening greeting, thanks to Dorothy, which I launched at each of my front seat copassengers. And then, as best as possible, I tried to twist in my seat and greet those behind me. As it turned out, three out of the ten people in the van spoke some English, and we were able to have somewhat of a conversation as we rattled down the mountain. As so often happens in such surreal circumstances, I quickly learned that one of the passengers seated in the back of the van, and one of the three who spoke English, was a man I had intended to seek out in the village where I planned to settle and conduct research.

Of People, Place, and the Gwembe Tonga Research Project

Part of the clarity of purpose I had since my arrival in Zambia a few weeks before, and my subsequent determination to get to the valley quickly, came as a result of serendipitous circumstances a month before my departure from the United States. My research plans for Zambia had been in process for three years prior to my departure in the Northern Hemisphere

Fig. 2.1. Southern Province, Zambia. Detail, map 3731 Rev. 4, January 2004, courtesy UN Cartographic Section.

spring of 1994. But a month before leaving, Thayer Scudder—one of the two anthropologists who had worked in the Gwembe Valley since 1956, had convinced me that I should shift my field site from Zambia's Eastern Province to the Gwembe Valley in Southern Province (see fig. 2.1). Part of the attraction in shifting to the Gwembe was simply the "infrastructure" for research.

Elizabeth Colson, the other, and first, anthropologist working in the region since before the 1950s, and Ted Scudder had been continuously working in four Gwembe villages since their first study on the consequences of resettlement of the Gwembe Tonga people caused by the building of Kariba Dam on the Zambezi River.[1] When Scudder encouraged me to consider working in the Gwembe, he offered me the choice to work in any of the villages where the project had been based, and he also offered me access to the village census material that he and Colson continually update. (See fig. 2.2 for a map of pre- and post-resettlement villages where Colson and Scudder have conducted research since 1956.) Thus, when I decided to shift my field site south, I suddenly found myself with specific villages in which to work, names of people with whom Colson and Scudder, and other researchers on the project, had worked, and most importantly, a foundation of almost fifty years of knowledge from which I could begin my own research. After discussing the various characteristics of the different villages with Scudder and Colson, I decided to make my home base in the Gwembe Central village of Sinafala, about five miles south of Chipepo along the lakeshore. Sinafala was considered one of the "better-off" villages because of its proximity to the lake, where people could farm

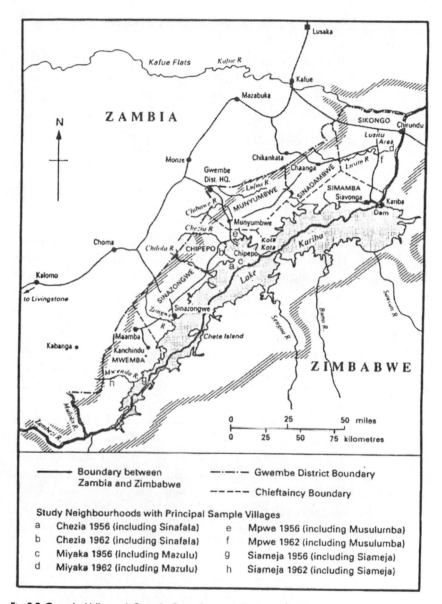

Fig. 2.2. Gwembe Valley, with Gwembe Tonga Research Project study villages.

the fertile shore land during the dry season and also benefit from the fishing opportunities.

For a second field site I chose a village at the northern end of the valley in an area known as the Lusitu, where living conditions were notoriously difficult. In the Lusitu in general, and Mazulu in particular, all useable land had been claimed, and for the most part the large rainy-season fields had been overused for such long periods that they barely produced any kind of harvest, let alone a sufficient one. The little bit of land along the Zambezi River, or tributaries to the Zambezi, allowed Mazulu villagers to farm small garden plots during the dry season, but those gardens did not produce sufficient harvests either. Using Sinafala village as a baseline for looking at intergenerational relations in relatively "good circumstances" would allow an effective comparison with Mazulu village, where people are forced to make even more difficult decisions about supporting dependents.

With the village census information that Colson and Scudder would share with me, I could arrive in both villages with basic information about each family, as well as the depth of knowledge available through all of their writing over the past four decades. From the census data, I was able to find all of the "elderly" people aged fifty-five or older in both Sinafala and Mazulu.[2] Thus, even before arriving in the village on this first trip, I knew that there were about 45 elderly people in Sinafala who I planned to work with, and 37 elderly people in Mazulu.

Also from the census material I learned that many Gwembe people had moved to other regions of Zambia, including not only towns but remote frontier farming areas, where many Gwembe people were moving in the hopes of better harvests. Since a primary component of my research interests was how adult children interact with their aging parents, even when they don't live in close proximity, the census information offered a valuable starting point for tracing migrants and exploring their relationships with village-based kin.

Using the census data, as well as conversations in the first few months with people in Sinafala and Mazulu, I decided to track down as many migrant children (of the 82 elderly people of Sinafala and Mazulu) as possible who lived in towns along the railway from Livingston (Zambia's southwestern border town and home of Victoria Falls) through Lusaka, the nation's capital, and north into Zambia's industrial Copperbelt region—a collection of six cities in close proximity. As I looked through the census material and talked with villagers, I was surprised that almost no "elderly" migrants from the two villages lived in any of the towns. One old and incapacitated widow, around age sixty-eight, lived with her son in one of the Copperbelt towns, and another widow, aged around fifty-two, headed her own household in a southern railway town. Other than that, the more than one hundred town-based migrant children of the elderly population in Sinafala and Mazulu were young and middle-aged adults working in towns either temporarily or at established careers.

As a result of looking through the census I also discovered that ten people above the age of fifty-five listed in the Sinafala census did not, in fact, live in Sinafala but had migrated to a frontier farming area known as Chikanta—a region bordering Zambia's largest national park, and about two hundred miles northwest of the Gwembe Valley. Because the census data recorded all people and families who had resided in the village in 1956, people who had since moved away were still considered part of the "village population." So although the "Sinafala census" is tied to a particular location, in practice it is a record of all people tied to the village from 1956, wherever they may live. In addition to the ten elderly people living in Chikanta, there were also nine children of Sinafala elders living in Chikanta. Thus, with the census I was able to identify an additional study site where I could explore intergenerational relations in a different context and also look at the ways extended family members interact over distance. In addition to containing extensive genealogies of all the families in Sinafala and Mazulu, and information about where each family member lived, the census material also included details about education, employment, marriage history, and sometimes other pertinent information (such as illnesses, religious affiliation, or unusual events that impacted an individual).

To have all of this information—specific villages, a total village census and extensive genealogies, locations of migrants, basic socioeconomic history, and potential research assistants—before arriving in country, let alone in the village, is extremely valuable for a PhD student as she sets about beginning her research. Still, although I had an unusual amount of knowledge about where I was going and what I planned to do, I felt the excitement and the anxiety of any first visit to a new and out of the way place.

So on this adventurous descent I was thrilled to have found one of my contacts, Maxwell. Despite the fact I couldn't see his, or anyone else's, face clearly due to the darkness inside the van, he introduced me to his wife, Martha. She did not speak English but greeted me in one of the few Citonga phrases I had learned, "Kwasya buti?" the evening greeting of "How is the night?" I answered with one of the ten other phrases I knew,

"Kabotu," "Good," and returned the question as proper Tonga etiquette requires. Maxwell and I, along with the two other English speakers, tried to chat during the hurtling descent, but the clattering toolbox sounds usually drowned out our voices, so within a half hour we fell mostly silent for the remaining two-hour journey.

Finally, in my haze of post adrenaline rush and pure exhaustion, I noticed the van was rattling less and that we had leveled off somewhat. In the dim illumination of the headlights (which had flickered on and off throughout the journey with each bounce), I saw that we were on a sandy road, and I could feel the van weave and snake as we lost and gained traction on the dusty track. Clearly, we were somewhere much different than we had been for the last two and half hours. The van veered to the left onto another sandy track, and we slithered our way for about a mile, finally coming to a stop in front of some official and dreary-looking buildings, from which a few people emerged. I was sure this was Chipepo, at long last. All occupants staggered from the depths of the van, some of us moaning as we tried to move limbs that had long since been numb with inactivity and cramped space.

Outside the van, and in the faint light cast by the front beams of light, I could see that we were indeed at some official location; next to the van was a flag pole, a primary signifier of a government institution. Maxwell and six of the other passengers were busy unloading their *katundu* and town-bought goods, including two huge sacks of maize seed. I also noticed that my bag had joined their pile. At this point, having regained some of my mental functions, which had shut down for much of the ride in an effort to numb some of the pain (and fear), I thought to ask what I assumed was the obvious, "So, this is Chipepo?" I did not want to hear the no that was given in response, and a flush of dread washed over me as I imagined another two hours in the rickety van bounding over potholes and boulders.

Slowly Maxwell and the driver clarified that this was not "the harbor" at Chipepo but a school and clinic where Maxwell and the others heading to Sinafala would sleep for the night. They told me the walk was shorter from this place to the village than from Chipepo, and since no motorized transport to Sinafala existed, walking was the only option. In my late-night, trip-weary, and increasingly hungry condition, I could not fathom an alternate plan to the naïve one I had laid out for myself more than a week ago. Although Maxwell and his wife explained that I could sleep in the room with all the other travelers and even offered me one of their blankets, I said that I needed to go to Chipepo before going to Sinafala because I had "business" in Chipepo first. It wasn't exactly the truth; I wasn't sure what I really needed to do in Chipepo. But I was sure that it fit with my vision of the orderly, step-by-step descent I had planned back in Lusaka, before I knew just how difficult it was to find public transportation in the valley. I had also been told there was a government guesthouse, like that in Munyumbwe, and I assumed that with the guesthouse would be a dining room. And since by now it seemed like almost twenty-four hours since I had eaten (although it was only about ten), I was fantasizing about *nsima* (corn meal porridge) with fish sauce—the meal I had subsisted on for five days in Munyumbwe.

With the reassurance of the van driver that Chipepo was "close close," and that I would see Maxwell in a day or so when I got to Sinafala, I forced my body back onto the wooden plank, next to the driver, watched the door get wired closed, and prepared myself for what I hoped would be a short journey but what I feared would take the rest of the night.

Happily, a half hour later the van pulled up to yet another dreary-looking building, but from which emanated the familiar sounds of Congolese soukous music, which is the preferred night club, bar, and restaurant dance music throughout Zambia. On the stairs leading up to the entrance, it appeared that a multitude of people, all men from what I could see, were standing, smoking, laughing boisterously, and holding brown glass bottles of Mosi—Zambia's Western-style bottled beer. I believed this must be Chipepo. But even if it wasn't, I was ready to stay for awhile. The beer looked especially great, but I also assumed that where there's beer, there's food.

Out of the crowd on the stairs emerged a man dressed spiffily in nice trousers and an ironed white button-down shirt. He descended the stairs and greeted me in perfect English, telling me that he was the guesthouse manager, and he confirmed that this place was indeed the Chipepo Guesthouse. With the crowd on the stairs, I feared that all the rooms might have been taken. Taxson, the manager said, "Oh no, these are teachers from the secondary school down the road. All of our rooms are available." My next question, "Can I get a meal tonight?" did not receive as positive an answer. "Ah, but our kitchen is closed. We do have some chips at the bar." That night, in my long-anticipated destination of Chipepo Harbor, I had a meal of two Mosi and two bags of chips, and proceeded to sleep for ten hours.

The Big and Little Questions We Ask

My arrival at the Chipepo Harbor guesthouse had been in the making for at least three years before I arrived in April of 1994. In fact, my research agenda and the topical focus of intergenerational relations had been in the works much longer. As my ideas about how people support and don't support the elderly in different societies developed during my graduate school years, I began to see that such questions become most pertinent in situations where people do not have enough resources to support all the people in their lives as comfortably as they would like. For this reason, it became clear that I would need to ask my questions in places where life is not easy. Such a place could have been Haiti in the Caribbean, where I had worked during the late 1980s and planned to do my PhD research. But when the political climate in Haiti worsened in the early 1990s, I needed to relocate my research to a more politically stable region. At the same time I was accepting this reality, serendipity came into play: I was offered a position on a survey research project on support systems for the elderly in Zambia's Eastern Province. Since I had always been interested in Africa, and had in fact taken many courses with African content, I decided relocating my research to Zambia was both practical and something I would enjoy.

After extending my graduate course work to cover the additional courses needed in order to focus my research in Zambia, and writing grants so that I would have independence in my research but could still collaborate with the survey project in Eastern Province, I ironically found myself funded but the project not funded and in a holding pattern. It was at this point that Ted Scudder learned about my plans to look at household economy and intergenerational relations in Zambia. On the basis of what he knew of my interests, he believed my theoretical lens and topical focus meshed well with the broad framework of the Gwembe research he and Elizabeth Colson had been conducting since the 1950s, and with crucial issues relevant to Gwembe people.

The ways that anthropologists develop their research agendas vary. At one end of the spectrum, some anthropologists are compelled by the love of a location and seek a way to conduct research in that place, no matter what the topic. At the opposite end, others find a compelling question and seek a place where it can be answered. Ideally, we would all like our research to emerge out of a mixture of love of place and compelling questions. My research plans, however, fell more into the "compelling-question/any-location" framework. Thus switching from research in Haiti to research in Zambia wasn't an intellectually huge leap. Theoretically, the issues were very similar. Of course, the context differed profoundly.

But no matter how an anthropologist ends up in her field site, the dynamic interchange between theoretical ideas and local context fundamentally shapes how she understands the issues and ultimately how she writes the resulting articles or books. In teaching graduate courses on field methods and data analysis, I find my biggest challenge is convincing students that theory, method, and interpretation are completely intertwined. In order to develop our research methods—how we go about getting the information we need—we must know what questions we are asking. And to know our questions, we must acknowledge where they come from—that is, we must acknowledge the theory that shapes our lens of inquiry. Inevitably students say, "I don't want to use abstract theory to determine my research. I want local people to tell me what they think is important." That statement alone emerges from a theoretical perspective of "action anthropology," in which local people play fundamental roles in shaping the research agenda. Alternatively, students sometimes have a phenomenal grasp of abstract theory and very little skill in translating those ideas to real-life situations.

In my case, my swirling interests in family dynamics, within-household (intrahousehold) decision making, and support for the elderly emerged both from my personal world and my readings in contemporary social science. As part of a family that I often describe as "volatilly close," I have always paid attention to the various social dynamics at play in our household and extended family. It seemed logical to me to consider those issues from a cross-cultural perspective once I entered graduate school. The vast literature in anthropology and other social science disciplines offered a huge array of perspectives for making sense of those dynamics.

Over time, both before leaving for the field and since then as I analyze the data I have collected, I have found myself increasingly attached to the ideas inherent in explorations of "household economy" and the "practice-centered" perspectives in anthropology and sociology. More recently I have found that the concept of vulnerable populations around the world and the political ecology that creates conditions of vulnerability offer a valuable framework for understanding the Zambian context. The dialectic (back and forth-ness) of theoretical development and actual lived experience means that although we set out to examine a topic from a particular viewpoint, that viewpoint shifts and refocuses as we gather information (see also Burawoy, Gamson, and Burton 1991 for discussion of this process). Thus, the ideas I set out with initially have been molded and reshaped into something quite different than what they were ten years ago. Nevertheless, some of the core ideas of household dynamics, individual action, and political ecology remain the primary framework for understanding the Gwembe situation.

Personal Agency and Household Economy

Theoretical movements in anthropology and sociology during the 1960s and 1970s highlighted the importance of individual action within social structures. The practice-centered approaches of Giddens (1976) and Bourdieu (1977) give individuals an active role in the formation of society. Both theorists suggest that individuals and social structures participate in a feedback system, changing and maintaining each other simultaneously. In their formulation, rules and norms shape and constrain behavior. However, each individual tests the boundaries of those rules and norms through their individual actions. The tension between the individual and these boundaries results in changes for both; people respond to their circumstances, and circumstances change through the energies of people's practice. The sexual revolution of the 1960s in the United States is one example of how individuals can push, and ultimately shift, the boundaries of social norms. In Zambia, clothing styles, a somewhat superficial example, have undergone rapid transformation in the decade I've worked there. In 1992, during my first visit to the country, when I pursued research in Eastern Province, a woman wearing a miniskirt on a main street in Lusaka had been attacked and stripped for dressing immorally. Only six years later, young sophisticated women walked Lusaka's downtown with confidence and no fear of such attacks. And even in the rural villages, young women wore all styles of trousers—a truly profound shift in the range of tolerable dress for women in village life (the most private body region for Zambian women is between knees and waist).

Taking these ideas of agency and joining them with economic and materialist interpretations—that is, looking at how individuals and social systems interact in the sphere of making a living—allow us to examine how individuals act and influence the fundamental process of daily survival. Household processes gained a solid place in anthropological research during the 1980s. These studies focused on the domestic mode of production and paralleled the "practice theory" movement in their examinations of the individual motivations inherent in household processes (Netting, Wilk, and Arnould 1984; Guyer and Peters 1987; Guyer 1986; Dwyer and Bruce 1988; Wilk 1989; Netting 1993; Clark 1994). Human agency allows for conflict and negotiation within the social structure. As a result, domestic settings—or households—are not simply homogeneous units but dynamic collections of individuals working both together and apart. My understanding of Gwembe Tonga domestic life, and particularly how the elderly in the Gwembe Valley manipulate their social worlds, reflects these theories of agency within the domestic setting. In my interpretations, I view the elderly as one set of players within their families and households, in the game of acquiring basic necessities of life.

Early work conducted by anthropologists and social scientists affiliated with the Rhodes-Livingston Institute (RLI) in Zambia (at that time, Northern Rhodesia) and its British counterpart, Manchester University, gave an intellectual foundation to the Zambian context of my focus on kinship and household dynamics. Research sponsored through the RLI and Manchester University revealed the complexity of African social systems and the ways individuals operated within those structures. The plethora of literature emerging from the RLI documents social, political, economic, and religious facets of life in southern Africa throughout the period of increasing colonial impact and intersection with Zambians lives. Gluckman's efforts at understanding African social systems included using situational analysis and the study of social dramas to emphasize the role of conflict in communities (Gluckman 1942, 1955, 1962, 1965), including contact between European administrators and both rural- and urban-based Africans. Paralleling Evans-Pritchard's discussion of fission and fusion (1940), Gluckman, using a case-study approach to look at a complex society, argued that conflicts themselves bind groups together (1958). Other anthropologists from the British school carried on with Gluckman's program by focusing on changing societies and the conflicts inherent in change. Barnes (1967), Colson (1958, 1960, 1971), Epstein (1958), Mitchell (1956, 1969), Turner (1957), and Van-Velsen (1964) all helped to illuminate the role of conflict, change, and adaptation in African social organization.

In addition to the insight drawn from the earlier research of anthropologists and sociologists in southern Africa, ideas emerging from broader and synthesized perspectives in anthropology have helped in interpreting what I have seen in Zambia. Wolf's treatise on world social history (1982) outlines the importance of kinship in understanding economic processes. What he calls the kin-ordered mode of production is a system in which kinship ties control labor. Marriage and descent are the primary forces shaping groups in kinship-based societies. As Wolf describes this kin-ordered mode of production, access to labor, and consequently resources, in such societies is determined by group membership, fertility control, and the ability to recruit new members. His ideas parallel discussions of "wealth in people" systems (Kopytoff and Miers 1977; Bledsoe 1990; Moore and Vaughan 1994), in which a group, or individuals within groups, has rights over other members' labor and resources through age, gender, and kinship. As the stories I relate throughout this book suggest, in Gwembe communities, individuals, and particularly men, struggle to draw together dependents and supporters in an effort to guarantee their position within their communities. Men have rights to children's and other relatives' labor as well as a portion of their property, thus setting the stage for tension within the kin group.

Colson's and Scudder's work in the Gwembe provides detailed ethnographic descriptions of people's strategies for coping with localized conflict (Colson 1973, 1979, 1995; Colson and Scudder 1981, 1988; Scudder 1983, 1984) as well as with external forces of change (Colson 1960, 1964, 1971; Scudder 1962, 1966, 1980). Their original focus on the effects of development-induced resettlement led to the formulation of a relocation theory that emphasizes a community's and an individual's ability to adapt to change (Scudder and Colson 1982). Throughout their work, both scholars have stressed the importance of adaptation and decision making, arguing that people make choices despite profound limitations on their options (Colson 1973, 1979, 1995; Scudder 1976, 1980, 1983, 1984; Scudder and Habarad 1991). Their description of old age in the Gwembe suggests that the old and young compete for resources, and the elderly are especially subject to stresses of relocation and changing social structures (Colson and Scudder 1981). They also suggest that one of the most important resources available to Gwembe Tonga is their dependents, because production, reproduction, and social relations are so closely intertwined (Colson 1960, 1971; Scudder 1962; Scudder and Habarad 1991).

With that detailed background to draw from in planning my own research, I knew that in order to explore the microdynamics inherent in relationships between family members and people living in close quarters, I would need to accept the fundamental role that conflict, big or small, plays in people's lives. In moments of conflict it is possible to see more clearly how individuals struggle with pressures of social norms and values. As a result of that conceptual preparation, I wasn't surprised during my second month living in the village when I learned that the son in a neighboring homestead, Turner, had fought with his father over a small income he had earned—a portion of which Turner's father demanded because he said his son used his oxen for drawing the load that earned Turner the income. As a result of that conflict, Turner not only moved out of his father's homestead but left the village entirely, moved to the frontier farming region, and apprenticed himself to a matrilineal cousin. By paying attention to that conflict, I learned of one strategy that a child can employ for coping with the authoritarian relationship between fathers and their children. That pattern of intergenerational relations has in fact repeated itself in numerous instances over the years I have visited with Gwembe people.

A Living Method: Participant Observation and Becoming Family

I was not surprised by the conflict between Turner and his father, and I was interested to learn that Turner resolved the issue by migrating. This was the kind of event I had hoped to discover in my research—an event in which individuals act in a way that shows me the rules and choices. Simply leaving the village, and the father, is one option for coping with conflicts over resources. Knowing some of the key events to look for, such as moments of conflict, was the beginning point in establishing my research methodology. The theoretical model I employed at the outset of my research—agency (individual action) within household economy (a kind of social structure)—shaped my research design entirely.

A core component of my research methodology, and a cornerstone of anthropological research, is participant observation. If I hadn't been living with a family in their homestead, I would certainly have missed the moment when I heard Turner and his father engaged in heated argument. Although I didn't yet understand the full content of their words—my Citonga-language acquisition required more than the six weeks of village residence I had under my belt—I understood the emotion behind the words and was able to talk with both Turner and his father, as well as with neighbors, after the passion had simmered down. If I hadn't been around to hear the incident, it might have taken me much longer to put together some of the pieces of father–son negotiations over resource access.

Living with a family in the village allowed me many opportunities to witness events and behaviors that informed my understanding of Tonga social dynamics and family interactions. And although each family in any given location has unique social dynamics, the family in whose homestead I resided was fairly representative of families in the central Gwembe.

My first visit to Kaciente's homestead came the day after my dinner of two Mosi beers and two bags of chips. As I drank my dinner in the bar of the Chipepo Guesthouse, one of the three women in the crowd approached me and began what I had come to anticipate during the week-long journey: the series of questions about my purpose in Chipepo, and the valley generally. And once again, Lady Luck played her hand. Maggie, my new friend and self-appointed assistant, was the niece of Kaciente, one of the research assistants Elizabeth Colson had worked with, and the man whose homestead she had lived in during her field visits over the past three decades. Although I had not yet decided where I hoped to live, Kaciente, along with Maxwell, whom I had met in the van ride to Chipepo, was one of the main people I planned to visit on this first journey to the village.

The day after my ten-hour sleep in the Chipepo Guesthouse, Maggie led me on the three-hour hike to Sinafala. Our first stop was her uncle's homestead, where we found Kaciente and all three of his wives along with an assortment of his nineteen living children sitting in the shade of one of the five one-room houses that made up their residence.

The Gwembe Tonga practice polygyny, the marriage system in which a man may marry multiple wives. In addition to polygyny and matriliny, mentioned already in chapter 1, the Gwembe Tonga social order is shaped by clan and lineage systems that group people into different levels of "extended families." In the case of Tonga clan membership, it is believed that everyone with the same clan identity has descended from a long-distant clan ancestor, much like the American notion that the same last name indicates some kind of kin relationship. Lineage identity involves a more defined group of people who can identify a specific ancestor (for the Tonga, traced through the female line), usually within three or four generations.

The way this social organization plays out can be seen in any homestead such as Kaciente's. Kaciente, sixty-three-years old as of 2003, has so far married five women. Since the first marriage to Malia in 1961, a marriage that is still intact, two of those marriages ended in divorce within three years. Marriages, and separations or divorces, are much more fluid in Tonga society than they are in Western societies, due in part to the matri-

Fig. 2.3. Kaciente's extremely extended family in 1995, including the author.

lineal system that allows women somewhat more autonomy than they would have in a patrilineal system in which women are more formally incorporated into their husband's family at marriage. In a matrilineal society like the Gwembe Tonga, women do not change their family identity upon marriage; instead, they remain part of their natal family throughout their lives. Thus, if a marriage poses too many difficulties, a woman can leave the marriage with relatively little penalty. The primary formal component of marriage in Tonga society is payment of bride wealth, almost always cattle along with cash, from the husband's family to the bride's family. If a marriage dissolves, a portion of the cattle payments must be returned to the husband's family. Marriage systems and bride wealth are discussed more in chapter 4 on village livelihoods. But the fact that Kaciente has divorced twice is not unusual or particularly noteworthy. Most Tonga men have had a number of significant relationships by the time they reach their senior years, and if they are lucky, some relationships will have endured so that by old age, a man still has at least one wife resident in his homestead (an issue addressed in detail in chaps. 4 and 5).

The longest-remaining marriage after that with Malia is Benedetta's. She and Kaciente married in 1972, when Benedetta was close to eighteen-years-old and Kaciente around thirty-two. Most recently, in 1989, Kaciente married Serida, when he was almost fifty and she was a mere, in comparison to Kaciente, seventeen. Because of the matrilineal and lineage/clan system, Kaciente's homestead consists of at least four distinct "families." Each wife is the household head of her own lineage (each of her children belongs to her line and not her husband's), and Kaciente himself is not a member of any of his wives' (or his children's) lineages; rather his lineage is that of his mother's family (including his sisters and brothers). The consequences of men being outnumbered by other lineages in their own homestead and the often great age difference between men and their younger wives contribute to the dynamics of securing support from relatives as men age and is discussed throughout the remainder of the book.

Over the decade I have worked with Gwembe people, I have based myself in at least seven families' homesteads, although my most permanent home was with Kaciente's family in Sinafala. Living in these various homesteads provided me with some of the most important insights I gained during fieldwork, but it also tested my patience and challenged my Western upbringing. As any fieldworker will admit, living with a family is both a highpoint and a daily struggle in the fieldwork experience. In one of his famous quips, Evans-Pritchard referred to the experience as promoting "Nuer-osis" (Evans-Pritchard 1940). By living within a family, a researcher subjects herself to "local rules" in a way that would not occur if she were living in her own house and space. Although I did have my own one-room, clay-brick, thatched-roof house within Kaciente's homestead (or tents and "base camps" in other homesteads)—so that I could have quiet time to write field notes for a few hours every day, and so that I would have a little privacy to maintain my sense of self—I was still called on as a member of the households and extended family. Also, as with any close living situation, and especially when so much of daily life takes place out of doors, "my family" had the opportunity to observe virtually all of my activities and behaviors, from teeth brushing, walking to the latrine, sitting in the shade while trying to read a book, or chatting with a visitor; sometimes I felt I was "living television."

Beyond the discomfort of having every move observed, however, there are more substantial facets of living closely with a family. Early on in my village residence, Kaciente incorporated me into his family through a fictive kin relationship. After I had spent about a week getting settled in the homestead, Kaciente began joking with me that my name was Lisa Munsaka Munsanje—a play on the name of one of his nieces living in the city, but also the name of Kaciente's clan, Munsanje, and that of his second wife, Benedetta's clan, Munsaka. As a result of that teasing, many people in the village and beyond now know me as Lisa Munsaka Munsanje, and it is believed that my matrilineal clan is Munsaka (thus I am a daughter to Benedetta) and my father is a Munsanje, presumably Kaciente. In assigning me clan identity, Kaciente incorporated me into his family, and the community in general, making me feel somewhat more a part of the village social world and also allowing me to be more easily welcomed into distant relatives' homesteads in a variety of migrant destinations. But in this incorporation, Kaciente also created official pathways that he, his family, and other villagers could use to gain access to me and my resources. And because I was "kin" I was expected to adhere to the various obligations and responsibilities inherent to kinship relations. Whether I liked it or not, I became part of the family and had to behave appropriately.[3]

Out of a sense of obligation that came with my fictive kin relationship, I have done things that I never expected would be part of my fieldwork experience. Sharing what food I have, with whomever is around, is a given, although I eat most of my daily meals with the family in whose homestead I'm living at a particular moment. I give gifts and loans of cash for the purchase of everything from a bit of tobacco for an old woman, a bit of drink for a senior man, medicine for a child, to notebooks and pens for schoolchildren. In exchange, these "extended relatives" endure my endless questions and idiotic Citonga-language constructions, tolerate my shadowing of their every move, and simply protect me as I live amid them in what must appear as a ludicrous life choice to forsake what they believe is modernity for life in their rural homes.

The most emotionally intense experience that resulted from being "kin" over the years has been helping to transport four corpses to their funerals in home villages. While retrieving the bodies from distant homes, city morgues, or the district hospital, I discovered the journeys also included carrying bereaved relatives who wail their laments continuously as we return to the village for burial. Initially, I found onerous the requests that I use my vehicle to provide transport of a corpse back to the village for burial. In a typically Western "work ethic" mentality, I thought, "I have work to do in the village; I can't just put things on hold and take fifteen hours out of my time to drive to town and back." However, after working through the initial feeling of resentment that I was being forced into a task

I didn't want to perform, I came to realize that, in addition to allowing me
the opportunity to participate in an extremely important life-cycle rite as a
family member, providing transportation was one of the most valuable
things I could offer "my family" and the community that was so patiently
putting up with my questions and presence.

That first public transport journey into the valley, and then the six-hour
round-trip hike to and from Sinafala, convinced me of two things: food
was not easily available for purchase in the valley, and public transport
barely existed (and when it did, there were issues of safety and reliability).
On that first trip to Kaciente's homestead, when I found the whole family
sitting in the shade, Malia, Benedetta, and Serida had been profoundly
generous, but I was too new to the circumstances to understand just how
generous. They cooked a meal for me that included two kinds of porridge—both cornmeal and millet—and three different sauces, including a
meat sauce from a chicken they slaughtered on my behalf. It was April, just
after what should have been the harvest. But the drought that year had
been severe, and I learned later that they had virtually no harvest at all;
thus the food they shared with me came from a quickly dwindling reserve
they had procured from selling some of their cattle. Realizing that food
was even more scarce than I originally assumed—there were no markets
where one could buy the staple foods of grain for porridge and other produce for sauces, and trying to purchase maize and produce from local
people would be almost impossible because they did not have enough for
themselves—forced me to accept that I needed a vehicle (rather than the
motorcycle I had anticipated purchasing) in order to bring food from outside the village. Owning and driving any vehicle, let alone one of the 4×4
pickup trucks that so often reek of "status symbol," was never part of my
plan for research (in fact, I had never owned a vehicle in the United
States—I was one of those "peddle power people," riding my bike to the
grocery store and laundromat). However, just as the reality of life in the
Gwembe Valley shaped the way I ask questions and apply theoretical models, the reality of food and transportation scarcity shaped the practical
issue of owning a private vehicle.

So it was, early in June 1994, after my vehicle had finally cleared customs from South Africa, and after two other return visits to Sinafala by
public transport and a borrowed vehicle, I drove into Sinafala and moved
into the little one-room house that had been built for me in Kaciente's
homestead. I was now finally, and officially, doing research.

The Asking: Theory-Driven Method

In addition to finding Kaciente and his family on that first walking visit to Sinafala, I also met Drivas "Willy" Chikuni, another Sinafala resident who would have a profound impact on my research and, indeed, on my life for at least the next year and a half. When I met Drivas on a path returning from his field, as Maggie continued my tour around the village, he greeted me politely and confidently in English. Although he had been working in his field and was hot, sweaty, and appeared rather disheveled, during that first conversation Drivas impressed me as intelligent, intuitive, and as capable of the abstract pursuits of anthropological inquiry as he was of the grounded hard work of village subsistence. As Maggie introduced me to Drivas, she explained to me their kinship relationship—he was in fact a cousin to her, the son of her mother's sister—and consequently they chatted for a few minutes about their various relatives. It was only after a bit of small talk about how I found Maggie, and what I thought of the hike to the village, that I learned Drivas not only knew of the work of Colson and Scudder but had in fact worked as the research assistant to one of the anthropologists who had worked in the valley in the late 1980s. When I learned this bit of information, I quickly put the pieces together and realized that this was one of the assistants Elizabeth Colson had mentioned to me, but who had been living in town the last time she visited. Having found yet another person on my "list" of contacts, we arranged to meet up a little later in the day and talk about my research in more detail.

That afternoon, Drivas found Maggie and me sitting with Kaciente and his family, making plans for building a small house that I could live in for the next year. With my housing arrangements under way, I moved on to talking with Drivas about acting as my translator and assistant, at least for the beginning of my time living in the village, until we knew how we worked together. Drivas's homestead neighbored Kaciente's, so it would be easy for me to find him for brief consultations as well as for the extended workday as we hiked through the village interviewing people.

The clincher for me came when Drivas began talking of the "village checklist," the census data that Colson and Scudder had given me. As it turned out, Drivas had worked with the checklist extensively in the late 1980s and knew by heart on which pages to find particular individuals and families. I was in awe. I had been working with the checklist over the past few months, so I was astounded that someone who had not seen the list in more than five years could remember code numbers and page numbers for particular individuals. I felt as though I had hit the jackpot: in approximately four hours in the village, I had settled on a family and homestead where I would live for the next year, and I had found a competent and, I hoped, reliable research assistant.

Although I always worked with Drivas in conducting interviews, walking the village, and often simply "hanging out," his role went far beyond interpreting conversations—although during the first six months or so I was virtually completely dependent on him for translating any meaningful conversations. His participation in the research was more of a partnership in discovery; I think we taught each other. He inevitably clued me in to issues and nuances of village life that I would have missed were it not for his awareness. For my part, I reinforced in him the importance of paying attention to the "who did what, where, and when," and most importantly, "why." Since the first year and a half of our working together in the mid-1990s, Drivas has taken on more of a leadership role in the Gwembe Tonga Research Project. We often depend on him to help train other village research assistants, and we still rely on his insight into village events when we aren't there to witness them ourselves. Indeed, I was lucky to find him during those first hours in the village.

With the core backing of Kaciente and his family, a small house to call my own in their homestead, and the guidance of a social science–savvy village research assistant, I built my daily routine of asking questions and collecting "data" in the village and in neighboring communities. My work schedule while in the field over the past decade always included daily hikes through the villages or towns to homesteads and fields or houses and workplaces, in search of individuals and families with whom I could discuss particular issues I've explored during particular field visits.

During my first year of residence in the Gwembe Valley, I sought out all of the 82 elderly people resident in what I called "greater metropolitan Sinafala," an area with a total population of around 960 people, and Mazulu (population approximately 420). While I considered Sinafala my full-time home, I frequently visited Mazulu for a week at a time during 1994–96, and also went in search of the migrants in Lusaka and Chikanta. My conversations with the elders, and with their families, centered on how the elderly obtained food and basic necessities, how they perceived themselves in relation to the aging process, and how they interacted with their relatives and other generations within their communities. I pursued these lines of inquiry in stages during the fieldwork period, with each stage of questions building on what had come before.

Drawing on my theoretical background, my questions and topics for exploration often started from the perspective that each household member operated independently as well as cooperatively within the domestic sphere. Consequently, when I talked to an elderly woman living with her married son, I asked her how *she* got her food that day, not how the family got food that day. Certainly, living in association with a married son influences how an elderly woman accesses resources. But assuming that because she lives with a son she will be cared for completely is naïve. In this way, the background perspectives of agency and household economy "drove" my inquiry and methodology.

In addition to the semistructured and open-ended interviews I conducted during the past decade in four regions of Zambia where Gwembe people live (I conducted approximately five hundred formal interviews over six field trips), I also gathered more quantitative information about property holdings, gift giving, and links between migrants and relatives at home. The actual data collection methods of participant observation, various styles of interviewing, and survey and quantitative measures are fairly standard in most anthropological field research. What links the method to the theory driving it is the conceptual component of the research design. A theoretically driven method is not just "doing participant observation"; it is also paying attention to particular issues, like conflict, individual action, gaining access to resources, and the like. An anthropologist exploring belief systems and meaning would be more likely to concentrate her attention on behaviors associated with taboos ("unmarried women should not straddle a log for fear of becoming sterile") or proverbs. Ideally, anthropologists will remain open to all that they see and hear—in the great tradition of our intellectual forbearers and "total ethnography." However, recent discussions in social science have recognized that capturing the vast "imponderabilia" of life (Malinowski 1961) is not practical, or possible. Consequently, these days when researchers set off for fieldwork, they take with them a mental map of their project—their research design. That mental map of the theoretical models that might inform the questions, the framework of questions, issues to pay attention to, and ways of getting at the issues make up the research design, and ultimately it assists researchers in focusing their gaze in the face of the vastness of life in another culture.

In my case, personal experiences from my own life and academic training with attention to household economy and individual agency shaped the lens through which I observed, asked, and counted. In the process of making sense of the data I collected and writing this book, I have returned to social science scholarship, picking up on the earlier models I employed but building on them with ideas drawn from political ecology and discussions of vulnerability. In the end the story I tell has emerged from the dialectical process of theory building, data collection, lived experience, reexploration of conceptual models, and facing the interpretive dilemma I mentioned in the preface of the book.

During sleepless nights in the village, lying on my steel frame cot beneath the wispy mosquito net, I often experienced a strange mental process bordering on physical sensation. While rehashing the day's conversations and the week's activities, I would feel my mind sliding "up," away from the precise conversations I had had, to a bird's-eye view of what I had learned, what I "knew." Along with the high-altitude vision, ideas about gender politics and generational strife would float by like clouds, making the vision fuzzy, and then focused again. The next morning, while drinking my tea in the moments of quiet before visitors arrived or I headed off to an interview, I would feel my mind slide "back down" and focus on what questions needed to be asked that day. The distant vision from the night before had clarified my immediate tasks, and both viewpoints shaped my days in the field. I came to refer to this recurrent mental exercise as "up and down the microscope," because it did feel at times like I was down there, on the glass slide with the observed, and then suddenly I was the observer, making sense of the dynamic patters I saw from afar. Intensive, long-term, field-based research and the subsequent analysis and write-up is not a simple linear task in which the researcher asks a list of questions chosen at the inception of the project. It is a method of inquiry that meanders through daily lives and intellectual ideas and ideally emerges as a meaningful and accurate description of life on our planet.

- Colonialism

Vulnerable.
- Scarce resources
- Fragile economy
- Poverty

- Copper

3. The Space and Time of Vulnerability

In 1956, the Gwembe Valley was a region most of us would not have chosen to live within, given its heat, its droughts and frequent famines, its endemic diseases including bilharzia and malaria, and the difficulty of communication with other regions. The Gwembe people were exposed to frequent times of hunger, to much illness, and to an appalling mortality offset only by a very high birth rate, which meant that its women spent much of their time in pregnancies whose outcome was uncertain.

Elizabeth Colson (1973, 90)

More than 10,000 people are homeless as flooding swept away homes, roads and maize crops in the hunger-stricken Gwembe district south of the capital, Lusaka, officials said. Prolonged heavy rains have also damaged electricity and telephone poles, and many roads have become impassable. Zambia was already facing huge food shortages affecting more than a quarter of the population of almost 10 million.

Reuters (2003, 6)

Meaningful and accurate description of life anywhere on the planet, let alone in rural Africa, is a daunting challenge. How can we balance the reality of the many horrible events with the beauty of human creativity and generosity? In our contemporary, highly connected global life, we see images of poor people around the world practically on a daily basis. The most vivid images coming at us through television and print media often emerge from Africa. On the eleven o'clock news we see a starving mother in Ethiopia, with a comatose baby in her lap, flies stuck in the corners of their eyes, waiting for relief food from a Mac truck that is surrounded by unruly crowds, their hands in the air grabbing anything they can. In Sierra Leone we see child soldiers, expressionless, with eyes glazed, carrying automatic weapons almost as tall as themselves. In the Democratic Republic of Congo we see bodies uncovered in mass graves and machete-wielding farmers amassing in the dusty roads that take them through the jungle-covered mountains. During the 2001 floods in Mozambique, newspapers and television news repeatedly followed the story of a woman giving birth in a tree, with a river torrent below and a rescue helicopter approaching—an ideal image for news producers—thus capitalizing on Western fascination with exotic others (woman delivering baby in tree), the spectacle of a natural disaster (the flooding and resulting refugee problem), and the drama of a rescue, all intoned with the joy of motherhood and the gift of life, despite dire circumstances.

For those of us who have had any direct experience of the world outside the comfortable life that a majority of Americans enjoy, we know that these images tell only a small part of the story. Anyone who has lived in, or worked with, or visited for more than a few days a low-income community or neighborhood, in the United States or elsewhere in the world, knows that life in those circumstances is comprised of more than what the news tells us. In the United States we know that although some low-income communities may suffer from chronic problems of drug-related crime, we also know that in those very same neighborhoods we find hardworking and churchgoing women, men, and families who help their children with homework and pride themselves on the sense of community they have established, despite the existence of the problems the media may have captured. In Africa the situation is similar. While crowds of hungry Ethiopians may chase food-relief vehicles in a refugee camp established for famine victims, in a neighboring community families may be farming and producing food for themselves, and even for the refugees.

At the same time, as those of us who have been exposed to the complexity of such lives know, these images do not tell the whole story, and although we, as informed and thoughtful individuals, try not to succumb to the drama of media visuals and storytelling, these images carry some element of truth, and they trigger awareness of problems that many Westerners would never otherwise envision. In some cases, the drama of media presentation catches the eye of someone previously unaware, who, with the general knowledge the media provides, may at least begin to realize that his or her comfortable life is not a given and that there are profound inequalities around the world that have very complicated sources. Yet if the only knowledge a person has consists of the generalized drama and stereotyping of the African region, then that knowledge is incomplete and can ultimately lead to misdirected efforts at "saving victims" and "fixing problems"—an attempt at band aid solutions that do not address underlying causes of the chronic problems.

More Than Skin Deep: Challenging Generalizations with Attention to Difference

One way to resolve the problem of broad-sweeping, generalized visions of poverty, the third world, and disaster-prone regions is to think about which people may be at greater risk of suffering from such problems. Which groups may be more vulnerable? Young? Old? Landless farmers? Herders with only particular breeds of animals? Small-business owners? Female-headed households? The types of groups to consider are almost limitless. In the past two decades, scholars, policymakers, and aid workers have increasingly devoted attention to the questions of where to find the vulnerable groups, who is at risk, and why some people may be at greater risk than others. The framework of vulnerability, emerging out of research and policy focused on environmental crises, famine, and food security, facilitates the exploration of what might have been considered in the past a poverty-stricken community or disaster-prone region without lumping everyone in the community or region into the same circumstances—thus perpetuating the problem of presenting only one generalized image.

In the 1980s and early 1990s, social scientists casting their gaze toward the developing world increasingly wrote of populations vulnerable to famine and food insecurity caused by a range of factors, including climate change, human-induced environmental change, and political turmoil (e.g., Sen 1981; Chambers 1983; Watts 1983; Blaikie and Brookfield 1987; Vaughan 1987; Berry 1989a, 1989b; Swift 1989; Watts and Bohle 1993; Blaikie et al. 1994; Scoones 1994). Over the past decade, the concept has moved beyond the boundaries of food insecurity, hunger, and famine into the terrain of health, nutrition, disease, and poverty in general (e.g., Guyer 1995; Apt 1996; Kilbride and Kilbride 1997; Peachey 1999; Coutsoudis et al. 2000; Ogunseitan 2000; Van Der Geest et al. 2000; Agot 2001; McCarthy 2001; Nomdo and Coetzee 2002).

A recent World Bank report specifically identifies the elderly as a group particularly vulnerable to poverty in general and needing the attention of health and social services specifically (World Bank 2002, 46). Adger (2000) argues that ecological and social resilience (and by association, vulnerability) are closely linked and together impact a community's ability to withstand external pressures to social systems. In these discussions of vulnerable groups and how vulnerability is created, we see that different communities, and individuals in communities, have differing capacities and tools for coping with both sudden shocks (such as political upheaval, floods, currency deflation, epidemics) and longer-term pressures that impact livelihood (such as climate change, progressive environmental decline, chronic disease). The concept of vulnerability offers us an analytical framework for unraveling the stereotypes and generalizations that so often blur our vision of real life.

In terms of theoretical modeling, Michael Watts and Hans Bohle (1993) offer a thorough discussion of factors involved in identifying and explaining vulnerable populations. In their article, Watts and Bohle argue that "vulnerability is fundamentally relational . . . and hence the space and shape of vulnerability is given by its social relations" (1993, 54). They identify three factors that structure a group's or a region's likelihood of experiencing vulnerability: entitlement, empowerment, and political economy relations. In more applied terms, entitlement refers to "command over food" or the economic capability to access enough food—that is, the economy of food production, markets, and income generation that allows people access to enough food. Empowerment refers to people's *ability* to get access to sufficient food—either through actual property rights and the ability to enforce those rights, or through other coping abilities, such as social support networks, that ensure access to sufficient food. Political economy refers to class relations and the power dynamics inherent in relating with different groups or regions. Do some groups or regions exert more power over another group or region, and consequently have more control of labor and resources, leading others to have insufficient resources and food to sustain a livelihood? According to Watts and Bohle, "the complex configurations of these three causal processes . . . define . . . a space of 'vulnerability'" (1993, 54).

Employing a framework of vulnerability allows us to move away from broad generalizations and instead examine the processes that make some groups suffer more than others. In many media reports, and increasingly in scholarly and applied studies, we see that children bear a disproportionate amount of suffering when resources are scarce. Although the elderly may not appear in the media or formal research as frequently, they too, like children as a group, tend to be more vulnerable to food scarcity and poverty because of their limited physical capacities and the likelihood that they depend more on others for their daily sustenance. By integrating the framework of vulnerability with notions of household economy in which individuals, with differing desires, abilities, and power, determine who gets which resources and how, we can better explore the reality of aging and daily life in Africa.

Making Real-Life Sense of Vulnerability

We must go beyond the scholarly discussions, development applications, and media representations and ask what it means to be vulnerable and how vulnerability is created.

In the last chapter I revealed some of my thought processes for developing my research focus: issues of household social dynamics interested me both from a personal and a scholarly point of view. As I conducted my research the ideas I had used to frame my questions shifted, swelled, dissipated, and reformulated in response to information I was gathering "on the ground." My thoughts about vulnerability as a way to discuss the reality of life in the Gwembe Valley have also meandered through my personal and scholarly consciousness in a similar way. Although I didn't employ the word *vulnerable* at the time, I have been concerned with marginalized people and poor communities since my adolescence, when I worked in an after-school tutoring program in a low-income community near my hometown in Northern California, and after college when I worked in an office of consumer protection for low-income people. In both of these instances my consciousness was raised about how variable the experience of being American, or the experience of being poor or low income, can be. Even in low-income communities, some people have choices and others do not, and people experience hardship differently depending on the range of resources at their disposal. A working single mother with a tightly knit family of siblings often fared better in terms of material and psychological well-being than did a married mother who did not possess a well-developed social network and who relied more heavily on her husband's limited income and volatile companionship. When networks are limited and choices are few, crises take their toll more acutely than when many pathways offer alternatives for coping.

Consequently, when I began exploring the concept of vulnerability, I thought of the term in relation to specific problems. When a small U.S. town loses a manufacturing company to Mexico, who suffers the brunt of the factory closing? While the town's professional elite, such as doctors and lawyers, may experience a business slowdown as a result of a decreased cash flow from the unemployed workers, their livelihood remains stable compared with that of the blue-collar workers, who virtually overnight lose all of their income. When a family of eight, whether in the United States, Africa, Asia, or Latin America, has only enough food to feed five, which family members go hungry? These are the types of problems I apply to the notion of vulnerability. Individuals in households can be vulnerable to resource shortages; communities and social classes can be vulnerable to imbalances in resource expenditures and power plays; and indeed, towns and regions can be vulnerable to market fluctuations and changes imposed from the outside. From a global perspective, nations can be vulnerable to the vagaries of the global economy.

To understand the experience of the elderly in rural Africa as a potentially vulnerable group, we need to explore the context, at both a national-global level and at the regional level, in order to see how global and regional history can converge to create a space and time of vulnerability for the old who live their day-to-day lives in rural villages.

Locating Zambia through Time

Zambia, landlocked by eight other southern central African nations, has been known by numerous names since Livingstone passed through the region in 1856 (for a map of Zambia's current political boundaries, see fig. 1.1). In the mid- and late 1800s, Europeans lumped the region with southern Africa or central Africa because most travelers arrived by trekking north from the coastal regions of the British and Dutch colonies in the south, or from the Portuguese colonies to the east and west. By the 1890s, Cecil Rhodes, a British industrialist based in South Africa who became rich from diamond mining in his new home region, was given power by the British government to stake claims, under the name of his mining company, the British South Africa Company, in new territories. In effect, a private mining company had power to extend the domain of the British Empire. Rhodes wanted to claim rights to the vast copper deposits north of the Zambezi River before King Leopold II of the Belgian Congo (deep in central Africa) or the Portuguese colonists from the east and west gained control of the region. Through the process of signing treaties with African tribal leaders and colonial powers in neighboring areas, the borders of what is now Zambia were fairly well established by the mid-1890s. Under management by the British South Africa Company, the territory became a British protectorate, known by 1897 as Northern Rhodesia. When the British officially established the region as a colony in 1923, the tri-colony area—including Nyasaland (now Malawi), and Southern Rhodesia (now Zimbabwe)—became known as British Central Africa and remained under British colonial rule until the African independence movements of the 1960s.

The approximately one hundred years of European presence in the form of industrialization and colonization of the region (and before that, at least a hundred years of slave trade and exploration) profoundly impacted all layers of society. The encounter with Europeans and their goals of exploration, extraction, and control triggered upheaval in African social, economic, and belief systems, and in many cases new forms of social organization, ownership, and management emerged in response to the European presence. These changes touched to varying degrees systems of indigenous kinship and political organization, gender dynamics both within families and within the broader society, language and belief systems, access to land and regulation of human movement across the landscape, and local economies and changing subsistence and cash-crop activities, to name only a few.[1]

The era of African independence movements (the late 1950s to 1980) signaled another series of societal changes. With independence in 1964, Northern Rhodesia became Zambia, and its southern neighbor lost its regional identifier and became simply Rhodesia until 1980, when the liberation war ended and Zimbabwe was born. Rhodes's nineteenth-century quest for minerals throughout southern Africa profoundly shaped the history and the economy of the region. Throughout the early and mid-1900s, Northern Rhodesia was the primary industrial zone of the British territories north of South Africa, while Southern Rhodesia offered vast farmlands to which ambitious and adventurous British citizens flocked with the expectation that they would feed the vast human labor force on the Northern Rhodesian Copperbelt and South Africa's diamond and gold mines. The intentional development of Northern Rhodesia as an industrially based nation and Southern Rhodesia as the "bread basket" to feed the industrial bases of southern Africa has played out ever since in the histories of these two nations, most recently seen in the Zimbabwean land redistribution crisis of 2001–3.

At independence in 1964, prices for copper on the international market were high, giving the newly formed Zambian government optimistic views of the future, as well as a GNP with which to establish top-heavy government-owned "parastatal" companies (companies run for profit, and owned and operated by the national government) and assist urban populations with fixed pricing of food staples and other necessities (Scudder 1985). Throughout the 1960s and early 1970s, national economic policies continued to favor the elite minority, urban industrial areas, and commercial farming, at the cost of the poor urban and rural majorities (Scudder 1985). These policies led many rural small-scale farmers to seek wage labor, thinking that with hard work they could earn more than they would by selling their crops at the government-fixed prices. Although town wages were not high, the government's emphasis on urban services such as medical care and education, and the availability of goods in markets and shops provided a benefit for those leaving the neglected rural areas (Ohadike 1981). In this way government structures created rural populations with few options for resource access. Using Watts and Buhl's framework for "the space of vulnerability," we see that rural populations were vulnerable to economic shocks and environmental fluctuations due to lack of entitlement—they had little control over the price of their agricultural produce. They were also made vulnerable through a political economy that favored urban dwellers (with low, fixed prices for staples and social services) over the unseen rural residents.

In 1974 when international copper prices crashed, Zambia's economy took a steep downturn, and consequently national spending for services and goods declined. At this time urban dwellers began to feel the pressure of an increasingly unstable economy. As staple goods became unavailable because of lack of foreign currency for imports, rioting became a mechanism of political expression for urban people. Rural populations adjusted to the economic downturn as they adjust to all pressures, by mobilizing survival strategies, limiting their consumption even more, and struggling along as they had during other hard times, albeit with less cash (Scudder 1993).

Reliance on a "mono-economy" of mining placed Zambia in a position of global economic vulnerability when its "entitlement" to the profits of production—revenue from copper on the global market—collapsed. Zambia then fell into the position of a struggling, poor, third world nation with a new reliance on international donors from the East and West (Scandinavian, European, North American, and Asian). While Kenneth Kaunda, president since independence, courted the World Bank and the International Monetary Fund in an effort to harness monetary and development resources, the Zambian government's commitment to demands for privatization, government restructuring, and democracy was inconsistent.[2] When Zambians protested publicly about rising prices and economic austerity, Kaunda reneged on the international guidelines and returned to subsidizing basic goods and industry. The economic fluctuations and policy flip-flopping fed continued inflation, top-heavy bureaucracies, and inefficient production in the industrial sector.

In 1991 Kaunda stepped down after twenty-seven years as the president of Zambia. He had been known informally as "president for life" following the 1973 constitution that established a one-party state, of which Kaunda was the head officer. Political unrest in the mid-1980s led to the creation of a new political organization, known as the Movement for Multi-Party Democracy (MMD); it could not be called a political party at that time because Zambia was a one-party nation. Throughout the 1980s the angry Zambian population, joined later by the MMD, called for democratic reforms, and in 1991 their efforts resulted in multiparty elections. International observers called the elections open and fair, and Frederick Chiluba, of the newly legitimate MMD party, became Zambia's second president. With a new president open to democracy and political liberalization, Zambia embarked once again on national economic and political reform guided by the World Bank and the International Monetary Fund. Since 1991 the Zambian government, under the guidelines of these donor agencies, has instituted an austere structural adjustment program (SAP) to which it has remained true (see n. 2). This commitment to the SAP, along with the involvement of Zambia's private sector, has led the World Bank to call Zambia one of the "success stories" of privatization in sub-Saharan Africa (World Bank 1996; Campbell White and Bhatia 1998).

Although in political and macroeconomic terms Zambia's structural adjustment program may be a success, the effect on the majority of the Zambian population is not so positive. During the 1990s, in the process of downsizing government, privatizing business, and increasing efficiency in those areas, the program led to the firing of formally employed Zambians as well as removal of housing subsidies, education and medical services, subsidized agricultural inputs, and guaranteed prices from which both the poor and working classes had benefited (Craig 2000; Scott 2002). Jobs became scarce, services expensive, and prices for staple goods soared. Urban dwellers who used to make a living above the poverty line found themselves in increasingly insecure positions, struggling to feed their own immediate families (*Post* 2002, 2003b). Stretching resources to provide economic support for the extended family was virtually impossible for most town residents during the mid-1990s.

In addition to the challenges of economic and political adjustments, the Zambian population, as well as most of sub-Saharan Africa, is faced with the horror of the AIDS pandemic. According to some sources, one out of every five adults in Zambia is HIV positive (United Nations Development Program [UNDP] 2001). In Zambia, and most of Africa, AIDS is transmitted through heterosexual contact. In a region where fertility, virility, and sexual activity are sources of pride, respect, social position, and often income, AIDS is a death threat for everyone, regardless of income, education, or family name. Indeed because educated and middle-class young adults travel more, and often postpone marriage until establishing a career, they have been more likely to succumb to AIDS than have subsistence farmers from rural areas, who typically marry local partners by their midtwenties. In 1994, Barclays Bank of Zambia was training twice the number of managers it expected to hire in order to assure that it would have enough qualified individuals at the end of training. Some recent studies suggest that HIV infection rates among some demographic groups in urban areas have leveled off, and there is evidence that HIV/AIDS is moving more rapidly into rural areas (UNDP 2001; Greene 2002; Population Services International 2003; Saluseki 2003). At a time when Zambia's economy is causing general hardship for the majority of the population, including the working classes, AIDS is a second blow to families, whether rural or urban based. People with HIV/AIDS, usually young adults aged sixteen to forty-five, are often the most able-bodied and productive segment of the population.[3]

Early into the twenty-first century, Zambia continues to struggle with an old problem but with a new twist—economic volatility is more tied to global systems of intervention (the World Bank and International Monetary Fund's structural adjustment programs), political maneuverings are tied to the new processes of democratization (rather than to African big-man leaders), and ever-present poverty is tied at different moments to urban and rural populations, as formal-sector jobs ebb and flow like the tides of a great ocean.

More than a decade down the road of structural adjustment in Zambia, critiques of the program suggest that the desired outcomes have not yet been achieved (Craig 2000; Scott 2002; *Post* 2002, 2003a, 2003b). Some may argue that these are still the early stages of SAPs, when the majority of people suffer the most difficult conditions as prices rise and incomes drop. As time passes, so the model predicts, the benefits of decentralizing the government and privatizing the economy with goals of political accountability, industrial efficiency, and free market competition, should trickle down to the poor majority. That trickle has not yet begun in the Gwembe. The problems of past decades have left the streambed very dry, so those at the end of the trickle, the poor majority of Zambia, will be a long time waiting. Throughout this book I discuss some of the options that people have amid these precarious living conditions.

Regional Vulnerability in Southern Province

When Zambia achieved independence in 1964, people's aspirations for improved quality of life were high. And during the postindependence honeymoon period, Zambians did in fact realize a better quality of life than they had had under colonialism. But quality of life for most Zambians began to decline in the mid-1970s when the price of copper crashed. Using a variety of measures, the United Nations Development Program documents the decline in what they call "human development." Combining measures of life expectancy, education, and per capita income to generate the composite human development index (HDI), a 2001 UNDP report states, "of the 79 countries for which HDI data are available since 1975, Zambia is the only country where the HDI value for 1997 is lower than its 1975 value" (UNDP 2001, 1). They go on to attribute this decline to the following: (1) life expectancy in Zambia dropped from fifty-five years before 1990 to thirty-seven years in 1998, due largely to HIV/AIDS; (2) approximately 15 percent of all children have no access to basic education, a figure tied both to economic conditions and household chronic illness and death; and (3) from 1976 to 1997, per capita income fell 1.7 percent, from US$451 to US$300.

While statistics and indicators should be viewed with caution, other reports and research suggest similar trajectories (Ferguson 1999; Craig 2000; Scott 2002; Saluseki 2003). In this case, the trajectory is not the result expected by residents in the developed world when they think of developing nations. The Zambian story suggests multiple patterns of nonlinear development, including falling indicators of quality of life and increasing vulnerability to global economic systems, climatic fluctuations, and disease outbreaks.

Within Zambia itself, however, regional differences create pockets of better-off and worse-off populations. At the very least, Southern Province has experienced some of the greatest climatic fluctuations in Zambia over the past two decades. Additionally, with the building of the Kariba Dam on the Zambezi River in 1958, and subsequent relocation of 57,000 valley residents, Southern Province has been a target of external interventions that impact a broad swath of the population in a way that other regions in Zambia have not been. These combinations of factors make people in Southern Province, and the Gwembe Valley in particular, extremely vulnerable to food shortages and poverty.

The middle Zambezi River valley forms Zambia's southern border with Zimbabwe. The portion known as the Gwembe Valley extends from the confluence of the Gwaii and Zambezi rivers in the southwest to the confluence of the Kafue and Zambezi rivers 230 miles to the northeast (see fig. 2.2). Descending 2,000 feet (and higher on the Zimbabwe side) from the neighboring plateau is a rugged escarpment, which levels off at the valley floor at approximately 1,500 feet above sea level. In 1958 the Central African Federation (comprised of Northern and Southern Rhodesia and Nyasaland, now Zambia, Zimbabwe, and Malawi) completed the building of Kariba Dam at the northeast end of the valley; the dam was designed to provide hydroelectric power to the Copperbelt mines and the quickly growing national capital of Lusaka. Before the building of the dam, the Zambezi River flowed through the lowest points of the valley and offered valuable bottomland for river basin agriculture, on which the valley Tonga relied for their primary subsistence. Once completed, the dam caused the Zambezi River to back up, flooding the lower regions of the valley and creating Lake Kariba, at that time the largest artificial reservoir in the world.

At the creation of Lake Kariba, 57,000 Tonga people from both the Zambian and Zimbabwean sides were relocated to higher ground, or downstream of the dam, from their original settlements along the shores of the Zambezi River. Approximately 34,000 of these people lived on the Northern Rhodesian (Zambian) portion of the floodplain. In planning for relocation, the Northern Rhodesia government hoped to move Tonga communities as short a distance as possible, attempting to keep families and villages intact. However, last-minute engineering changes resulted in a higher than expected lake level. This necessitated relocating more villages than originally planned, including more than 6,000 individuals from the central portion of the valley. This Gwembe Central population was resettled downstream from the dam to an area known as the Lusitu. In addition to settling one hundred miles downstream from their original home and families, these Tonga people found themselves living among a different ethnic group, the Shona-speaking Goba people. Many Tonga families were also geographically divided when they were forced to establish permanent homes on either the Zambian or Zimbabwean side of the lake. Before the Kariba Dam, there had been easy and regular contact across the Zambezi River, with families marrying to the other side and people farming in gardens across the river from their residence. Families were now physically cut off from many kinship and community links that had been a part of daily life.[4]

Survival and Scarcity in the Gwembe Valley

The Gwembe Valley is known throughout Zambia as a drought-prone, isolated, and impoverished region of scarcity. The difficult living conditions in the Gwembe are linked closely to the local changing environment, agricultural practices, and changing social institutions. Although the Gwembe climate and ecology have always challenged local people's food procurement strategies, the resettlement in 1958 caused additional pressures for both the Tonga and their hosts in new areas. People were forced to compete for the same limited resources, and in most cases, resettlers had access only to poorer-quality soils than their hosts had in the new areas, and than what they had had before resettlement.

Changing weather systems signify three distinct seasons in the Gwembe Valley. The rainy season, *mainza*, usually begins by late November, and rain becomes sporadic by March or April, with the heaviest rainfall in January and February. Following the end of the rains is the dry cold season, *mpeyo*, when night temperatures drop into the forties (Fahrenheit) and occasionally lower, and daytime temperatures average in the seventies. During this season the wind picks up, and dust combined with cold wind gusts make everyone suffer, particularly the old who are more sensitive to the cold. People often sleep around a fire in their clay-brick houses, which increases the risk of burns as well as respiratory and eye infections from poor ventilation. However, without the benefit of warm clothing or blankets, a fire offers much-appreciated warmth.

In mid-August, day- and nighttime temperatures begin to rise again. By October and November, nighttime lows are often in the eighties or higher, and daytime temperatures can soar to 120 degrees Fahrenheit and higher. During the hottest months, people sleep outdoors—on the ground or in raised shelters—because their houses become clay ovens during the day and retain heat until early the next morning. By sleeping outdoors, people feel whatever slight breeze may blow and avoid the smothering heat of clay-brick houses with few or no windows. According to Scudder (1962), the Tonga people divide the dry hot season into two periods, which are related to the agricultural work they perform in preparation for the rains. The first period, *cilimo*, begins when the temperatures begin to warm in August, while the second period, *kumwaka*, begins when people clear and burn the stubble from their fields and ends when the rains fall consistently (see Scudder 1962 for details of climate and environment).

Food availability fluctuates seasonally. In the middle of the rains a variety of fruits and vegetables becomes available. These are used to make the sauces that add taste and nutrition to the hearty staple, *nsima*, a porridge made from ground millet, sorghum, or maize. The meali meal, as Zambians call the ground grain, is boiled into a thick paste the consistency of heavy mashed potatoes. To help this starch slide down, people dip a small handful into a sauce, usually made from vegetables grown in gardens or gathered from the surrounding bush. When fish from the lakeshore are available, people eagerly make a sauce to supplement the vegetables, and occasionally a chicken or goat is slaughtered; when available, eggs are added to the variety of sauces eaten with nsima. Cattle are common in the Gwembe, and their milk adds another element of variety to the basic diet. People occasionally slaughter an old cow or ox for food, but they are most often considered a method of saving. The most common time for eating beef is at funerals, when families are expected to demonstrate their respect for the deceased with the resources they invest in the funeral.

As the season progresses and fresh produce from gardens decreases, particularly from August on, food availability and variety plummet. People may still have grain during this time, but supplies for sauces are minimal. By the end of the hot season, hunger often becomes acute, with both grain and sauce in short supply. From at least November until the first harvest of green mealies (fresh maize to be eaten off the cob) in February, people complain about "the hunger" (*nzala*). In addition to these annual and expected "hunger seasons," the increasingly regular drought years of southern Africa have accentuated these hunger periods so that they become "hunger years" (*mwaka nzala*). During these drought years, even the carbohydrate staple of nsima is scarce. People rely on famine foods collected from wild grains and greens, famine relief supplies from international donor agencies, and sale of their livestock to purchase grain from town.

The Gwembe has historically been a famine-prone area (Scudder 1962, 1985). Gwembe communities have adapted to these regular droughts in their use of lakeshore and tributary gardens, their livestock savings, and their complex social ties, which act as a web of support in times of need. Siamwiza (1993) describes the history of famine in the Gwembe and addresses the variety of people's coping mechanisms as well as the government's participation in the phenomenon (see also Vaughan 1987 for a description of similar practices in other regions of Zambia and in Malawi; Moore and Vaughan 1994). In later chapters I discuss details of these coping mechanisms in the Gwembe and how they relate to survival of the elderly.

Although drought and famine are not unfamiliar in the Gwembe, the frequency of these phenomena is increasing. In a good harvest year, grain supplies last until people begin to harvest again, in late February. In the past, two out of every five years were good, and two were adequate; during the other year, crops failed (Scudder 1985). In a bad year people will exist without grain supplies for three to eight months. However, if bad years come in succession, as they have in the past two decades, real hunger sets in. In at least half of the past twenty-five years, Gwembe people have produced less than their needs demand for the year, and in 1992, 1994, 1995, and 2002 the Gwembe Valley suffered the worst four droughts on record. Decreasing rains and rising temperatures for southern Africa have been linked to global warming and El Niño, which influences climates across the globe (Gantenbein 1995; Dilley 2000; Oba, Post, and Stenseth 2001; Anyamba, Tucker, and Mahoney 2002).

Land degradation, changing social institutions, and localized overpopulation also contribute to decreasing food security and conditions of scarcity in the Gwembe. Before construction of Kariba Dam, the Gwembe population was estimated at 86,000 people, with a population density of approximately eight residents per square mile (Scudder 1962). Of these, 52,000 lived on the Zambian side of the river. Upon resettlement, some communities were forced into population densities three times the density of their previous communities (Scudder 1985), and by 1987 the Zambian population of the Gwembe Valley was approximately 125,000 (Scudder and Habarad 1991). Although portions of the Gwembe remain forested and uninhabited, some areas, especially land close to the lakeshore or tributaries, have become densely populated. Lack of water in the less-populated uplands, which are distant from natural springs and river tributaries, is the primary problem that prevents people from dispersing.

Fig. 3.1. One of the agricultural fields that has been in use since relocation in 1958. In 1995, with the severe drought, the field produced no wild grasses, let alone a crop of maize or millet.

Relocation to distant farming areas on the plateau where rain and virgin soil are plentiful has become the most common choice for those farmers who do not want to struggle with the Gwembe Valley's harsh conditions.

Farming practices in these conditions contribute to the stress on productive resources. When the river communities were moved from the alluvial plains, they were forced to rely on rain-fed agriculture, thus removing one of the primary options for coping with drought: dry-season river gardens irrigated by hand. With control of tsetse fly in the Gwembe, emphasis on ox-drawn plows increased and allowed for cultivation of larger tracts of land. This change in agricultural production, in conjunction with growing populations, which limited field rotation and fallowing, hastened the decline of soil fertility and increased erosion.

In addition, many ritual activities and beliefs, such as neighborhood rain shrines and prophets, were decreasing in popularity since the resettlement (Scudder 1962; Colson 1971). These institutions had influenced the communal management of land and agricultural practices. Ritual leaders coordinated a community's use of natural resources; they also initiated agricultural activities such as clearing fields, planting, and harvesting, and the community was expected to comply. These leaders also directed village resettlement when crop yields at old sites declined (Scudder 1962, 115). Resettlement to new areas drastically changed people's link to their land, resulting in decreased importance, and effectiveness, of the ritual institutions and their leaders. People increasingly preferred to make independent decisions about planting, pest control, field rotation, and use of wild resources (Colson 1971). As recent research suggests, the combined effects of decline in community integration and community institutions, not simply population growth, contribute to land degradation (Agrawal 1995; Turner 1995; Gibson, McKean, and Ostrom 1996).

Seasonal scarcity and periodic famine years were familiar to Gwembe communities. However, the changing relationships of these communities to their environment, global processes of climatic change, and socioeconomic processes all contribute to the increasing hardship of daily life and the vulnerability of much of the Gwembe population. It is in this context of vulnerability that Gwembe people make their living.

The Creation of Gendered Vulnerability in Old Age

In addition to increasing the vulnerability to environmental crises and economic upheaval for the majority of Gwembe people, processes of the relocation affected different groups of people in very specific and meaningful ways. Although the old suffered more than the young at the time of relocation, a number of other factors tied to changes in farming practices, changes in value of land, increased preferences for cattle, and particularly changing differential access to resources ultimately resulted in different kinds of vulnerability for older women and men.

In discussing old people's experience of vulnerability in southern Zambia, we need to recognize differences in women's and men's resource base, styles of interaction, and repertoire of coping strategies, all of which influence their well-being. Part of grasping the range of elderly experience of vulnerability requires exploring how a matrilineal social system establishes who is family and who is not, rules of property ownership and inheritance, and notions of duties, rights, and responsibilities toward family members. In the following sections I offer the history of changes in access to fundamental resources that impacted old women and old men in meaningful ways. In these discussions, the matrilineal backbone of Tonga social systems remains a strong force in how people strategize. But at the same time, contrary to textbook kinship models, the way people negotiate relationships within the matrilineal scheme draws on creative and independent choices that often challenge the tidy matrilineal kinship model.

Some of the changes we see in resource access, coping strategies, and styles of interaction come about when people push the boundaries of their kinship system to their own benefit and in order to enact a sense of control over processes that spiral endlessly out of reach. By providing the history of these changes, I set the stage for the discussion in the remainder of the book, which focuses on the differing strategies of women versus men in how they negotiate their relationships with their family and their communities. Because of women's increasing alienation from important material resources, they have developed highly creative social strategies for securing their well-being as they age. Older men, on the other hand, have managed to accumulate wealth as they age, which they can then translate into resources for old-age support. But in order to explore the range of strategies men and women employ for securing old-age support, we should first understand an important component of history that contributed to the development of these differential gendered strategies.

The Changing Value of Land

Before the forced relocation of the Gwembe Tonga people, the majority of the population farmed on the alluvial soils of the Zambezi River, using the horticulturalist technology of handheld hoes and digging sticks. Cereal crops (predominantly millet and sorghum, but increasingly maize), vegetables, and tobacco made up most of their crops.

On portions of this land, both dry- and rainy-season harvests were possible. Alluvial gardens on the riverbanks maintained their fertility over time because of annual flooding and generally allowed two harvests a year. Consequently, these riverbank gardens were highly valued. Corporate matrilineages held communal access rights to this land, but individuals within lineages and clans often competed for the same land, particularly as the population grew. Colson and Scudder document many dramatic stories of witchcraft and murders attributed to disputes over land from that time period (Colson 1960, 1963, 1964a; Scudder 1962, 1969).

In the 1950s, a few men began clearing bush areas so that they would have larger fields, which they planned to plow with oxen. These fields allowed for more extensive cultivation of bulrush millet and also solved the problems of decreasing fertility of some fields and population increase (Colson 1960, 1971; Scudder 1962). In contrast to the alluvial gardens that did not require clearing, these "bush fields" required extensive woodland clearing. The men who cleared them had rights over the land. Upon a man's death, the matrilineal inheritor of the man's property expected to claim rights to the land. The sons of a man's brothers and sisters were the most common matrilineal inheritors of a man's fields (and of his property for that matter).

The same matrilineal inheritance distribution occurred with river land, except that whereas only men had rights to the large cleared fields (because they had done the work of clearing), women as well as men had rights to the alluvial gardens, and daughters and sisters as well as sons and brothers could inherit these riverside gardens (Colson 1966). In the Tonga inheritance system, men are primary inheritors of men's property, and women usually inherit from women. The growth in bush fields meant that men gained access to land that women had little chance to inherit or clear on their own, and men continued to be the primary inheritors of that land.

After relocation in 1959, the imbalance in women's and men's access to land increased; the preference for ox-drawn plows increased also because people were forced to rely more heavily on cleared fields. Most women depended on their husbands for fields and plows in the new location, rather than clear bush themselves and plant such large areas with a hoe (Colson 1999a). In effect, the Tonga agricultural system changed almost overnight. Close to 60,000 people replaced intensive agriculture on alluvial soils with extensive farming on fields cleared from the bush, using ox-drawn plows.

Communities that resettled close to the lake dug gardens along the lakeshore. Some of the older women informants described to me how they "grabbed" garden plots next to the lake when they found them and used the familiar hoe to plant. However, because the lake level can change unexpectedly due to variability in rainfall and inconsistent water releases downstream, these lakeshore gardens, although more fertile than their counterparts on higher land, can be precarious. With little warning, a rising lake will drown grain seed, and a retreating shoreline can reduce the groundwater table, thus drying out germinating seeds. These days people rely more on rainy-season fields, cleared from the bush and ploughed with oxen, for their subsistence. Shore gardens, usually planted by women, are most often used during the dry season to grow the vegetables that supplement sauces eaten with the carbohydrate staple.

Although Tonga are matrilineal, and inheritance ideally follows through the matrilineage (*mukowa*), there is also a patrilineal link (*lutundu*) between fathers and their children that provides the basis on which a father claims his sons' and daughters' labor. This link also allows children to make claims to their father's property upon his death and inheritance of his property. Since relocation, the tendency to inherit from fathers has increased, particularly since the passage in 1989 of the new inheritance laws, which give children and wives more legal access to a deceased man's property. The fact that the men who cleared the fields from the bush in the resettlement areas owned those fields facilitated this transition to patrilineal inheritance. Children could expect to inherit land from their fathers because the fathers held original, and individual, rights to that land. However, the rights to land could fall to the clan if a man died without allocating the fields he cleared to his children before his death.

In addition to increased reliance on large, rain-fed fields and an increasing tendency to inherit from fathers, the growing reliance on cattle and plows for farming accentuated the ties children have to their father. A father depends on children's labor in his fields. In exchange he gives them land and lets them use his plow and oxen for their own farming. The increasing importance of huge cleared fields made plows and oxen critical resources for farming, so young men were willing to work for their father in exchange for access to farm implements. In effect, the role of patrilineal ties grew in importance, as plow farming became the norm. This echoes other Africanist scholars' work suggesting that matrilineal societies often rely on hoe farming, whereas patrilineal societies are plow based (Murdock 1949; Goody 1976; Schneider 1979).

Most adult women did not have their own fields after relocation both because clearing the bush demanded male labor and because local gender perceptions allowed women to expect that husbands would provide fields. Although a woman could gain access to land through her husband, both before and after resettlement, a field was not allocated to her as owner but merely as a wife farming on behalf of her husband (Colson 1999a, 32). Upon the death of a man, relatives can challenge his wife's right to use his land. A son can claim his father's land on behalf of his mother, but if there are no sons present to help a mother, she risks losing access to the fields completely. In these cases, an old woman becomes dependent on her kinsmen and community for productive land.

One elderly widow in Sinafala village told me about her annual practice of "begging" for land from different relatives and villagers, four years in a row. She said that people were willing to lend her a field once in a while, but that after she had used the field for one year, the owner would say, "oh, I'm going to plant that field this year," and they would tell her to ask someone else for land. Her two sons lived in the capital city, and without their support, she had little help in advocating for extended use of any land.

Over the past four decades, men have continued to clear new fields because of the decreasing fertility of the land originally cleared at resettlement. Gwembe people do not use fertilizer on their fields, but they do have a good sense of how long particular fields require fallowing in order to restore fertility. However, fallowed fields are vulnerable to requests for use from kin and neighbors. For this reason, men are likely to keep rights to older fields, whether fallowing or not, which they can lend to relatives, including children, wives, aunts, and cousins. One result of continually clearing new land while simultaneously farming old fields is the increasing loss of soil fertility and the growing problem of erosion, which can be seen as one walks through the village and surrounding areas (Cliggett 2001; Petit, Scudder, and Lambin 2001). The changing environment plays a part in the current role of land in the Gwembe.

In the past, land was highly valued, and conflict over land was common. Today in some communities that have no remaining woodland to clear, land is still worth fighting for. Colson (2000) tells of a recent death caused by witchcraft between two half-brothers over rights to an unclaimed field. But conflicts like this are not as frequent as they used to be, particularly in Sinafala, where some virgin woodland remains.

During my visits of the past decade, people have repeatedly told me that land is not as important as it was when they first settled in the relocation areas. Village fields have become less productive over time because of overuse and erosion. In some cases young men don't want their father's fields because they are too small for their dreams of cash cropping. When villagers decide they want new fields, they either clear a bit of remaining woodland or migrate to the frontier, where they can claim up to a hundred hectares of virgin woodland.

Unless they are clearly high quality, rainy-season fields in the village have become less and less desirable to new generations of farmers. For communities in which land used to be highly valued and desired, these changes suggest that the importance of village land has decreased. The increasing presence of development aid in the Gwembe Valley (usually in the form of food handouts), people's well-developed ability to plead for food assistance from relatives and neighbors who have a surplus, and the possibility of selling cattle in order to buy food offer Gwembe people a range of options for obtaining at least a minimal amount of their food staple. The energy to extract a small harvest from poorly producing fields may in fact be equal to the energy and cost expended in mobilizing food from other sources. In this way, then, rights over land in the Gwembe these days do not guarantee a secure, reliable, and sufficient food base. For these reasons, and unlike the generations before them, young adults have told me they were no longer concerned about land inheritance. During the past ten years, when I asked people what they hoped to inherit from elders now, they all agreed: they want cattle.

The Importance of Animals

Owning animals is both an investment strategy and a symbol of wealth for Gwembe Tonga people. This point became clear to me when I learned that many people in Sinafala do not view one of the local shopkeepers as wealthy. Jackson has two wives, which is a sign of prosperity, children in secondary school, a cinder-block home, and at least three small businesses, which he runs out of his home. In my subjective opinion, Jackson is very well off; he has a steady income, and he could feed and clothe his family better than most other villagers could during the drought of 1994–95. But he did not have any cattle at the time of my fieldwork. For this reason, I was told, Jackson is not a wealthy man. Although cattle don't provide a regular income, like a business would, they do provide security for financial emergencies, including the purchase of food when needed and a respected social position.

All Tonga desire cattle, but access to animals is not equal. Women and young people experience more difficulty in accumulating cattle than do older men. This is largely the result of the bride-wealth system, which gives the majority of cattle to the father of a girl, and the men's historical wage-earning possibilities, which gives men access to cash with which to buy cattle.

In the current bride-wealth system of the Gwembe Tonga, husbands increasingly make payments in cattle, most of which goes to the father of the girl. In the past, such as during the period when Colson and Scudder first began research in the Gwembe Valley, bride-wealth payments were divided more equally between the matrilineage and the father of the girl who was marrying, with the matrilineage often receiving the major part, at least in some regions of the valley. However, at that time, the payments included symbolic gifts such as a hoe and cooking utensils as well as a small number of goats or chickens. A maternal uncle to the girl (a brother of the girl's mother) usually received the lineage portion of the payment. In the

Fig. 3.2. A herd of cattle at the time of a wealthy man's inheritance. While the primary inheritor selected the majority of the best cattle, other relatives waited on the sidelines for a chance to benefit by at least one head.

1960s, when cattle became a more common part of the bride-wealth payment (although the number of cattle was still small—between one and three head), a tradition of a more equal distribution between the girl's matrilineage and her father was strengthened. However, by the 1980s, the imbalance between the father's and the lineage's shares of cattle was well under way, as was the inflation of payments. By then, four cattle were commonly required for full payment, plus increasing sums of cash.

According to field notes from Colson's files, a few men in the 1990s explained their argument that a father should receive more of the payment than the lineage because he ate only once, from the daughter, whereas the matrilineage would continue to collect bride wealth from that woman's daughters. Thus, to be fair, according to these older men, if a young man paid six cattle to marry a woman, her father should receive four of those cattle, and the majority of the cash, while the lineage should receive only two cattle and a token portion of the cash. During the 1990s this imbalance of payments was considered the norm, with the maternal uncle still receiving the lineage portion. However, in the late 1990s a few mothers began receiving the share that would have gone to a mother's brother, largely because mothers have increasingly taken on the specific matrilineal burden of assisting a young man in obtaining cattle to make the payments. In the past, it was the maternal uncle who gave the most assistance to a young man hoping to mobilize cattle and cash for marriage payments, and uncles consequently claimed the "profits" when their matrilineal nieces married. With mothers taking on the responsibility, they are more able to claim rights over the payments made when their daughters marry.

In addition to the recent changes in which mothers assist sons in making marriage payments, fathers have also begun to assist their sons. Since the 1990s, it is more common to hear that a father has assisted his son in making bride-wealth payments, particularly for his first marriage. This is especially true if the son has worked for his father extensively.

As all of these details demonstrate, the content and amount of payment have changed over time, as have the division of payments among recipients and the assistance that young men may receive. Such dynamic shifts in important institutions like marriage arrangements indicate that, indeed, following a population and systems through time provides the best information on how people adapt and trigger new social and cultural forms.

Nevertheless, even with the changes in who helps make payments and which representatives of the matrilineage receive a portion of the payments, the system is somewhat unbalanced; fathers can increase their cattle herds by three to five animals through the marriage of a daughter. Mothers and their brothers may receive one or two cows for the same marriage. At the same time, fathers infrequently help their sons with marriage payments, but mothers and their relatives are expected to assist a young man if possible.

In contrast to men's ability to accumulate cattle quickly, women usually obtain cattle through inheritance or as a gift from a matrilineal relative. Brothers can give a woman a cow as his investment toward a marriage payment of his nephews (the woman's sons). These days it is more common for a mother to be given a share of the marriage payments for her daughter, so that the options for women acquiring cattle may be increasing. But for the population of senior women during the mid- to late 1990s, obtaining cattle has been difficult throughout their lives.

In effect, men have more, and more lucrative, options for accumulating cattle than do women. In Sinafala during mid-1995, senior women (those above age fifty-five) on average had fewer cattle than did men of the same age group (table 3.1), and women also had fewer goats (table 3.2). In addition, homesteads with any resident man over age fifty-five had more cattle and goats than did homesteads with women but no men over fifty-five (table 3.3).

What does ownership of animals mean to daily life in the village? Cattle owners are respected within their community, and they have a secure savings account. I saw distinctions made within the village in the various types of assistance offered to respected women versus women who were pitied for their poverty. When I noticed one young man giving one aunt only a plate of meali meal but giving her sister a whole bucket of maize, he explained to me that the first aunt was poor, and he gave her that plate out of charity. The other aunt, a relatively wealthy and respected woman, had the potential to help him in the future, so he was willing to give her more maize now. This example supports the argument that material resources influence who supports who in the village; the change in the value of land and cattle plays a significant role in who has access to what resources.

TABLE 3.1
Cattle ownership in Sinafala, by gender

	Women (%)	Men (%)
Total population (age 55+)	33	10
No. who owned cattle	13 (40)	0
No. who owned more than one head of cattle	20 (60)	10 (100)
Average no. of cattle per capita	4	8

Source: 1955 data.

TABLE 3.2
Small livestock ownership in Sinafala, by gender and animal

	Women (%)	Men (%)
Total population (age 55+)	33	10
Goats		
No. who owned goats	24 (73)	6 (60)
No. who owned more than one goat	9 (27)	4 (40)
Average no. of goats per capita	5	10
Chickens		
No. who owned chickens	14 (42)	8 (80
No. who owned more than one chicken	19 (58)	2 (20)
Average no. of chickens per capita	10	4

Source: 1995 data.

TABLE 3.3
Homestead animal holdings in Sinafala, by gender and animal

	Women (%)	Men (%)
Total no. of homesteads with one resident age 55+	28	10
Cattle		
Homesteads with any cattle	24 (86)	10 (100)
Average no. of cattle per homestead	9	14
Goats		
Homesteads with any goats	15 (54)	6 (6)
Average no. of goats per homestead	9	12
Chickens		
Homesteads with any chickens	25 (89)	9 (90)
Average no. of chickens per homestead	12	12

Source: 1995 data.

The Land-for-Cattle Exchange

As I've described, after relocation, land started to lose value. At the same time, cattle ownership increased and became one of the major local currencies. These changes occurred from the late 1960s into the 1970s. Most of my informants agreed that by the end of the 1970s and early 1980s, cattle ownership was the number one source of wealth and desire for land was not so frequently an area of conflict. The exception is ownership of lakeshore or tributary fields that still exist in some communities; the fertile soil of the lakeshore and riverbank fields makes them highly desirable and worth an argument.

Two of the major differences between land ownership and cattle ownership are mobility and gendered access. Cattle, a highly mobile form of property, can be hidden, sold for cash, and given to relatives and friends nearby and far away. In fact it is common practice to distribute your herd of cattle among relatives in different regions as part of risk management in drought-prone regions. Additionally, what makes cattle accumulation possible at all are communal grazing lands. People do not need their own land in order to graze cattle but rather access to the communal lands that everyone can use for animal grazing. In Gwembe villages, some areas are set aside specifically for cattle grazing, especially along the lakeshore, where the unpredictability of the lake levels makes planting a precarious option, and along small tributaries or areas in which soils are known to be poor for farming. After fields are harvested, young boys herd cattle through them, where the animals eat the grain stubble and other wild plants that grow among the main crop. Although herding cattle requires access to land, the necessary land does not require the same type of fertility as does land for farming, which makes cattle accumulation a logical adaptation when farming lands decline in quality.

Other benefits of cattle ownership include issues of conflicts that may arise over who should donate animals for slaughter at a funeral. A man who has spread his herd out among a number of relatives in different areas will be more able to claim poverty because the community will not know exactly how many animals he truly owns, and thus he can avoid obligation to slaughter more animals than he feels is his share. The ability to keep your wealth somewhat hidden is a primary benefit of animal ownership.

Animal ownership can include other benefits: income can be garnered from the sale of milk or the rental of an animal for plowing, and loan of an animal can encourage the establishment of support networks and cooperative relationships over distance. A number of men in Gwembe villages periodically give an ox to a brother or cousin in one of the distant frontier farming areas to help with plowing. The frontier area has frequent outbreaks of cattle-borne diseases, so maintaining a herd in that region is impractical. But using one or two cattle at a time permits completion of farming tasks without risking loss of a herd. And in the sharing of the cattle, brothers reaffirm their supportive relationship. That relationship often benefits the cattle owner in the form of food assistance during droughts and poor harvests. Because of better rainfall patterns and good soils, the frontier region produces a larger and more reliable harvest. Gwembe villagers with links to the frontier know they have a form of insurance through those relationships, and providing use of cattle strengthens those links.

In contrast to cattle, land is fixed in location and, in effect, fixed in social relations. Land, although used and managed by individuals, belongs to a broader group of relatives—usually the matrilineage. Land should not be sold for cash or given for permanent use to someone outside the defined kin group, although it occurs and is disguised as "sale of improvements" such as clearing. A particularly disturbing exception to this rule is the increased sale of valuable lakeshore land by chiefs to outsiders, such as Afrikaners or Europeans, for commercial development, including fishing enterprises, crocodile farms, and tourism. In the past, Zambian law prohibited sale, rental, or mortgage of communal land. However, under new legislation, an individual can have a plot of land within a communal area surveyed and receive a title deed, making the plot subject to the laws applied to land outside of communal areas. With this new legislation, a chief does not actually sell a plot of land to an individual, whether an outsider or a subject; rather, the chief can allocate a plot, which the recipient can pay to have surveyed and then purchase a title deed from the government. In such instances, the chief is likely to have received a nice gift for his assistance in allocating land, but technically his involvement is not considered a sale.

Aside from this kind of alienation, for the most part land remains in the hands, and in the sight, of owners and users. Land cannot be hidden when conflicts erupt over use or wealth, and land cannot be used to establish insurance networks over long distance.

The other key difference between land and cattle is women's versus men's access to these resources. Over the last forty years, women's access to cattle has been limited by a male-focused bride-price system, lack of significant cash-earning options (compared to those available to men, which include migration to find wage-earning jobs, the ability to grow cash crops, and the control of resettlement compensation payments), and gendered inheritance practices that keep cattle in the hands of men. In contrast, before relocation, women had relatively open and equal access to land that was highly valued. In contrast to Schneider's (1979) argument that land-based societies are more hierarchical than cattle-based societies, the Gwembe Tonga scenario suggests that the transition from wealth in land to wealth in cattle fostered gender inequality and increased hierarchy.

In this cattle-for-land exchange, increasingly men own cattle, and owning cattle is increasing in importance for both wealth and status. Land, which used to be a source of women's wealth and status, has lost both its real and perceived value: land is losing fertility, and young people do not value it in the same way that their parents did.

If we consider what these differences in resource accumulation mean for an older person trying to mobilize support from a child or nephew, we see that older men have the material advantage. In Caldwell's (1982) study of intergenerational resource flows, he suggests that it is the potential to inherit from a parent or other elder that motivates young people to provide support. Among the Gwembe Tonga, children typically stand little chance to inherit much wealth from their mothers but potentially quite a bit from a wealthy uncle or these days, with changes in inheritance systems, from a wealthy father.

As of the late 1990s, the majority of Gwembe women aged fifty-five and older did not have easy access to cattle or other forms of substantial material wealth with which to influence their personal relationships. However, with changing patterns in bride-wealth payment and inheritance, younger women in the Gwembe may have more options for cattle ownership throughout their lifetimes, which consequently will improve their ability to control important material wealth by the time they reach their senior years. As the opportunities for women to control property increase, certainly their options for mobilizing social networks will also change, raising the possibility for new styles of gendered strategies of elderly support that will deserve additional investigation.

Ultimately, the analysis of historical changes in access to resources suggests that senior women exist in a much more vulnerable space than do senior men. Returning to the Watts and Buhl (1993) framework, we see that senior women have been made more vulnerable than men through all three of the relational processes Watts and Buhl outline. Simply through age and decreased physical ability, women (and many older men) do not participate in food production, marketing, and income generation—things that would ensure their entitlement to food and material security. Because of lack of material resources with which to bargain, senior women are less empowered than men to negotiate for that food and material security. Gwembe people generally, as inhabitants of a rural and difficult-to-reach region, and Gwembe women in particular, as a group that has little access to wage employment and systems of regional and national governance, have less power in the systems of political economy that shape resource availability both locally and regionally.

Despite women's very marginal "space" in terms of resource control and access, they have found extremely creative ways to negotiate their relationships with children, relatives, and neighbors in an effort to ensure their security as they age. Examining the outcomes of differential access to wealth in men's and women's later life reveals important understandings of the life cycle, extended family support systems, and the creativity inherent in women's and men's negotiations within their social networks. In later chapters I explore the various arenas in which these gender differences in intergenerational relations play out.

Tying It All Together: A Framework for Exploring Aging and Vulnerability in Africa

By identifying differences (gender, class, generational, or historical differences) in the face of generalizations, i.e., poor and disaster prone, we develop a much more complicated, insightful, and reality-based understanding of our world. In the last chapter I suggested that anthropological fieldwork aims at producing meaningful and accurate descriptions of life on our planet. In the case of my work, I aim to reveal the complexity of aging and family relationships in conditions of scarcity as a way of deconstructing stereotypes of poverty in Africa. A framework that integrates notions of individual agency and household economy with an analytical focus on vulnerable populations provides a toolbox of theoretical concepts that give broader meaning to the basic events and behaviors I witnessed. Theory is, after all, a tool to assist in explaining the reality of lived experience.

As this chapter suggests, however, understanding contemporary reality requires acknowledging the history that helped to create current circumstances. Zambia has been incorporated into the global political-economic systems for at least the past two hundred years, through trade, exploration, and resource extraction. The relations of that political economy have always placed Zambia in a precarious position in relation to more capital-heavy and power-filled nations or political bodies. Zambia's industrialization, which privileged a mono-economy based on copper extraction, perpetuated the nation's vulnerability in the global sphere. Within Zambia, the case of the Gwembe Valley in Southern Province offers an extreme example of how outside forces can trigger a cascading series of changes that lead to the exaggeration of some group's vulnerability as compared to others. The marginalization of Gwembe women over the past forty years from important material resources has resulted in their need to develop alternative strategies of securing support as they age—strategies that do not depend on control over wealth or property.

When we give close attention to the various ways different groups of people negotiate their day-to-day lives at the local level, we challenge the media's tendency to portray poverty as affecting everyone in a community, or region, in the same way. Poverty affects different people in different ways, and some are better able to cope than others. Once we, as educated and concerned Westerners, realize that very real differences exist in how people respond to stress and external pressure (whether droughts, economic crises, development projects, or international relief aid), we will be better prepared to offer useful assistance or simply to better acknowledge people's capacities to withstand and overcome adversity.

The remainder of this book explores a range of arenas in which senior men and women negotiate their relationships with relatives and neighbors in an effort to secure their own well-being, in a region where food and scarcity of resources are the norm. The differences in women's and men's styles of interaction give insight into both the history of gender differences in access to resources as well as the gendered nature of intergenerational relations in rural Africa.

4. Making a Village-Style Living

I once planted cotton. My husband said I could try to plant, but he wouldn't let me use his animals [for plowing]. So I planted by hand, and I got ten bags of cotton. But my husband had planted [cotton] using his animals, and he also got ten bags.... So he was jealous and told me that I shouldn't be planting for myself, and that I should help him in his fields.

Belinda, August 1995

Whenever I meet people from other regions of Zambia and explain that I conduct research in the Gwembe Valley, and with people who have moved from the valley to other places, the responses are almost always the same: "Ahk, the Gwembe Valley, that is a rough place. There is always hunger there, and the people are very backward. Why do you go there? It would be much better to work in a more civilized place like . . ." and inevitably they mention their own home region, or a town along the main roads, as a much more hospitable location in which to base myself. For Zambians in general, almost all of whom have had to cope with volatile economies and climates themselves, the Gwembe Valley carries the stereotype of a harsh environment, where making a living is even more challenging than in other places. Zambian newspapers and radio briefings regularly carry stories about rains failing, floods washing away a year's harvest, disease outbreaks, people starving, and relief food being insufficient for the valley residents' needs.

Although the stereotypes and prejudice are often painful to hear, both for me and the Gwembe people who must listen to these perceptions each time they venture from their homeland, there is some element of truth to the headlines. As the previous chapter explained, rains do fail regularly, and those failures seem to be increasing. Floods do occur, washing away crops and roads. With poor infrastructure such as washed-out roads and bridges, people do experience isolation, compared with the intense activity of big towns and markets that exist along main thoroughfares. And of course, where infrastructures are poor, education also suffers. Schools are few and far-flung, and resources such as books, paper, and pens are nonexistent. Teachers' salaries throughout Zambia are not sufficient to sustain a lifestyle that some perhaps imagined for themselves. And teachers posted to a rural village in a region like Gwembe, where roads are bad and transportation is lacking, may be unable to easily retrieve their meager paycheck. Teachers in the bush regions north and south of Chipepo, and into the hills from the lakeshore, often leave their post for a full week, due to transportation difficulties, in order to pick up their monthly paycheck in town and purchase supplies. During their absence students may attend school, but often they spend their time weeding another teacher's field, or they double up in another classroom, where a lone teacher may attempt to guide students of vastly different levels through a math lesson.

In a setting such as this, where climates are unpredictable and the local economy does not offer many options for vibrant livelihoods, people must develop a variety of techniques for piecing together their sustenance. The broader context of the local economy influences the ability of elderly people to secure their material well-being, and consequently we must explore the range of livelihoods available to Gwembe people in general. Middle-aged men, those above the age of forty, have usually accumulated cattle over time and are willing, though often reluctant, to sell off their herds and other small stock, such as goats, when a food crisis is acute, or for particular cash needs. Older women with animals will also sell a goat or a chicken in order to buy maize meal for her family. Younger people usually do not have such resources and frequently opt for migration and wage labor in town or in rural agribusinesses.[1] Increasingly, young and middle-aged adults migrate to frontier farming areas, where the land is more fertile and the rain more plentiful. When life in the home village seems tenuous, migration appears to be a logical choice.

But relocation is only one option for coping with the stresses that the local ecology poses. Flexibility of social systems and the creativity of individuals have proved to be, as anthropology has shown, the most effective and enduring facets of human survival. As Netting (1981, 1993; Netting, Wilk, and Arnould 1984) described in his work in both West Africa and Switzerland, social groups adapt and change in response to their surroundings, both environmental and human (see also Colson 1979, and Colson and Scudder 1988, for Gwembe examples). His ethnographic and theoretical work demonstrates that household units in particular are sustainable social groups because they adapt and respond to changing conditions (Netting 1981, 1993).

A focus on the household as the smallest unit of analysis may give the impression that household members operate with common goals. However, individuals within the unknown "black box" of the household often compete with each other for resources and employ varying strategies to achieve their differing goals, as the description of women's alienation from valuable property in the last chapter demonstrates (Dwyer and Bruce 1988; Wilk 1989, 1991; Netting 1993). In the case of Gwembe elderly, the social mechanisms employed to cope with limited resources are vastly different from those of other age groups, and women employ different strategies than men. These differences can be seen in agricultural and income-generating activities, residential arrangements, socializing, and invocation of traditional beliefs.

This chapter explores the resource base and economic activities from which Gwembe people generate their day-to-day livelihoods. In addition to ownership of important resources, all Gwembe villagers have access to a range of small cash-generating options. Government assistance and wage employment also play roles in providing villagers with cash and basic necessities. All of these resources can be used by individuals and families to increase their security when times are rough. The ways people use these different resources reflect their gender and their generation, as well as their social networks and their capacity to negotiate relationships to their own benefit. But before discussing how women and men, old and young, use resources to ensure their social security, we need to see the range of methods of income generation available to Gwembe people.

The Illusive Market

Gwembe people identify themselves as farmers. But when rains fail and fields don't produce harvests, they get busy (or rather, busier) and find ways to get by until the next year. Old women and children will collect famine foods, such as the grains from grass I described in the first chapter, when the need arises. Other villagers will collect on old debts, start petty trade, or hand irrigate a small lakeshore garden in order to sell vegetables.

Gwembe people are indeed farmers, but they have always engaged in a variety of nonfarming activities, and investment in those activities expands and shrinks depending on the moment in time. Gendered differences in activities are to be expected, and the outcomes of the gender divisions ultimately impact women's and men's material security as they move through their lives.

During my first visits to villages in the Gwembe, I was surprised that there appeared to be no system of markets where local people met to sell their produce and supplies, and to buy things not available in their own area. In other rural areas of countries or regions where I had worked or visited, including Haiti, Mexico, other parts of the Caribbean and Central America, and also the Middle East, a market often rotated village locations throughout a rural district on a weekly basis—each day the market taking place in a different village. It seemed an efficient way for people to exchange goods not available to them in their own village and to earn a small income from their own produce. These markets also facilitated socializing and business communication. I was astonished to learn that the Gwembe had no such system of rotating markets. How did people get food that grew in other places? How did they get town-produced cooking supplies? How did they maintain communication with other regions? The absence of a formal market system led me initially to the impression that Gwembe people were indeed quite limited in economic activity and isolated from the rest of the country.

Attending my first village funeral exploded that impression. During my first month living in Sinafala village, Drivas suggested that we visit a funeral—on its second of five days— to find some of the old women I still needed to meet. Older women are fundamental to any village funeral, and because funerals last five days, most old women are found there rather than at their homes or fields during those days. It seemed like a reasonable suggestion to me, so off we went to the neighboring village, about an hour's walk from my homestead.

As we arrived at the homestead hosting the funeral (for one of the senior men in that village), I had my first realization that funerals were something to which I would need to pay attention. Here, clearly, was a gathering of more people than I had seen in one place since visiting the central market in Lusaka. The crowds on the periphery of the funeral reminded me of crowds in a parking lot at a big-ten university football game—lots of drinking and loud conversation that at times became even belligerent. Because it was my first visit to a funeral, I had no idea what to expect, and I certainly didn't expect to "walk the gauntlet" of a drunken melee, with me the prime target for derisive shouting. Over time I learned that these verbal assaults were not targeted at me personally; rather, anyone traversing any drunken event is a likely target. After a few more funeral visits, I learned how to cope, largely through learning to joke with the overzealous drinkers, but this first experience was a shock and made me dream of the peace and quiet of anonymity in the United States.

As I forged on through that first "layer" of the concentric circles around the funeral homestead, I found in the next ring the group of beer-brewing women who sold the drink to the drunken welcoming crew. And inside that layer I began meeting roving salesmen carrying various bundles, including bananas grown almost sixty miles south of our village, wood carvers selling wooden plates and dishes, and one woman selling homemade buns (baked in a "ground oven" made by digging a hole and placing a sheet of metal over the top, on which coals were placed to warm the oven below). At the core of the funeral grounds the different matrilineages and clans had their "camps." At these camps women cooked the meat and cornmeal porridge that had been distributed in the morning by the funeral leaders as part of the required daily ritual offerings.

As I moved through each layer, discovering a system of activities I had not known of before, I realized I was at a market of sorts. Not only did people exchange and sell goods, but everywhere I looked women and men, old and young, sat in clusters, some chanting the funeral songs, others simply chattering, catching up on events that had occurred in other places, and telling stories. Others, exhausted from drumming and dancing through the night, slept in small patches of shade, under a grain bin or at the corner of a house. The atmosphere resembled a music festival in the United States, where people eat, sleep, and party together for days on end and various stands and kiosks offer goods and services to the festival goers.

I had found what would turn out to be one of the illusive markets of rural Zambia. At these funerals, and other large gatherings, villagers and visitors always find a range of goods for purchase and exchange. And the local villagers themselves look forward to the event as an opportunity to sell some of their wares and earn an important bit of income. But nonfarm economic activity exists outside of large gatherings as well. Gwembe women and men, faced with the fact of regularly occurring insufficient harvests, have a wide-ranging repertoire of complimentary income-generating activities from which to choose when needed.

Gender and Generating Livelihoods

Men in the village can earn small amounts of cash by carving stools, axes, and mortars and pestles. They can sell milk from their cattle (see chap. 5, the section on boys and milk sales), produce from gardens, especially to-bacco, and they can perform manual labor such as building houses, molding bricks, or hauling supplies. If a man owns a valuable resource such as a plow, bicycle, or sledge (an ox-drawn sled used for hauling), he can rent these out in exchange for cash or something in kind. Oxen are often lent during the planting season. It is common for two men with one ox each to join together and plow their fields, or for a man with two oxen and another with a plow to cooperate in plowing. Men with a variety of resources, typically older men who have had time to make such investments, can generate an income by allowing others to use their wealth. Some men will pay a bag of salt to another man for use of his plow. In the village, assets are highly commercialized; any useful property can become a source of supplementary income.

As mentioned in the previous chapter, women typically lack resources that can generate an income in this way, but they have a variety of craft and service-oriented skills. Baskets for household use, especially for winnowing grain, are necessary in any rural home where grain is pounded by hand in a mortar. Most women know weaving techniques, but some women are more skilled than others. Their baskets are prized for their durability and good form, thus fetching a good price. Clay pots are still used by many villagers who don't have the cash to buy metal pots from town. Women make their own Tonga pipes (*mfuko*) from a calabash and a ceramic pipe bowl, which the local women potters produce for sale, along with pots and dishes.

Women also travel into the bush to collect tall grasses for thatching roofs. They tie the grass with a vine and then balance the huge bundles on their heads as they hike up to three hours back to the village. You can easily mistake a woman for a moving haystack until you see the bit of colored fabric above her bare feet. One bundle of grass sells for between fifty and eighty cents (US) in the village. Roofing a new house requires approximately ten bundles of grass, thus providing a useful income to a woman with the energy and time to spend hauling bundles.

Benefiting from Brew and Other Cottage Industries

Brewing beer is the most lucrative of the cottage industries available to women.[2] The markets for baskets, pottery, and grass may be constant, but these goods endure over time, so selling crafts is never a thriving market. Beer, however, is often finished in a day, and the men who drink it, after a day or so to recover, are ready to drink more. The market for beer is almost insatiable.

Women most often use their own grain for brewing the traditional seven-day beer, *gankata*. They then sell 2.5-liter units to village men for approximately fifty cents (US). Women who sell *gankata* beer at funerals, times of heavy drinking and a good market, can make a profit of approximately ten dollars from one batch. Of course women do not often see the profit at one moment because the brewer is frequently forced to give credit to her drinkers. If she is a good businesswoman, she learns how to collect on those debts quickly or, better yet, avoid the pressure to give credit in the first place.

In the past two decades a "wine" (*kapindula* or *njungula*) has become popular. Said to have come from the Bemba people of Northern Province, this brew is made from tea, yeast, and sugar. It is especially popular during drought years, when there is not enough surplus grain for *gankata* beer brewing. Wine takes only a day or two to ferment, and my friends who brewed told me that with a four-dollar investment in supplies, their profit could be almost ten dollars. Finding the capital for the first investment is always a problem. Sales of less-capital-intensive products, such as baskets, grass, or garden produce, can provide women with the initial investment. Husbands, brothers, or other matrikin sometimes lend women cash, but they expect a free portion of the final liquid product as payment on the debt.

Colson and Scudder's (1988) book on the role of beer in Gwembe communities points out that beer sales are an efficient way of redistributing men's income to women. They also describe a rapid rise in the amount of beer produced for sale, versus the amount for ritual purposes, from the mid-1960s until the late 1970s—a rise due primarily to the boom in the fishing industry after relocation. The creation of Lake Kariba produced a short-lived abundance of food for fish in the newly formed lake and consequently caused a rapid increase in the fish population. (New lake ecosystems provide substantial food sources due to the submerged biomass at the time of flooding. But following the initial wealth of nutrients during approximately the first three years, food sources decrease to what the annual climate systems create through rainfall and runoff. At that time fish populations also drop to more typical levels.) Local men capitalized on this boom by initiating small-scale fisheries, through which many men earned a good living while the boom lasted. Women used this moment of increased male wealth to initiate their own small-scale businesses in order to harness some of the profits men were making through fishing. Brewing beer for sale was one of the most lucrative options women had. During this same period, when cattle were becoming the major source of men's wealth, beer brewing gave women a source of cash income independent from that of their husbands. As with the difference between land and cattle, discussed at the end of the last chapter, cash income and cattle ownership are resources with different potentials for investment, a key issue that is explored at the end of the chapter.

Other cottage industries such as making buns or fritters (fried sweetened dough) are similar to beer brewing in their need for capital investment. My young female friends often asked me to bring them flour, vegetable oil, and sugar from town as a gift so they could start their own business. Luxury food items are especially popular around holidays like Christmas, New Year's, and Zambian Independence Day—as I learned my first Christmas in Gwembe.

By the time Christmas rolled around in the village, I had long since developed a thick skin and an effective technique for dealing with funeral drunks—based on a core of good humor and the ability to joke in Citonga. I attended the Christmas celebration of 1994 with anticipation and curiosity to see how villagers interpret this "Western" holiday. As with other daytime village celebrations I had seen, people congregated at crossroads between neighborhoods, and the scene resembled a small market, much like the funeral described at the outset of this chapter. Adolescents and children gathered around the one or two cassette players and danced to the ever-loved Zairian pop music, sometimes competing for the award of best dancer. Young adults, especially unmarried or recently married women, danced and sang in this group, or visited and joked around the perimeter. Many young men, and older people of both sexes, were drinking in nearby homesteads or weaving their way between the two places. On the periphery of the dance area, local businessmen, whom I had learned to expect at any village gathering, set up their stands, where they sold bath soap, petro-

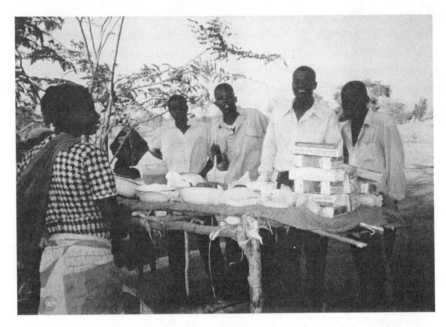

Fig. 4.1. One of the outdoor village "shops" where local businessmen sell basic supplies they have bought in town. For sale here are soap, salt, and cooking oil.

leum jelly, plates and cups, laundry detergent, vegetable oil, salt, chewing gum, and other small items they had carried from town. Unlike men, Gwembe women usually do not make a business of selling goods bought in town to their fellow villagers, largely because they lack the initial capital required to start such petty trade.

Businessmen must purchase sufficient stock and bring large quantities of supplies to the village in one trip in order to make a profit beyond the sometimes hefty costs of transport. Men, with their profits from cash cropping and sale of animals, are able to start small-scale businesses that demand an initial cash investment. At the Christmas celebration, I saw Gideon selling town goods (plastic plates and cups, sweets, and soap) for the first time. A man in his forties, and the son of one of my favorite "old women," he told me that when he saw 1994 was going to be a bad harvest, he sold all of his pigs in order to start his business. Rather than just sell animals to buy food, he thought it was better to start a business selling things from town. This way his money would last and he could buy food all year. And his strategy not only worked that year but benefited him over at least the next four years. When I saw Gideon in 1998, his business had moved in a new directions—he was selling secondhand clothing as well as "town goods," but he told me the business still fed him, his two wives, their children, and his aging mother, who, I was happy to learn, was still alive.

Working for Relief and Wages

During droughts people rely heavily on government-sponsored food-for-work programs. These are not permanent village programs but appear as the potential for famine increases. Food relief programs provide bags of grain (usually maize) for those in the most severely drought- or famine-stricken areas. In Zambia the relief program is managed at the international level by the United Nations World Food Program. Once supplies are shipped from donor countries, Zambian government agencies and non-governmental organizations (NGOs) distribute relief food. At this stage, some supplies are designated for disabled and elderly people through government social welfare departments, while the majority of grain bags are given in exchange for community work programs such as improving roads and building medical clinics or schools.

Supplies are limited, and handouts are small. In Sinafala in the mid-1990s, an adult would receive one bucket (approximately fifteen kilograms) after ten days of work. Once a person received a bucket of grain, that person was ineligible to work for the second bucket until the whole community had had the opportunity to work for the first bucket. Food supplies also arrived at distribution points late, so that although a group may have completed their ten days of work, they often had to wait another week before receiving their ration. During the 1995 food relief program in Sinafala, an adult who participated in "food for work" could expect one bucket of maize approximately every six weeks. For a family of five, a bucket of maize might last a week if used sparingly. In addition to these limitations, only one adult from a family could work during a given session. Although each wife of a man could work (since the relief program defined families as units of a mother and children), the husband himself could not work unless one of his wives declined. Women's adult children sometimes replaced their mothers so that the women could work in their fields or perform household duties.

People with physical or mental handicaps, as well as those too old or frail to work for their rations, received a bucket of maize through the social welfare program. Again, supplies for this segment of the needy population were small. Those elderly people eligible for social welfare distributions in

Sinafala received only four distributions from October 1994 to June 1995. In two instances when the supplies were not enough to give full buckets to all workers and social welfare recipients, the ration was decreased to half or three-quarters of a bucket so that everyone would receive something.

In addition to the problem of limited grain supplies from the relief agencies, villagers believed that continual illegal siphoning of supplies contributed to insufficient food distributions. Gwembe people tend to suspect corruption and theft in all activities that are out of their control. Grain bags were usually brought to the African continent by ship to the port at Durban, South Africa, or Dar es Salaam, Tanzania. From there supplies were transported by train to government store houses in Lusaka, where local NGOs and government agencies divided the shipment for further distribution to the needy districts. The last two stages were distribution by local development groups to different villages, followed by the final handout in the village.

Local people spread rumors that workers in the distribution centers, especially the points of distribution in their own district, took portions of the food relief. One rumor suggested that during a delivery of approximately a thousand bags of maize to the government center in Gwembe Central District, close to a hundred bags went missing. Villagers suspected the NGO workers and government administrators of taking these bags for their own use or to sell at a profit.

In one Gwembe Central village, local gossip identified a village NGO worker, Thomas, as a primary benefactor of misdirected resources. Thomas was a full-time employee of the NGO, and he lived in a nice house with many luxuries. One rumor credited him with taking building supplies meant for the village clinic to build and improve his own home. During the maize distribution of February 1995, villagers suspected that Thomas and a few other NGO employees stole bags of maize during the night. Cases of theft and corruption are taken to the village committee that administers food relief. However, people believe that committee members also profit from the relief program. People told me that for each distribution period, when workers receive one bucket each, committee members will get two or three buckets. Villagers commonly assume that by maintaining the status quo with the NGO employees, committee members continue to benefit.

Rumors and gossip reflect villagers' beliefs and suspicions about each other. However, villagers seemed to accept the perceived corruption as if such inequality is part of life. People assumed that as long as thieves were local people, there was a chance for redistribution of those resources. In the case of Thomas, everyone knew he was wealthy and assumed his wealth came from stealing supplies. But Thomas had a large network of extended family in the village, so when people needed food or assistance, they often went to him to plead, using their kinship and community ties as justification. Committee members and others believed to surreptitiously benefit from assistance programs were also approached in the same way. Although individuals may act to benefit themselves, the community counters by using culturally sanctioned paths of redistribution.

Formal employment for locals within the village, such as Thomas's position, were rare. Schoolteachers and administrators were usually outsiders to the village. Most were Tonga, but from different areas, and did not have relatives in Sinafala. Because they were "proper family" to no one, they were not subject to the same pressures from residents as were villagers who held such positions. Two of the three NGO employees were local, however, and committee members for a variety of groups (development and relief groups, political parties, and church and women's groups) were always from the local villages. A person with any position is likely to receive some kind of material benefit, whether it is a bucket of maize at distribution time, cash stipends for attending meetings, or access to special resources, such as a grinding mill.

The local Movement for Multi-Party Democracy (MMD) political representative, Mixon, was made responsible for a grinding mill given to a Sinafala women's group by the Hope Foundation, an assistance program sponsored by President Chiluba's wife, Veera Chiluba. Mixon wanted to keep the mill in his yard so that people would come to his homestead to grind. The community believed he would benefit by having the mill in his yard—at the least he would be able to grind his own grain on the sly, but he might also siphon off some of the income generated from the mill, which should go to the women's group. The community was in an uproar over Mixon's idea to keep the mill in his yard, and they finally installed it at a central location in the village. In this case individual will was overruled by community consensus.

The Gwembe Tonga Research Project is another formal employment option within some of the Gwembe villages. In addition to multiyear, part-time employment for one or two scribes in each village, there are assistants who work with any researcher while in the field. Perhaps initially these jobs were seen as temporary and unique. But the duration of the project has lead people to believe that part of our purpose is to bring "development" to the villages, or at least to bring tangible benefits in the form of employment and gifts. Colson's field notes from 1996 reveal that our presence in Gwembe communities is contributing to social differentiation. Some community members see employees of the GTRP as taking resources that should be given to the villages as a whole. Conflicts between employees, who are now visibly better off (with their new clothes and household goods) than the average farmer, are increasing. Employees are sometimes guilty of spending their salaries on luxuries, such as many changes of clothes for babies or new and expensive clothing for themselves, which can give them a "flashy" appearance. However, like Thomas and other resource-rich people in the community, neighbors and kinsmen exert pressure on those with wealth, and eventually those with less will have a bit more, while those with more will have a bit less.

Parallel Frontier Livelihoods

In the rural frontier region of Chikanta, where so many Gwembe people have migrated, the livelihoods of the inhabitants echo many of those in the valley. However, because harvests usually surpass those of the valley, people tend to have more surplus food and income than their relatives at home, which generally promotes more local and regional exchange and marketing. In fact, during the late 1990s a small permanent market area emerged in the most densely populated area of the frontier. The migrants have dubbed this market "first class," a pun on the colonial-era name of the main shopping district of Lusaka, and often tell me they are going to drink or shop at "first class."[3]

Over the years of visiting this "shopping center," I have watched the variety of goods available for purchase increase exponentially. On my first visit in 1994, the only market I saw consisted of a traveling salesman selling brightly colored plastic wares such as plates, cups, covered bowls, and basins for hand washing. He told me he stayed at that location for a few weeks and then moved on to his next destination. In 1996 I found an actual structure in which another man sold sugar, tea, yeast, cooking oil, hand soap, batteries, and a few other household items. By 1998, at least two more buildings had popped up, with merchants selling similar wares, along with an expanded inventory of used clothing and *chitenge*. In 2001 the market had indeed become "first class," with offerings of cold bottled beer and cokes from a refrigerator powered by a solar panel and battery, small ready-to-eat food items such as potato chips and other snacks, and an even larger assortment of household items such as towels and kerosene lamps. A local entrepreneur had also built a block of rooms behind the shopping center, which he rented out to the traveling sales people, and probably also to participants in the growing sex industry, which unfortunately tends to follow vibrant market areas, contributing to the increasing rate of STD and HIV infection in migrant areas.

The maize surplus in the frontier region is a key component of this thriving market. That so many goods are available in the shops suggests that local people have cash with which to purchase or goods for exchange. Along with this transformation in the market area, I have also watched the maize and cotton harvests thrive. During that first visit to Chikanta in 1994, I was distressed to see massive piles of ninety-kilogram bags of maize—piles the size of a two-bedroom house in the United States—sit waiting for buyers from town. I had come from the Gwembe, where the food shortage was at critical levels, and here in the frontier—about a ten-hour drive from my home in the valley—bags of maize were at risk of spoiling from pests and weather. As the market center has developed, migrants have begun trading their surplus maize with buyers who travel to the frontier from town. Migrants also grow cotton through a contract system with one of the cotton buyers in the region. Through this system farmers get seed, fertilizer, and pesticides on credit and a guaranteed price for their cotton. This is also the contract system Gwembe farmers use to grow cotton, but in the last decade there has been little reason to attempt it because the rains have been too sporadic and people prefer to grow food instead. When the rains are favorable, however, as they are more frequently in the frontier, farmers can make a good income from their cotton-planting labor.

In addition to the expanding market center in the migrant destinations, other cottage industries also thrive. In one of the migrant villages, a homestead composed entirely of four divorced or widowed sisters (ranging in age from thirty-two to forty years' old) and their divorced mother (approximately age fifty-eight) had established the equivalent of a full-time bar. Men and women from all the neighboring villages spoke of this homestead as the local watering hole and told me anyone can get wine there on any day. Compared to the pattern of beer brewing in the valley, where women usually sell beer only one or two days at a time, and only two or three times a month, maintaining an on-going supply of wine or beer is quite unusual. But like the market in this frontier region, which is permanent, a permanent beer hall makes sense given the economic vibrancy of the region.

In the summer of 2001, on all four of the occasions I happened to pass by or actually went to visit, the homestead had at least two well-established visitors who were obviously planning for a day of relaxation and drinking. And the wine continued to flow throughout the day. Men of any age and older women made up the clientele, and the hostesses took their roles of greeter and bartender quite seriously. This bar scene, like much of the Zambian frontier, has an atmosphere that reminds me of the American Wild West as depicted in Hollywood films: hearty women running the local establishment who can control the often rowdy patrons and making a good living in the process.

These women in the migrant frontier did indeed appear to make a decent living. The structures in their homestead were well kept, meaning they had resources to hire someone to make roof repairs when needed, and they had a good collection of small livestock, including a few pigs and goats, and at least ten chickens. Of course, like their frontier counterparts in the American West, such women may have other sidelines, including selling sex to their customers. Although some of the men I spoke with in the frontier told me that these women were prostitutes as well as beer businesswomen, I never confirmed that information.

Another facet of the economy in the frontier migrant area that differs from activities in the valley is the assumed but undocumented trade in "bush meat"—meat derived from wildlife in the neighboring national game park. Conversations throughout the region bordering the park abound with rumor about a group of armed young men who hunt animals and sell to local traders. But like questions of prostitution on the frontier, the pursuit of this topic demands a longer period of immersion with the local people than the few months at a time I have spent over the past decade. However, a number of different men and women I spoke with suggested to me that if the various government controls on illegal hunting were enforced in the area, then the "first class" market would fall into decline. According to their view of the local economy, many of the traders from town (including businessmen trading secondhand clothing for the surplus maize of the region) come in part because of the game meat market. If, according to those I spoke with, availability of game meat dries up, then local farmers will loose their ability to sell the maize surplus.

Although differences exist in the range of economic activity seen in the frontier and valley, the core components of farming when possible, cottage industries, sale of labor, and exchange of goods make up the repertoire of livelihoods for all rural Zambians. Beyond these basics lie subtle differences in economic activity consistent with gender and generation, and these differences add particular dynamics to how people invest their labor and resources.

Collecting Grains from Grass: Productive Activities of the Elderly

Anyone can engage in the economic activities I've mentioned. However, young to middle-aged adults are the most common participants because they have the physical strength that is often needed and access to capital. Men's need for a small income often decreases with age because by the time men are older, they usually have resources or dependents (daughters of marriageable age and sons running a small business) from whom they can anticipate an income. Older women, on the other hand, do not accumulate valuable resources in the same way as men, nor do they exert the same control over their children as do men. Elderly women usually do not have access to surplus grain or cash for brewing beer and wine, or for purchasing baking supplies. Older women's most common cash-earning activities are basket weaving and pottery. In the few cases where they still have energy to plant a good garden, they can sell vegetables and tobacco, which offer a small and irregular source of cash.

In addition to the typical food procurement activities that all Gwembe people use, such as collecting foods like wild okra and other green leafy vines that grow throughout the area, and catching small birds and mammals such as squirrels and field rats, older people often expand the range of foods gathered during periods of extended hunger. For example, collecting grains from grass is one strategy, but it is highly labor intensive and does not provide much in the way of sustenance. Another famine food choice of older Gwembe people is the hunger-season beverage of boiled tamarind paste mixed with ashes from a wood fire. The women I saw making this meal told me that it takes a lot of work to process the tamarind pods into paste, but worst of all is the stomachache they get after drinking the mixture (a result of the ash content)—yet they all said it makes them feel full, the primary goal in consuming most famine foods.

Beyond these more extreme examples of coping with extended hunger seasons, older Gwembe people have a battery of options for sustaining themselves on a day-to-day basis. Older women's choices for supplementing their daily needs include activities that are not typically seen as economic production but are nevertheless productive strategies. Eating at a neighbor's homestead, pleading for meali meal from relatives and friends, and collecting food relief are all key components of an elderly woman's survival in the village. In December 1994, the beginning of that year's acute hunger problems in the Gwembe Valley, I collected information about productive activities of the elderly from 29 homesteads. The people I talked with described fourteen types of activities that I considered to be productive for food procurement. These activities were brewing beer, producing crafts/pottery, making baskets, fishing, practicing traditional healing, selling/exchanging cattle, selling/exchanging chickens, pleading meali meal from the community, getting food from children, getting food from siblings, eating meals with other homesteads, working/laboring for other people (for example, weeding fields or scaring birds), and availing themselves of the government's food-for-work and social welfare programs.

Of the 29 homesteads with which I worked, 23 consisted of widowed or divorced women living alone or with their sons. Of the remaining 5 homesteads, 4 consisted of elderly couples, and the last homestead consisted of a widowed man. The single elderly women used an average of 4 of the 14 strategies during December, whereas elderly married couples used an average of 6 strategies. The most common activities for single elderly women were getting food from children (78 percent), pleading meali meal from the community (52 percent), and exchanging work for food (52 percent). Making baskets (43 percent), trading fish (35 percent), and eating with neighbors (30 percent) were also common productive activities for single women. Married couples sold or traded animals, both cattle (3 of the 4 homesteads) and chickens (2), traded fish (2), made baskets (2), exchanged work for food (2), and practiced some form of traditional healing (2) for their daily needs.

Although the number of elderly married couples in the village is small, it is logical that when there are more people able to participate in productive activities, a homestead will have more options to draw from. This is especially true in multigenerational homesteads, where elders benefit from the increased number of "productive" adults and older children, a topic that is addressed in the next chapter.

Investing in Mothering and Other Intergenerational Livelihoods

Clearly, the myriad ways to make a living suggest that Gwembe people in general have a highly developed capacity to cope with their difficult living

circumstances. Producing food directly by farming and exchanging produce are preferred methods for self-provisioning. But given the changing
climate, ecosystem, and economy, people find themselves more often than
not unable to produce enough food to sustain themselves for a given year.
In such circumstances Gwembe people, both in the valley and in the frontier, engage in a mixed economy composed of some self-provisioning,
some trading, and some wage employment. Probably most important,
however, they build social networks that provide access to food and resources. It is this last component, building social networks, that has become the primary "productive" activity for elderly Gwembe women.
Women make small investments in social relationships as they move
through their life cycle, so in their old age they are able to mobilize support in the form of food, household assistance, and general care.

In the previous chapter I outlined how changes in resource ownership
in the Gwembe Valley over the last half decade, particularly ownership of
land and cattle, have led to a situation in which older women have become
marginalized from prestigious and highly valued material wealth, while
men of the same generation have increased their holdings—which is not
such a new story (di-Leonardo 1991; Mikell 1997; Robinson 1998). But the
important questions in this dynamic then become the following: how do
these differences in access to important resources play out as men and
women negotiate relationships with children and relatives, and how do
men and women mobilize support as they age?

If a father hopes to keep his children near him and extract some of their
labor, he is wise to allow controlled use of his equipment. His best strategy
for security in old age is to have amassed enough cattle that he can still attract his younger wives and their children. As men move through their
young adult years into middle age, they have a broad range of income-
generating options, including the marriage of their daughters, which allows them to accumulate cattle. By the time they have reached their senior
years, most likely they have amassed enough resources to attract younger
dependents—younger wives and adult sons, whose productive activities
depend on the resources the senior man owns. In exchange for allowing
these dependents to make use of his equipment, cattle, and general material base, a senior man receives the kind of support he requires to live into
his senior years.

If they do not own cattle, women have little material base from which to
encourage an adult child's support at the time she most needs it—in her
own old age, when she is often divorced or widowed. Although women

have far fewer ways of generating an income than men, they have demonstrated their energy and creativity in economic activities such as beer
brewing, bun making, and other crafts. Over time women can purchase
cattle from the profits of these cottage industries and attempt to join the
men in accumulating material wealth and status. But it is more common
for women's cash to be invested immediately into family needs such as
school fees and uniforms, medical costs, clothing, or household supplies.
Through their less visible and less prestigious material wealth, women
continually participate in behaviors that reinforce the cultural construction of the nurturing, protective mother. That is, they invest their income
in "mothering" (Clark 1999, 720), one of the strategies that elderly women
rely on as they attempt to harness support in their old age.

As the descriptions in this chapter reveal, making a living in a rural village poses severe challenges to everyone, young and old. As I tried to make
sense of people's behavior in 1996, I wrote in my field notes that "no one
here has enough, everyone has something, some have more than others,
the rest are struggling for more . . . and everyone schemes to their best
ability." After my field trip in 2001, this remained an apt description of life
not just for the elderly but for everyone in the Gwembe, and even in the
migrant destinations. Suspicions of corruption in relief programs, fights
between salaried workers and other villagers at beer drinks, and social
pressures to give assistance to kin are all part of daily survival for rural
Zambians.

In a crude breakdown of class in rural Zambia, women typically lack
material resources, whereas men accumulate wealth through wage employment and property ownership. From this fundamentally different material base, older men and women then move through their daily lives and
years with a clearly different repertoire of strategies for securing support
from their relatives and communities. In other words, older women's and
men's "spaces" of vulnerability are vastly different and result in profoundly
different relationships with other generations. The arenas in which elderly
women and men employ those repertoires are explored in the following
chapters.

5. Mother's Keepers, Father's Wives, and Residential Arrangements of the Old

If my son weren't here I'd be suffering. My clan won't help me, they believe everyone
should be helped by their sons. . . . A clan can help, but not like a son.

Sarina, March 1995

A son can't chase you [from his homestead], or throw you like a stone, or chase you like
a dog, because he's your relative. If he's a reasonable person he will take care of you.

Malala, March 1995

For everyone living in the Gwembe Valley of Zambia's Southern Province,
household composition and living arrangements play a vital role in subsistence because they affect the redistribution of resources that occurs in the domestic unit. Most homestead members bring some kind of productive capacity to a homestead, whether agricultural labor and produce, material wealth,
cash-generating activities, or domestic chores. Through the redistributive
processes typical of most domestic groups, members generally benefit from
some element of the group's productive energy. In this way, residential
arrangements shape and fundamentally influence support for the elderly.

This chapter examines the critical issue of how Gwembe elderly organize their residential arrangements. The domestic setting forms the locus
of fundamental social and material reproductive activity. In the Gwembe
Valley, as in other regions of Africa (Draper and Keith 1992; Hakansson
and LeVine 1997; Smith 1998; Ferreira 2000; Tengan 2002) and elsewhere
(Domingo et al. 1995; Lee, Lin, and Chang 1995; Aytac 1998; De Vos 1998;
Lam et al. 1998; Knodel and Saengtienchai 1999), living arrangements influence the ways elderly people harness resources. While extended family
and community members often participate in support networks reaching

beyond the residential domestic setting, the elderly most often gain access to the majority of their food and basic necessities through their residential arrangements. (For a discussion of nondomestic support, see Knodel and Saengtienchai 1999.) When a widow lives with a successful farmer son, she will most likely eat better than a widow who lives alone and cannot farm aggressively due to limits on her physical abilities.

The domestic setting, or homestead, also becomes the primary stage for elderly people to assert their identity as elders and to call upon obligations that are inherent to their position. Part of identity assertion among Gwembe elders centers on their gender and the ways that mothers and fathers differ in their relationships to children. Other studies of intergenerational residence patterns, particularly research in which survey methods provide the majority of data, tend to treat elderly men and women as one group (Domingo et al. 1995; Mehta, Lee, and Osman 1995; De Vos 1998; Lam et al. 1998). The story from the Gwembe Valley points out the different choices and strategies that elderly men and elderly woman employ as they interact in their domestic settings. Consideration of the different ways that aging men and women negotiate support with their children and relatives provides valuable insight into intergenerational relations. Recognition of this variety and subtlety of relationships in the aging process allows us to better understand the range of support systems and subsistence strategies in nonindustrial settings—important knowledge when our research provides a foundation for policy and development directed at providing for the needs of the growing elderly population of the world.

As I described in chapter 2, living with a family while conducting my fieldwork exposed me to the vast array of household activities and social dynamics that informs the more formal data I collected through interviews and surveys. Eating meals with Kaciente and his family, and other village families, offered me a multitude of opportunities to witness village life in action, including many moments of sharing food and other resources. In the sections that follow, I present components of the quantitative data I collected, but I also contextualize this information with more vivid stories of how elders and family members negotiate their relationships and resource access.

Daily Life in Tonga Homesteads

The village social environment consists of a variety of social groupings. The concept of village itself is subject to multiple interpretations. The

British colonial legacy throughout central Africa superimposed a political organization of chiefs and village headmen that was not indigenous to Tonga society (Colson 1960; Vail 1989). However, "neighborhoods" based on groupings of related families and collective ritual activities predated colonial transformations and have persisted to the present (Colson 1960). Villages, originally identified and created by colonial authorities, are smaller groupings than neighborhoods and generally consist of multiple homesteads of related families. As contemporary social and political groupings, villages play a roll in daily life, particularly in conflict resolution through "traditional courts" overseen by headmen and as sponsors of soccer teams. Villages are also the most immediate social environment beyond the homestead; they often consist of close relatives to whom individuals often will turn in times of need.

Another important social grouping for Gwembe Tonga is the matrilineal clan, which I mentioned in chapter 2, and the subsidiary matrilineages that comprise the clan.[1] Through the matrilineal kinship system people know their "proper family," a concept that plays an important role in who elderly people turn to for assistance. Exogenous marriage systems lead to heterogeneous family groups; men should marry women from different clans, and a man should not marry two women of the same matrilineage. Consequently, at the married "nuclear family" level, a man is alone in his clan identity. Each wife and her children share clan identity, but unless a man has brought members of his own matrilineal clan into his homestead, he represents an extreme minority within his own living area.

These heterogeneous families usually live in a homestead, defined as a cluster of houses in which an extended family lives. The term *homestead*, which in Citonga also means village, captures the layered and interwoven levels of people in each of those separate structures. As I described in chapter 2, using Kaciente's homestead as an example, the social composition of a homestead typically includes a married man, his wives—occasionally as many as nine—and their children, some of whom may be married sons with wives and children. A homestead may also include an elderly mother if the man is young enough to still have a mother living, perhaps an unmarried or divorced sister of the senior man, and in some cases other matrilineal kin of the man, such as a sister's son or daughter, or mother's sister. Only in these last cases will a man have another member of his matrilineal clan, that is, his primary kin identity, living within his homestead.

Each adult has her or his own house, although the senior man may simply use his wives' houses unless he has decided to have an "office," both as a symbol of his importance and as a guesthouse for visitors. In general, each wife has a house, each married son has his own house, and an elderly mother would have her own house, as would any other adult relative. Children typically sleep in their mother's or another adult's house, or in a boys' or girls' group house. As a result of these arrangements, one large homestead may have twenty buildings.

Of course there are variations on the composition of homesteads. In the case of elderly women who live alone, a homestead can simply consist of a single wattle-and-dab shelter, in which case the homestead is one house. Although Tonga men often claim they want to marry many wives, it is relatively uncommon for a man to have more than three wives simultaneously. Most homesteads in the villages where I have worked for the past decade consist of a man with between one and three wives, their children, often a nephew, niece, and other related children, and possibly one of the man's widowed sisters. With this kind of composition, most homesteads included between seven and fifteen people, at least four of whom were adults. However, people aged fifty-five and older were more likely to live in smaller homesteads, unless they had moved in with a relative's family. The majority (73 percent) of the elderly population with whom I worked during 1994–95 lived in homesteads with no more than four adults and four children.

In these social groupings of residence, the most basic elements of survival are played out in daily life (see Weismantel 1988 for a Peruvian parallel). Food is not produced and consumed at the homestead level but within a house—that is, each wife grows food for her children and her husband— yet the exchange between wives and other homestead members is a fluid process between individuals and groups. In addition to the fields owned by their husbands for which the women are responsible, wives have their own gardens and fields in which they and their children and matrilineal relatives will plant, weed, scare birds, and harvest. Upon returning to the homestead in the evening, each wife, or one of her daughters, prepares and cooks both nsima and an accompanying sauce on her own fire.

The three-stone hearth on which women cook is both a kitchen and a symbol of a woman's membership in the homestead. Women rarely share a cooking fire, so each homestead has as many hearths as there are wives and other adult women. A woman should not approach another co-wife's fire while food is being cooked for fear that the trespasser will be accused of witchcraft or using dangerous medicines against the other woman.

Fig. 5.1. One of women's and girls' daily tasks—cooking *nsima* for the family on the three-stone hearth.

Once wives or their daughters prepare the meals, men and boys cluster around the area near a man's gathering place, *igobelo*,[2] or near his grain bin, to eat the dishes served by all the wives. Women frequently sit together, near but not with the men, and taste each other's cuisine, feeding the young children from the bowls of various food. Although wives prepare food separately, they often taste what the others have cooked. Even during cooking, co-wives, daughters, and daughters-in-law often share and exchange their resources. A wife who just sold an ox to buy grain may give a dish of meali meal to her co-wife who has none. Or a daughter-in-law who just received a jar of cooking oil from her husband may give a small portion to the elderly grandmother cooking a small dish of wild greens on her own fire. It is clear that inclination toward self-interest and tendencies of cooperation are intertwined within the homestead (Netting, Wilk, and Arnould 1984; Guyer 1986; Guyer and Peters 1987; Dwyer and Bruce 1988; Wilk 1989, 1991).

Children supplement the family's diet by bringing fish, birds, or field rats from the surrounding bush. Although children frequently provide substance for the sauces in the family pot, particularly fish during the brief season of plenty, they do not always share the products of their labor. One of my favorite memories of eating with Kaciente's wives was the evening when Alice, a giggly little girl about five years old, roasted a field rat she had caught that afternoon and proceeded to scoot into the shadows beyond the fire light, away from the crowd of her brothers and sisters, to eat the critter gleefully.[3] Teenage boys often arrived in the homestead in the late afternoon, before others had returned from the fields, to roast and devour birds they had hit using their slingshots. Although Tonga adults spoke to me about "bush animals" that can be used for food, I only saw children actually making use of the resource. Perhaps these sources of food demand nimble bodies and quick hands, characteristics that the senior villagers no longer have.

Young boys also milk cattle, when their families are fortunate enough to have them. Even though the boys do not own the cattle, if they milk the herds they have rights to the product.[4] By selling the milk, boys can generate a small income to buy school supplies. Milk is also a favored sauce for nsima, and the guidelines for regulating its consumption were never clear to me. On a few occasions I heard a boy refusing to bring out milk to one of his mothers, but at other times a boy would spontaneously disappear into his house only to emerge with a quarter liter of sour milk (a favorite sauce to mix with nsima) for everyone in the family to enjoy.[5]

Homesteads have a complex system of regulating consumption and production activities. Production and consumption are also highly attuned to the composition of the group. The immediacy of daily life is played out in the homestead yards: children lick from the pots as meals are prepared; old women cook grains from their own kitchen garden over their own fire and then share with grandchildren; daughters-in-law borrow food from a neighbor and then serve a dish to an old woman; and a man sometimes returns from working on the road in a food relief program with a bucket of maize for all his wives to share. In addition, when free from the duties of herding cattle, sons may mold bricks and build their father a new office, and daughters carry buckets of water home after they return from weeding their mother's fields near the lake. While weaving baskets to exchange for a dish of meali meal, old women look after their grandchildren until the mothers return from the monthly visit by the government vaccine program.

Understanding basic survival for Gwembe villagers begins with the vast assortment of production options, both social and material, that individuals bring to the homestead. For the elderly, who often are physically limited in their mobility and self-sufficiency, residence becomes the most critical variable influencing well-being.

Elders' Residential Choices

Elderly men and women have very different living situations. In 1994–95, most men (89 percent) but only a quarter of the women lived with a spouse, reflecting the high rate of widowhood among older women and the necessity for women to find other residential options (see table 5.1). Only one man but half the women (51 percent) lived with or near a married son. Specifically, 26 women (40 percent) lived in a married son's homestead, and 7 women who headed their own homesteads lived near a married son's homestead. The other 49 percent of the women lived in various situations—alone (no men lived alone) or with or near a brother, sister, or grandson. Although children who have migrated out of the immediate vicinity (to rural areas nearby and afar, as well as towns) play a role in village and family life through their return visits, I save a discussion of their contributions until chapter 7, when I address migration and maintaining links with home communities.

Clearly, gender differences influence residential preference. Even though men may be in their sixties, a truly elderly age given Zambia's life expectancy of thirty-seven years, they are most often married and living with at least one wife. Widowed or divorced women most often live with or near a married son. Rather than depend on children for support, a man wants at least one significantly younger wife who will continue to work for him, and he wants to head his own homestead. Women prefer to live with

TABLE 5.1
Residence by gender and arrangement

Living Arrangement	Women (%)	Men (%)
Total population 55+	65	27
Married living with spouse	16 (25)	24 (89)
With or near a son	33 (51)	1 (4)
Alone	5 (8)	0
With or near a brother	5 (8)	0
With a sister	4 (6)	1 (4)
With a grandson	2 (3)	0
Other (matrilineal nephew)	0	1 (4)

Note: This table includes the total population aged 55+ in two Gwembe Valley villages and one rural migrant destination.

adult sons when they become widowed, and in many cases a woman will divorce a husband in order to live with a son, particularly if the husband is quite aged himself and cannot assist her with tasks that typically fall to men.

Living the Good Life

The gendered division of labor among the Tonga, the dynamics of power relations within the homestead, and instances of personal preference influence the variation in residential arrangements of the elderly. When I asked why an old woman prefers to live with a son rather than a daughter, the almost unanimous answer was that "a son can build a house for you." Indeed, male labor within Tonga society is largely centered on building structures—including grain bins, fences to protect gardens from invading cattle and hippos, and living shelters both in the homesteads and the gardens—and on the heavy work of clearing fields and plowing. A husband usually performs the men's work in a homestead until a son is old enough and strong enough to take over the responsibility. In the absence of a husband or a son, a woman's brother or sister's son may fulfill some of these needs.

The matrilineal system of the Tonga is somewhat contradicted by their bride-wealth system (*lobola*), in which young men pay cattle to their wives' families, thus transferring rights to female labor from one man to another through the payment of lineage property. I use the word *contradicted* in this case because in fact bride-wealth payment systems most frequently occur in patrilineal societies, not matrilineal ones such as the Gwembe Tonga. In a patrilineal society men use control over material wealth (cattle) to gain rights over a person and in effect incorporate a woman into their families. For example, among the patrilineal Masai of Kenya, when a man gives cattle to his wife's family in order to marry her, he then has rights of "incorporation" over that woman; she becomes, for the most part, no longer a member of her natal family but a new member of her husband's family, and the children she produces will be her husband's children, not children of her own natal family. In the Gwembe Tonga bride-wealth system, the exchange of cattle gives a husband rights to a woman's and her children's labor but not to their personhood.

Because of this focus on rights to a person's labor, the Gwembe Tonga system of bride wealth encourages reliance on sons rather than daughters for support in old age. The system underscores the exchange of labor between families: once a woman marries, the rights to her labor transfer from her father and natal family to her husband and his family, who paid for it with *lobola*. For this reason, both men and women agree that it is improper to live with a married daughter because the parents have "already eaten that man's cattle," despite the fact that the matrilineal identity will be passed through those daughters. So just as an aging mother would not live with her married daughter because she no longer has legal rights to the daughter's labor, she can easily live with her married son; in this arrangement a mother has rights to the labor of her son, and to the labor of her daughter-in-law for whom her matrilineage gave cattle.

Lazwell, a successful young man who had completed secondary school and teacher's training, described to me how his mother influenced his first marriage. While he was in secondary school, Lazwell's mother encouraged him to marry a woman from the village with whom he had had relations for some time, saying that she needed a daughter-in-law to help her with daily work while he was schooling. Despite the risk of expulsion from school because of the marriage (school regulations prohibit students from marrying or becoming pregnant), Lazwell married the woman, partly to satisfy his mother's pleading. He then sought a position at a secondary school in town, where he was able to conceal the illegal marriage, leaving his wife behind in the care of his mother. With access to both a son and his wife, an old woman benefits from the availability of male labor, and a daughter-in-law who can help her lighten her own load of drawing water, pounding grain, collecting firewood, and cooking.

For older men, the story differs significantly. While children grow up within the homestead, respecting their father as the homestead head and power holder and providing labor in his fields, cattle kraal, and home, they do not share a common matrilineal identity with him. A man is an outsider within his own homestead because of the matrilineal kinship system that emphasizes ties to mothers and their families. The matrilineage (*mukowa*), in addition to shaping property ownership through time and generations, plays a powerful role in individual, family, and kinship identity. Primary identity in Gwembe families derives from links to mothers and their relatives. As I mentioned in reference to Kaciente's family in chapter 2, for this reason, unless a man has brought his own kin (clan members), such as sisters or his mother, to live in his homestead, he is the only member of his clan in the homestead.

Recognition of the man's patrilineal line, the *lutundu*, helps to mediate a man's alienation in his own homestead. Although a person's matrilineage provides primary social identity, all children also carry a component of identity with their father's lineage, and this link provides the basis on which a father claims the labor of his daughters and sons. However, this patrifocal nuclear group lacks the strong source of identity that the matrilineage carries. As a true clan identity, the matrilineage links living members to long-deceased ancestors, whereas the patrifocal group survives only three generations; a man, his children, and their children constitute part of his *lutundu*, but the link ends there.[6] Children respect their mothers as parents and elders within the homestead, but children also draw their primary kinship identity from their mothers. Women can use this link of identity as a powerful tool when issues of loyalty and personal preferences surface.

Men must find some path other than kinship to provide for themselves as they age. Like aging men in societies throughout most of the world, Gwembe men choose marriage as the best possible option for old-age security. Once a man has paid *lobola* for his wives, he has the legal rights to their labor, and they are obliged to fulfill the role of wife for him, although these days women often begin working for their husbands before the marriage payments have been made. In the Tonga gendered division of labor, women and their children provide the bulk of domestic labor—the household chores of cooking, cleaning, and drawing water—as well as field chores of breaking hard soil with hoes, planting, weeding, and harvesting. Absence of a wife to do these chores marginalizes a man within his home and the community. Boys usually learn how to cook for themselves so they can survive if they go to boarding school or must live alone in town. But a man prefers, whenever possible, to have a woman do these tasks because "women's work" demeans a man, whereas having a wife bestows status. A man with a woman looking after him indicates his good fortune, while the community pities a man when he must care for himself. A man with wives working in his fields can produce more, thus ensuring that he will have food and increasing the possibility of surplus.

Under these circumstances, a wise man will marry younger women as he ages in order to guarantee that they survive until he dies. The complementary roles of men and women form the basis of a functional homestead. A man with one wife has at least her labor in addition to his own. If that wife has children living within the homestead, the aging man benefits from his sons' strength for the male activities of building and plowing, and he benefits from his daughters' skill in their female work, but more importantly he benefits from their bride wealth. A man with many daughters of differing ages has a guaranteed income well into his fifties and sixties.

Power in the homestead and respect within the community come with bride-wealth payments in cattle. The more wives and children a man has, the more he can improve his position at home and among his peers. Indeed, many men speak of their primary goal as establishing and then maintaining social standing within the community. Young men often told me that their dreams for the future consisted mainly of having many daughters so that they could "eat their cattle" (collect cattle from bride wealth), and they desired herds of at least thirty head. When a young man amasses cattle, he increases his ability to marry more and younger wives as he ages. Old-age security for men begins with increasing the number of his dependents who will ultimately provide him with more wealth. Women married to such a man benefit from his wealth and the respect he receives. In particular, an elderly woman still married to a husband with younger wives to perform the heaviest labor may find she has a relatively good living situation. If a woman has a decent husband who allows her to slow her activities in accordance with her physical ability, she may enjoy the security that marriage provides yet also benefit from assistance given by her adult sons and young daughters.

However, a man's character and his access to resources fundamentally influence the quality of life of an aging woman still married to her husband. One elderly woman told me that she divorced her husband in order to go and live with her son "because I didn't want to work for anyone any more." Other women spoke about the "ease of life" with no husband and said, "once you are old, that is when you rest."

Marriage does not guarantee security, however. If a man has wealth, an aging wife might benefit from it. But if a man struggles to support himself and his wives and children, an older wife might be more disadvantaged than if she were living with a son, as the story of Muchembele in the first chapter demonstrates.

These residential arrangements represent the best options for the village elderly. For men of any age, marriage is the only good option for acquiring necessary labor and wealth; for aging women, marriage also offers benefits, particularly when a husband adheres to the Tonga norms of support. In contrast to the relatively easy choice of marriage for men, women must more often make real choices between a variety of options in order to create a secure living arrangement in which to age. When a husband begins to avoid responsibility, or when he admonishes an aging wife for her decreasing productivity, or if she simply becomes a widow, residence with or near a married son is a secure and in some ways ideal residential arrangement. Living with a married son may provide an old woman with the first opportunity of her life to not work for someone else and to enjoy a rest.

Living in the Margins: Elderly Women and Proper Family

What happens to aging individuals, especially women, as their life circumstances and living arrangements change, for example, when a spouse dies or children migrate? Women almost always outlive their husbands. In some cases a widow has no son living nearby who will provide her with a home. Of the 16 aging women who were not married or living with or near a married son in 1994–95, 5 (8 percent of the total of 65 women) were heading their own homestead near no relations of any kind, 5 (8 percent) were living with or near a brother, 4 (6 percent) were living with sisters (two "pairs" of women), and 2 (3 percent) were living with grandsons. In the event that a man does outlive his wife and is unable to remarry, he must find an alternate place to spend his last years. Of the two men who were no longer married, one man was a leper whose previous wives had divorced him because of his disease; he was living with his sister. The oldest man in the sample, whose wife had died four years earlier, lived with his sister's daughter, who herself was part of my sample and lived with her married son (see table 5.1).

The most vulnerable position for an elderly woman occurs when she has no close adult matrikin, such as a son, brother, or classificatory father, living in the village.[7] Even a sister can provide a sense of emotional security at the least, and sometimes material security if she has children in the area or has some property. An old woman who lives alone in her homestead, even with small children, becomes vulnerable to theft of what few possessions she has, especially chickens or small livestock. In 1994, the year before my arrival in Sinafala, someone stole most of Lutinda's small heard of cattle and all of her chickens. Although the community mobilized to locate the thieves, they never formally accused anyone. However, local gossip attributed the theft to Lutinda's young nephews, her brother's sons, from a neighboring village. People believed the young men took advantage of her solitary living situation and also wanted to act out their own changing ideas of inheritance systems.[8] Until recently, Tonga property passed from an individual to her or his matrilineal heirs—most often a sibling or a sister's children. Over the past decade, attitudes about inheritance have been changing, with children increasingly demanding access to their father's property upon his death, and putting matrilineal relatives, particularly elderly women, in a difficult position.

In addition to the risk of theft, a woman or man with no matrikin in the village faces problems associated with a limited or nonexistent formal network; these social support systems become especially important during times of need. When I asked these women whom they turned to when they needed assistance, they often responded, "I have no proper family here." People employ the technique of begging, *kulomba*, or as I prefer to call it, pleading, as a standard means for acquiring necessities and at times luxuries.[9] This pleading mobilizes assistance from members of the community, usually in the form of food handouts but sometimes cash or material goods, such as an old shirt or *chitenge*, the women's waistcloth. But the practice most often targets kin; "proper family" answer requests for assistance more often than do nonrelatives.

Proper family resembles a kindred (Ferraro 1992, 185); each individual has a unique network of relatives whose members are called "proper family," and these can include people through a variety of relationships. While the kindred includes a bilateral social network, "proper family" emphasizes maternal ties, although a person's proper family sometimes embraces marriage links and paternal connections. Women's children, especially sons, constitute the most obvious members of proper family. This category also includes brothers of "one womb," *mwida l'omwe*.[10]

For the purposes of pleading, Gwembe people often ignore sisters, despite the shared matrilineal identity. Like mothers who hesitate to depend on a daughter for the needs of daily living, sisters usually do not depend on each other. Women say that a husband becomes enraged when his wife's relatives come pleading for assistance too often. Nevertheless, wives do receive family visitors, and visitors expect hosts to feed them while visiting. But upon departure, a visitor calling on sisters might not have as large a bundle of goods as someone mobilizing a fraternal link, because men's rights over land give them substantial rights to the grain harvest. Even in women's fields a husband can claim rights to the harvest if he plowed or provided seed. Women, who usually do not have a large supply of their own grain, do not have the freedom to give away food belonging to their husband. As all my informants asserted, when a husband is around, a wife is not the "owner of the homestead."

Over the past decade of my fieldwork, other proper family have included a mother's sister's sons, even a co-wife's son, and in one instance the "classificatory father" (see n. 7) of the woman. However, these instances of broadened kinship links make use of a highly flexible category and thus cannot be considered dependable options. The identification of proper family, and how and when people call on it, changes over the life course. When co-wives live together in the same homestead with their children and husband, co-wives call each others' children "daughter" and "son"; at that time children also call all co-wives "mother." Upon adulthood and establishment of an independent homestead, co-wives and the group of children lose that intimacy and call only their own children by the terms son and daughter. The rare act of calling on an elderly co-wife's son for assistance demonstrates the array of possibilities that an old woman can mobilize on her own behalf. Individual action, such as choosing support networks and mobilizing assistance from relatives, can be highly personalized, taking into account the social and material factors in people's lives (Bourdieu 1977). The individualized process of identifying proper family, or the kindred, often depends as much on the personalities of those involved as on obligations inherent in the actual kinship relationships and demonstrates that kinship models are just that, ideals for structure and behavior; real life offers far more variability than models can capture.

Although Gwembe people usually view brothers as proper family for the purposes of pleading, living within a brother's homestead is less than ideal for an elderly woman. Unlike his mother, a brother considers his elderly sister more of a guest, and she has few rights to the labor and resources of the homestead. A brother sees his sister as a guest because the sibling relationship represents a horizontal link within the same generation, whereas parent–child relationships move vertically, with the parent holding the position of seniority. An old woman has little claim to assistance from her brother's wives or from her brother himself. Yet if she possesses any strength and physical ability, her brother will often expect her to work in his fields, just as his wives do. Although she may work for her brother, he usually views the assistance he gives her as a handout, and the community pities her. One villager, commenting on an old woman living with her brother who had very little control over her food supply and no money for new cloths or luxuries like soap, told me, "when you live like that, it is just better to be dead."

Tonga custom prohibits living with a married daughter. Women speak of the possibility as a taboo: "You can't eat with the son-in-law, you have already eaten his cattle"; "if you live with a son-in-law, his family will become jealous because he is caring for you, and not his own family." The Tonga justly fear jealousy because it often forms the basis for threats of

Fig. 5.2. An elderly woman sitting with her great grandchildren, in front of the house her grandson made for her, in one of the migrant frontiers.

witchcraft, a very real aspect of village life. Colson (2000) has described cases in which men have been accused of witchcraft against both wives and sons because of a son's tendency to give more gifts to his mother than his father, indicating the reality of jealousy and the importance of egalitarian resource sharing. If a mother lived with her married daughter, her son-in-law's family could accuse her of using witchcraft to redirect the son's resources away from his own clan. Alternatively, if an old woman fell ill while living with her married daughter, the daughter and her mother could accuse the son-in-law's family of making her sick through witchcraft because they felt jealous of the attention she got from the son-in-law.

Given these circumstances, women do their best to find other residential options. Even if they feel emotionally close to their daughters, and those daughters bring them plates of food everyday, an older woman is more likely to live with a brother, if she has one, than to move to the homestead of her married daughter.

Despite this strong belief against living with daughters, one woman out of the sixty-five I interviewed from 1994–96 did indeed live with her married daughter. When I asked why she lived in this arrangement, Luwazo offered: "I have no family. My husband died. I have no brothers. I am an old woman; there is no one to care for me." When I pushed specifically on how it is possible that she can live with her daughter when everyone else says that it is not allowed, Luwazo told me that her son-in-law is a good man, "he won't beat me." Luwazo's daughter and son-in-law live in Chikanta, the frontier farming area to which Gwembe people began migrating in the 1980s. Luwazo became widowed in 1958, and joined her daughter and son-in-law in 1987 after shifting among the homesteads of various clansmen (her "classificatory fathers") in the home village. Perhaps within the migrant community people tolerate variations on traditional and normative behavior. It is also possible that once outside of the home village, the threat of witchcraft decreases; at least distance can buffer the immediate fear. Indeed, Scudder and Habarad (1991) speculate that migrants to Chikanta often move in order to protect themselves from such threats.

The Ambivalence of Grandsons and Rescue by Daughters

In some instances a woman whose best hope may lie with a daughter may live with a grandson, which maintains the image of normative behavior while allowing the daughter to play a significant role in caring for her aging mother. Another residential arrangement involving a daughter developed in Chikanta toward the end of 1996. On my last visit to the frontier region during that field trip, I discovered that Sala, an old woman who had lived in an isolated homestead in Sinafala, had just moved to Chikanta at the urging of her daughter and had taken up residence with one of her daughter's sons. Sala had matrilineal family in Sinafala, including men she called "grandson," who gave her much help in building her house and other structures, and in plowing her fields.[11] However, during the extreme drought, when she had little or no harvest from her gardens, and after losing most of her chickens and goats to theft, Sala chose to follow her daughter to better land and rains, giving up her small homestead in Sinafala where she had lived for all of her adult life. However, unlike Luwazo, Sala became a formal member of her grandson's homestead, not her daughter's, thus maintaining the image of normative behavior. Yet it was clear to me that Sala's daughter controlled this arrangement, not her grandson. In effect, Sala's daughter facilitated and oversaw the situation, and if any problems arose within the grandson's homestead, her daughter took responsibility for settling them.

The frontier migrant community in fact offers numerous examples of breaking with normative behavior. As I discussed in chapter 4, in one frontier migrant village I found a homestead in which four unmarried (either widowed or divorced) sisters and their divorced mother lived together. In addition to the noteworthiness of their homestead-based economic activity (they ran a local bar and, according to some, a brothel), the fact that all these women lived together *and* with the mother caught my attention. Although the women had origins in a different region of the Gwembe Valley, they were Tonga, and their customs of residential preferences were similar to those of the people I knew more closely. Nevertheless, two of the sisters and their mother explained to me that they shared a homestead because "they had no husbands or brothers who could help them, so they help themselves in this way."

It was also in the frontier where I found two co-wives working together—farming, harvesting, and selling their surplus of groundnuts and sweet potatoes, in a way that I had only ever seen sisters of "one womb" work together. The evidence from the frontier region suggests that, at the least, there is great variety throughout rural Zambia in the way people live out their daily lives, despite normative preferences. It may also be that in the frontier, migrants have limitations in their social networks—the proper relatives just are not there—in which case the migrants employ more flexibility in their preferences.

Back in Sinafala, in 1995, I witnessed yet another instance of individual action, despite formal statements of "respect for the elderly" and norms of caring for the aged. Like Sala in the frontier, Malala, the oldest woman in Sinafala, lived with one of her daughter's sons, Mister. In Tonga naming systems, people often call women in reference to their children—they say "mother of" and usually add the oldest child's name. BinaMister, that is, the mother of Mister, lived within a ten-minute walk of Mister's homestead, in the homestead of one of her other sons. Mister's "other mother" (meaning his mother's sister), BinaFosten, lived in the homestead just below with her own son Fosten. Another married daughter lived in a neighboring village, but she played a minimal role in caring for her mother, in part because she lived close to an hour's walk away. Thus, Malala had two daughters (both widows living with married sons) in the immediate vicinity, and indeed those daughters helped support Malala as much, if not more, than Mister and his two wives. BinaFosten brought firewood to Malala every few days so that she could keep a fire going in her small wattle-and-daub hut. BinaMister brought vegetables from her garden every so often. They also brought small dishes of cooked nsima and relish every few days.

In contrast to the attention given her by her daughters, the grandsons expressed much more ambivalence about their grandmother. During one of my visits with Malala we sat next to her house in the garden of bullrush millet that she had planted during the rainy season of 1995–96. Mister had decided that he would clear an even larger area adjacent to Malala's garden. Throughout our conversation, Malala turned to Mister and made comments about the trees he was cutting and threatening him with retaliation should one of those trees fall on her millet and crush it. Mister responded with sarcastic chuckles and teasing pleas for some of her tobacco. This grandmother–grandson relationship represents a common form of "joking relations," as research throughout Africa documents (Colson 1951; Murdock 1959; Stucki 1995). Yet despite the joviality of their exchange, Mister, as well as his "cousin" Fosten, frequently veered from the norm of respect for elders.

Fosten, the extremely active and vocal leader of the local Seventh-Day Adventist church, rarely visited his grandmother or gave her assistance (although the meals his mother brought to Malala came from Fosten's food supplies). However, he did make a trip to her hut one day. On one of my journeys out of the village I left a 2.5-liter jug of water for Malala. Malala already had such a jug from which she drank and bathed, but it was broken, so that at most it could contain only a liter and a half. One of Mister's wives had the responsibility of bringing water to Malala, but she thought it a great burden, and Malala received water perhaps once a week if she was lucky. Malala described bribing some of Mister's young children to collect water for her by giving them a treat when she had something (when I gave her gifts of sugar she could then use that to entice the children into helping her). So, according to the gossip, about an hour after my departure from the village, leaving the new jug with Malala, Fosten arrived at her doorstep and took the jug back to his own homestead. Malala, in her early eighties, almost blind and physically frail, could not defend her rights to the jug. Fosten added the jug to his collection of property in his homestead.

A few months later, deep into the drought of 1995–96 when it was clear that rainy-season fields would yield no grain, Malala experienced another crisis instigated by a grandson. Without any warning, or words to his mothers or brothers, Mister packed up his homestead, including both wives and all the children, and moved to their gardens on the lakeshore. During intensive weeding and bird-scaring periods, and especially in hunger years, villagers commonly move to their gardens. People often erect a temporary shelter in order to sleep in the fields at night to scare away hippos and intruding cattle. However, when a man has two wives, and dependents in the village homestead, one wife usually remains behind to keep house. This time, Mister's nuclear family abandoned the whole homestead, and Malala with it. Because BinaFosten and BinaMister were also living at their river gardens, no one knew of this abandonment for three days or more. Malala ate nothing and drank the few drops of water left in her cracked jug. BinaMister described meeting with her sister, BinaFosten, to decide how to manage the situation once word got out. BinaMister, because she had a particularly successful garden from which she ate even during the hunger, went to rescue her mother from the abandoned homestead. BinaMister carried the few possessions Malala owned, while Malala struggled the few miles to BinaMister's garden. According to BinaMister, a forty-minute journey took Malala close to five hours. When I found Malala at her daughter's garden a week after the abandonment, Malala appeared cleaner and more animated, mobile, and clearheaded than I had seen her in sixteen months, due to the improvement in food and access to water that BinaMister's presence mobilized. In this case, residence with a daughter raised her quality of living significantly and saved her from starvation induced by a grandson's abandonment.

The community condemned Mister's behavior, claiming that he was wrong to leave Malala alone in his homestead with no food and water. However, Mister suffered no sanctions or reprimands other than the stories that circulated. As Colson and Scudder indicate (Colson and Scudder 1981), Tonga eventually distrust the oldest old for fear that with their continued life, they rob children in a homestead of their health and well-being. Despite people's criticism of Mister's behavior, they seemed to tolerate and understand his situation; he had four young children to feed and protect. In a community living with frequent scarcity and appropriate conditions for belief in a "limited good" (Foster 1965), the continued existence of Malala means an unjust distribution of resources. Supporting a woman who has already lived eighty years robs resources from children who still have a full life to live. Perhaps this is why BinaMister, also an old woman, living alone in her garden, could care for her very old mother. Additionally, BinaMister, a widow herself, had no husband with a competing claim on her labor, making her free to give what she had, both in material and personal resources, to her elderly mother. In this way, two old widows living on their own, and feeding themselves, do not present a threat to the youngsters of any homestead, nor a challenge to any man's claim over them.

The stories of Malala, Sala, and their residential arrangements emphasize two points: residence is fluid, and individual action, within the limits set by gender roles and age structure, forms the heart of homestead composition. Some children decide to leave their grandparent's homestead to live with their father, who gives them more food to eat. An old woman may decide to visit a relative and stay for a few months because the area has harvested green maize, while her own son's field has burnt in the sun. A man abandoning his old and frail grandmother acts on a similar choice. All of these examples illustrate how individuals make decisions for their own benefit. During resource scarcity, people make choices to trim down their expenditures and increase their own access to necessities.

Homestead composition and residential arrangements comprise the cornerstone of daily life. Individuals act in reference to social groups and material limitations in their surroundings. People's actions shape group dynamics, but at the same time individual action responds to group dynamics. The range of options available for individuals to play out their choices and behavior links to the resources available to them—resources that are both social and material. It is much more likely that an old woman with a loyal son, and his wife within shouting distance, can harness small surpluses of food or labor than can a widow living alone in an isolated one-house homestead. The options for such a solo individual must, according to cultural and social forces, include a broader support net than those who can command their choices from their own doorstep.

In our endeavor to understand support systems for the elderly, we must recognize the important role that residence plays. We must also recognize that the elderly we speak of are not a single group but a collection of individuals, some of whom may share similar characteristics and strategies but others who may have different preferences and options available to them. In the next chapter I explore how these different preferences and options play out in older women's and men's spiritual lives.

6. Ancestors, Rituals, and Manipulating the Spirit World

You can't have a funeral without old women. A funeral without old women is like it was a dog who passed away; it's not very important.

Agnes, March 1995

Men are witches [sorcerers] because they witch their friends and talk about witch-craft more than women. They even feel proud and say they need to be feared because they can cut a person's life short.

Bina Sialuwa, July 1995

Walking through central Sinafala on a Saturday morning, visitors will hear the uniquely harmonic voices of attendees at the Seventh-Day Adventist church—harmonies that in a Western context would sound out of key but in the echoing open space of rural Africa sound inspiring and lyrical. The church gathering often lasts all day and resembles a village party, with parishioners moving in and out of the one-room, tin-roofed hall in a constant flow, chatting, singing, or resting in the shade. On Sundays, "downtown" visitors will find a similar atmosphere, but parishioners belong to the Catholic, Pilgrim Holiness, New Apostolic, and Apostolic Faith churches. At any school, clinic, development, or government-influenced village meeting, such as political rallies, meetings to plan bore hole drilling, or an "under-five" child vaccination day, organizers typically open the session with a prayer, and meetings conclude with another reference to the Christian God. Clearly, Christianity has a strong foothold in rural life. If you look closely though, you may notice that the majority of attendees at church gatherings are adolescents and young adults. The loudest voices in prayer at village meetings come from the same age groups. Although older adults and even a few "elderly" people may attend meetings, and occasionally church services, the most active Christian population in the village is below age forty.

Christianity arrived in rural Africa generally, and Zambia in particular, along with the industrialism that predated colonialism. In fact, historians can trace educational development for African populations and subsequent political movements throughout former British Central Africa to inroads made by a variety of Christian missionaries (Scudder and Colson 1981; Schuster 1987; Chipungu 1992a, 1992b; Carmody 1999). So although the heightened activity of young people in Christian religious life might suggest that Christianity is relatively new, the fact is that Christianity has played a role in all Zambian lives since at least the early twentieth century. Thus it would be only reasonable to ask, in reference to public religious activity, Where are the old people?

Alongside the strong Christian belief system in rural life exists an equally, and possibly more vibrant, indigenous belief system. Even the most active church leaders and attendees give legitimacy to the indigenous belief system, whether through their own participation in ritual activities or by their acknowledgment of the power of those systems. During my first visit to Zambia in 1992 I was amazed to learn that college-educated women with professional careers bought special medicines to make their husbands and boyfriends love them more. And in 2001 again I was impressed with the power of traditional belief systems when I learned that young adult members of a local development group in one of the migrant regions had participated in hiring a "witch finder" to cleanse the community of the "witch epidemic" they believed existed in their region. Although Christianity has a strong presence in all facets of Zambian life, indigenous belief systems provide the underlying foundation of belief for most Zambians. Consequently, it seems that as people move through their life cycle, they frequently return to a core belief in the power of the supernatural, including both the benevolent care provided through connection to ancestors and the more dangerous malevolent powers of the spirit world.

This chapter considers the role of the elderly in indigenous ritual and spiritual practices and the way in which these activities influence their social position in the village. Illuminating this facet of social relations reveals additional variations in men's and women's strategies for mobilizing support from kin. As with men's relationships to their children, men's participation in ritual and spiritual activity relies on their active manipulation of resources. At funerals men play managerial and organizational roles, whereas in regard to other aspects of Tonga belief systems, men's resources are a bit more illusory; men manipulate the spirit world to their benefit. Women play roles that are less dependent on control of resources. Their participation in funeral rituals emphasizes their close link to ancestors rather than their control over them, and their involvement with bad spirits, *zyelo*, is also based on more passive rather than controlling relationships. My discussion of these belief systems emphasizes the possibility that ritual and spiritual aspects of communities are manipulated by individuals in order to attain personal goals and security.

A Brief History of Ritual Life in the Gwembe

At relocation in 1958, some of the worst upheaval Tonga society experienced involved ritual institutions, particularly rituals and shrines associated with land and ancestors' links to specific localities. Colson (1958, 1960, 1971) and Scudder (1962) describe the complexity of the ritual institutions and their influence over agricultural activities and personal lives. A fundamental component of the indigenous Tonga religious tradition is called the cult of the shades by Colson and Scudder and follows a system of ancestor worship based on lineage and clan affiliations. Families appease the ancestors by brewing beer made from grain they cultivated and pouring it at the doorstep of their home. In the past, causes for death and illness were sought from diviners, and death was most often attributed to ancestors' displeasure. Since the 1980s, people have turned more often to witch finders to learn the cause of death, and accusations of sorcery by living relatives are increasingly common (Scudder 1983, 1984; Scudder and Habarad 1991; Colson 1995, 2000).

In addition to the cult of the shades, other ritual systems associated with annual agricultural cycles played important roles in Gwembe life. Before relocation, a local ritual leader (*sikatongo*) initiated agricultural activities each year and led the major rain ceremonies at the local rain shrines. The position of *sikatongo* was inherited through matrilineal ties traced to the founding lineage for the area. The activities under the jurisdiction of the sikatongo were completely intertwined with specific localities, because the sikatongo himself was a representative of the first lineage to cultivate that land. At relocation in 1958, the community's ritual relationship to the land was dissolved, just as the systems of land access and ownership were undermined (see chap. 3). Colson and Scudder (Colson 1971, 1973; Scudder and Colson 1982; Scudder 1985) have seen adaptation to these changes, with first a breakdown of the previous systems and then slowly the emergence of new institutions that build on past patterns but adapt to new conditions.

Some of the ritual activities that Colson and Scudder observed in the 1950s are still practiced in the Gwembe. However, they do not play as central a role as they had in the past. During the drought of 1994–95, I heard a few people discussing the possibility of "clapping for rain," the ritual performed to bring on the rains. But I was told that only a few old women knew how to clap these days and that most people don't rely on such beliefs anymore.

In some cases people appreciated the changes in ritual activity that resettlement brought. Colson (1971) suggested that one aspect of the relocation to new lands that people liked was the ability to make individual choices about agricultural activities. With the breakdown of the agricultural ritual traditions, people were free to plant and harvest when and where they wished. Scudder (1962) mentions shrines that some men established to give them special hunting powers. These days, with so little game in the valley area, few hunters are active, and I heard nothing about rituals or shrines for hunting. In the migrant destinations, where the abundance of game makes illegal hunting an attractive activity, people still do not discuss, at least openly, ritual activities to strengthen hunting skills. Quite likely, some people in the areas around the park have rituals or shrines for hunting that draw on practices of the past, and quite likely they have incorporated new traditions as well, but given the government's and NGOs' focus on ending poaching, these practices would be kept quiet except among those closely involved.

Although the cult of the shades (ancestors) is not as popular as it was before resettlement, it was the most active aspect of the indigenous belief system during my fieldwork. The cornerstone of the cult is grain and a house, symbolizing agricultural and social/sexual reproduction: beer brewed from a family's grain is poured on their doorstep. In this ritual, ancestors see that their lineage will endure. A person who inherits the spirit (*muzimu*) of a deceased relative should pour beer for the ancestor (*kupila muzimu*) annually. However, during the droughts of the early 1990s, most people did not pour beer for the ancestors. In my interviews, I learned that many old people with three or four spirits inherited from different relatives had not poured beer in the last three years. Sinafala people told me that the ancestors "know there is hunger; they look to see if there are rains," and they will be patient until the hunger is finished. Ancestors are tolerant of the difficulties of daily life, and living relatives have opportuni- ties for flexibility in their beliefs. Flexibility in fulfilling ritual obligations was also documented for past eras. Wild game populations dwindled in the 1950s, and the government prohibited hunting, so in order to appease the spirits of hunters, inheritors mimicked harpooning a hippo or they stalked and speared fresh droppings. These activities appeased the ancestors "since they are well aware that times have changed, and that it would be in no one's interest to demand the impossible" (Scudder 1962, 193; see also Colson 1971, 213).

Spirit inheritance is the other ritual still active in the cult of the ancestors and has been the most visible example of the indigenous belief system over the past decade. Elders, and especially old women, play important roles in the perpetuation of the system. In the following sections I focus on funerals as a framework for examining the role of the elderly in the contemporary spiritual world of Gwembe people.

Concerns about sorcery and malevolent spirits are also part of Tonga spiritual beliefs. Increasing social differentiation and the resulting jealousy fuels fears of sorcery and malicious intentions within Gwembe communities (Scudder 1983, 1984; Scudder and Habarad 1991; Colson 1995, 2000). In the final sections of this chapter I address witchcraft and sorcery, and the position and vulnerability of the elderly within these phenomena.

Funerals in Village Life

My friends in Sinafala repeatedly told me that "you can't have a funeral without old women." Elderly women are key participants at any funeral, and at children's funerals they usually manage the proceedings. The roles these women play during funerals for adults include leading mourning songs and dances, providing important information about kin relations to influence choices of spirit inheritors, and performing rituals; for an infant's burial they also dig the grave and bury the child.

The central role that elderly women play in funerals is clearly visible the moment you arrive at the homestead hosting a funeral. Elderly women cluster at the physical center of the event, the house of the deceased. If their numbers exceed the shaded areas around the house, they gather in the shade of any neighboring structures or sit on the ground in between.

Aside from the physical centrality of old women, their participation in the rituals associated with funerals is also fundamental. Indeed, a funeral is officially over only when the old women have swept the ashes from each of the cooking hearths, long after the guests have departed.

Understanding the part old people play in funerals requires some basic knowledge about funerals. For most deaths in Sinafala, a funeral takes place over the course of five days. Each day, different kin members and clans with kinship relations to the deceased have responsibility for slaughtering an animal, while the clan members of the deceased provide maize for nsima. The wealth of the family sponsoring the funeral, the season, and food availability can influence the length of a funeral. A poor family and clan are more likely to have shorter funerals. During famine, funerals are also likely to be shorter for the same reasons: no one can mobilize the quantity of grain needed to feed the funeral guests, who often include most of the adult villagers as well as clan relatives from other areas. During acute food shortages guests are often even more numerous simply because they are guaranteed at least a few decent meals at a funeral. Over the past decade, I have seen funerals shortened due to severe drought. Sometimes during the planting season, the funeral of a well-known or important person was postponed until harvest time in the hope that hard work would pay off and people would have sufficient grain to offer at the huge multi-day event that a respected elder deserves upon his or her death.

Funerals differ from burials in that family members organize the burial of the deceased as quickly as possible. When a person dies in the village, the burial usually occurs the same day. However, for those who die while living away from the village, other arrangements must be made. Usually bringing the body back to the village for burial is preferred. According to Colson (personal communication), before the 1980s, people were more willing to bury a relative in town, as long as the official funeral was held in the village. However, in the last decade families have gone to enormous expense and trouble to bring the body home to the village for burial. We are not clear about the reasons for this increasing preference. My Sinafala friends told me simply that the family wanted to see the deceased before she was buried and suggested that otherwise the family may not believe the relative has died. This idea compliments our impression that accusations of sorcery are on the rise (Scudder and Habarad 1991) and suggests that families want to see the deceased relative in order to determine the cause of death. I was also told that when someone is buried in another chief's area, the family must pay a fee of an animal to the chief or his representative. During the 1994–95 fieldwork period, three adults and one child died while living in towns on the plateau. All adults were brought back to the village for burial, whereas the infant was buried in an urban cemetery.

The burial event takes place during one day. Close relatives of the same sex as the deceased bathe and prepare the body for the grave. While men with affinal ties, or no close relationship, to the deceased dig the grave, relatives and community members lead the mourning outside the deceased's house. During this time a group of male relatives sit to set the date for the formal funeral and discuss the cause of death. These discussions usually include information obtained from a witch finder (*munganga*).

It is very common that as soon as someone dies, two relatives, one from the matrilineage of the deceased and one representing the father's lineage, are sent to the nearest witch finder to seek information about the cause of death. During the time between the burial and the funeral, relatives continue to gain information about the death from a variety of traditional healers. Villagers told me that there are different kinds of *munganga;* some have a license from the government to publicly state the name of the one accused of "witching" the deceased. I was told that there are fewer of these witch finders available, and their fees are much higher than a *munganga* who simply identifies the category of relative doing the witching (a father's brother or mother's father, for example), or a diviner who usually identifies displeasure of ancestors as the cause of death. However, I was never able to get reliable information from government officials about the existence of these licensed witch finders. There is also a "traditional healers union," which the Zambian government recognizes as an indigenous medical group. It is possible that villagers I spoke with were aware of this group and presumed that the official status gave clearance for making public accusations of individuals thought to be witches. Colson (1996, 2000) and Scudder (1983, 1984) suggest that increases in sorcery accusations and suspicion of individuals are part of the process of social unraveling occurring in Gwembe communities. The desire to know the name of specific individuals who are the cause of suffering could be an elaboration of the same process. Not only do people want to know that their daughter, sister, or nephew died wrongfully, but when possible they want to know the name of the perpetrator of the evil. In the past villagers more commonly sought out diviners (*musonda*) who identified displeasure of ancestors as causes of illness and death. But as Colson has pointed out, since at least the 1990s, witchcraft has become the primary cause of death, and people consequently search out witch finders rather than diviners (Colson 2000). In the following sections I talk more about suspicion and fear of individuals within the community and the ways in which these events impact the elderly.

At the moment of burial the spouse of the deceased is expected to perform a few tasks, such as sitting at the edge of the grave to dislodge some of the earth, which signals the death of her or his partner and the end to their marriage. Once the grave is filled in with earth, mourners dance and sing on the grave, sharing their emotions and pounding the earth to prevent the grave from collapsing at a later date. The main participants in this mourning are women, both old and young. Men may join in initially, but after a brief period they move to the side and under the shade of a tree continue the discussion of the death and the imminent funeral.

Relatives set the date for the funeral after considering a variety of factors that influence the ease with which the funeral will be carried out. The time needed to inform distant relatives of the death is an important factor. People also express concern about the time needed to acquire supplies, including grain, salt, and vegetable oil for cooking. The rain and agricultural cycles also influence funeral times; I was told that during heavy rains it is difficult for people to travel through the valley because of flooded river crossings, and if there are labor demands in the fields, people will choose not to attend the funeral.

Ascot, an older wealthy man with extensive kinship and business relationships over the whole Gwembe Valley, died in November 1994, but his funeral was scheduled for the end of March 1995. People hoped to be finished with the heaviest work of planting, and they needed this much time to make sure that the news of Ascot's death reached distant relations. They also had to accumulate all the food needed for what was going to be a large funeral. About a week before Ascot's funeral began, an old Sinafala woman died. Her funeral was scheduled to begin the day Ascot's funeral ended so that people traveling any distance would not need to return to Sinafala at a later date. Obviously, funeral decisions are made with concern for convenience as well as material constraints.

Siabulungu: A Funeral Elder

In describing village funerals and elderly women's roles during the event, I focus on the experience of one woman who played many active roles and taught me much about the importance of old women in village ritual. Siabulungu is of the Mukuli clan and the sister of the senior headman of Sinafala. I was told that in the past the Mukuli clan had strong male members who amassed wealth and power within Sinafala but that these days those lineages in the Mukuli clan have lost much of their wealth, and with it, prestige. Despite the changing social rank of her clan, Siabulungu is still respected in the community as one who knows the history and kinship links of many generations. She is sought out as a leader for funerals of her clan members because of her wisdom and her strong character. As a leader of these funerals, she performs key roles in the rituals and activities throughout the five days.

Siabulungu lives with a widowed son and his children in a small homestead near the center of Sinafala. Her younger son is a teacher at a primary school on the plateau, where she visits occasionally. Neither she nor her elder son, Scott, have much wealth, but she and the family in the homestead benefit from the assistance given by the teacher.

Siabulungu was a central figure at every funeral I attended. Upon arrival at a funeral homestead, I found her sitting at the home of the deceased, singing the funeral songs or leading songs as the group of elderly women moved throughout the homestead. At the funeral of her classificatory sister, Lutinda, Siabulungu was the leading clan elder and responsible for a variety of tasks directed at both the deceased and the community. Her jobs included laying grain on the grave at the start of the funeral, giving the spirit of the deceased to the spirit inheritor, breaking down Lutinda's grain bin to expose all the contents, and pouring the funeral porridge (*kabelebele*) on the grave during the wee hours of the funeral's last night.

The grain placed on and in the grave are offerings to the deceased to satisfy their hunger and to prevent them from returning to the homestead in spirit form, demanding to be fed, which is believed to cause harm to living relatives. As part of feeding the ancestors, *kabelebele* is poured at the end of the funeral; Siabulungu told me that "before the ancestor can drink the first beer [ritual beer which is brewed and poured about two weeks after the funeral], she must first drink this porridge." Old women make the porridge from grain remaining in the deceased's grain bin. They also make the miniature pots, from which they pour the porridge, from the clay of the deceased's grain bin. In this way the deceased is buried with both her grain and her storage bin. The clay for making the pots is taken from the walls of the bin at the time it is broken, revealing the contents inside. By opening the bin for the community to peer into, relatives are satisfied that no property has been hidden, and the spirit of the deceased is also appeased by seeing that no grain remains.

The overseer of inheritance is one of the most important roles at a funeral. This role is taken by someone of the same sex as the deceased, although clan elders of both genders are vocal participants throughout the inheritance discussions. Inheritance of *mizimu* (plural) is an important decision for the clan and often a source of conflict. The inheritor becomes responsible for the annual feeding of beer to the spirit and for the living relatives.[1] A man's *muzimu* is usually taken by his brother or a sister's son. A man who inherits the spirit of a brother with many children is entitled to the labor of those children and any bride-wealth payments that come from marriage of a daughter, along with a large share of the deceased's property. The inheritor is also expected to provide for dependents as the biological father would have done. These relationships between children and their father's inheritor can be volatile, with older men hoping to extract as much as possible from the children while avoiding investing much of their own resources. As with a biological father, children are not of the same clan, so the kinship and emotional link is less than it is with a mother who is of the same clan as her children. A father's inheritor is that much more distanced from the children; not only is he of a different clan, but the children are not even his own biological offspring. At two different funerals of important and wealthy men, the conflict between the inheritor and the sons of the deceased led to the children hiding property (bicycles and plows) and cattle so that the inheritor could not lay claim to them.

A woman's inheritor is often a sister or a granddaughter. When a sister inherits a *muzimu*, the inheritor is already a classificatory mother to the deceased's children, so the conflicts that can occur with male inheritance are not as common. In addition, women typically have less property to inherit, and the potential for conflict is lower. At her sister's funeral, Siabulungu performed the actual ritual of installing the *muzimu* in Lutinda's granddaughter: touching the soft spot of the throat of the inheritor and saying the phrase, "Lutinda, now you live here." I was told that by placing the *muzimu* at the base of the throat, it is sure to taste the beer that the host drinks on behalf of the ancestor. In addition to conducting the inheritance ceremony, Siabulungu participated in the decision of who should be given the *muzimu*. Before Lutinda died, she requested that her granddaughter inherit her *muzimu*. However, Lutinda had many granddaughters, which prompted me to ask how they chose Margaret. Siabulungu told me that she chose Margaret because she was the granddaughter who most

Fig. 6.1. Dancing on the grave as a five-day funeral is just beginning.

often visited Lutinda, especially when she was sick. In this case, an inheritor was chosen at least partly because of her actions in relation to the deceased, not simply because of kinship links. Margaret's investment and care gained her the honor of inheriting her grandmother's spirit.

Old women have many roles at funerals. Siabulungu was a key participant in her sister's funeral not only as an old woman who led mourning through song and dance but also as a respected lineage member who had responsibilities for decision making and ritual. The other aspect of elderly participation at funerals centers on their sheer numbers and their treatment by the other funeral participants.

Funeral Room and Board

During the five days of an average funeral, at least three cattle and as many goats will be slaughtered in honor of the deceased. The meat is handed out to all funeral attendees to cook as their sauce to eat with nsima, also provided by the funeral hosts. Each community (kin group, village, neighborhood) in attendance has its own cooking hearth where members prepare all their meals. The spatial arrangements at funerals are usually circular. The home of the deceased, where all the old women cluster, forms the focal center of the funeral. Spiraling out from them are the homestead relatives, who live and sleep on the homestead grounds, outside of their own houses, during the entire five days. Other funeral guests settle on the uninhabited areas of the actual homestead, on the outskirts of the homestead, and so on until all guests have found a place for a hearth and temporary shelter. People choose a location in relationship to the road or path on which they arrived from their own village; I was told that people choose a camping spot close to the road back home in case a fight breaks out and they need to run away (see also Colson 1960, 183). Such conflicts never arose at any of the funerals I attended. In the past, however, funerals included drum competitions (*ingoma*) between neighboring communities as well as heated warrior competitions (*budima* dances) that parodied battles and highlighted men's fierce strength and power. Communities still compete at funerals of important people, and in the past the competitions sometimes resulted in real conflict between communities.[2]

Each kinship group, village, or neighborhood attending the funeral establishes a camping spot and builds a cooking hearth. The funeral hosts typically harvest enough firewood from the bush for all guests to use throughout the five days. Each day relatives appointed by the owner of the funeral (*mwini waidilwe*) distribute meali meal, salt, cooking oil, and portions of meat from the slaughtered animals to the cooks at each hearth. A funeral guest who has personal food taboos, sometimes expressed as an "allergy" to goat meat, might receive chicken, which he cooks on a separate fire in order to prevent contamination by the other foods. Conflicts over food distribution are common. Women often insult those distributing cooking oil, arguing that their group is larger than their neighbors and they should receive a larger portion. During some of the most severe periods of drought, I saw mothers take portions of meat and meali meal back to their homesteads to feed their children who did not attend the event. At the planning of one of the largest funerals in Sinafala history, elders warned that "we need to watch the maize distribution carefully—because we don't want people to take maize in a *chitenge* [woman's cloth wrap] to cook at home—there's hunger this year."

For hungry people, funerals are good opportunities for a decent meal. I was told that more people than usual were attending Sinafala funerals during the 1994–95 drought, and in at least two cases the "owner of the funeral" asked close neighbors to return to their own homesteads so that relatives who had traveled from afar would have enough to eat.

Because of their ritual and spiritual importance and their close link to the ancestors, old women are fundamental to any funeral; they can always

TABLE 6.1
Food resources consumed at two Sinafala funerals

Data	BinaJohn's Funeral (female)	Ascot's Funeral (male)
Funeral date	April 1995	March 1995
Approx. age at death	72	68
Approx. no. of attendees	150	700
No. of animals slaughtered		
Cattle	4	21
Goats	17	8
Chickens	7	4
Amount of other food items		
Maize (kg)	320	1,440
Salt (kg)	11	NA

NA, not available.

find a place to sit for mourning at the center of the homestead. Food is prepared by relatives of the deceased specifically for the old women, and once seated among the group of lead mourners, a woman is guaranteed nsima with sauce at least three times during the day. This is more than most old women ate in their own homesteads during the 1994–95 year of fieldwork.

Families invest massive resources in funerals. Reflecting on the funeral traditions in the village, some young people expressed their dismay at the obligation to spend so much wealth on a dead person. These young people told me that they hoped to channel their resources into their children while they were alive, rather than have their relatives "eat the wealth" during a funeral.[3] Indeed the great expense of funerals appears to many outsiders, and apparently some locals as well, as an extreme contradiction. At two different funerals I was able to collect information about the total amounts of maize and animals consumed during the five-day events (see table 6.1).

At the funeral of BinaJohn (female), who died in early April 1995, at about age seventy-two, relatives slaughtered four cattle, seventeen goats, and seven chickens. Hosts distributed approximately 11 kilograms of salt and 320 kilograms of maize for cooking nsima. BinaJohn's funeral was slightly better attended than most of the other funerals I witnessed; approximately 150 people came to mourn her death.

The largest funeral since the death of the previous headman of Sinafala in 1982 (and some said that that funeral actually had had fewer people) was given for Ascot at the end of March 1995. Approximately seven hundred people came to the funeral, and seven drum teams competed with their *budima* dances. Ascot died when he was about sixty-eight. For this well-known and respected man, with kinship relations throughout the valley, twenty-one cattle, eight goats, and four chickens were slaughtered. Hosts distributed 1,440 kilograms of maize to funeral guests, and they also gave an equally large amount of salt and cooking oil to participants. My queries to funeral participants about why people spend so many of their few resources when someone has died were answered in various ways: "because the man had made a name for himself"; "he used to go to funerals in Sina-zongwe [Gwembe south area]"; "he would take animals to help his friends . . . so his friends, when they heard about the death, they came here with animals to help." People also said that you must slaughter animals to honor the deceased and to tell people that you loved him. In addition, hosting a funeral with lots of food and many people reflects well on the family of the deceased and makes a good impression on both the living community and the ancestors. This huge investment in funerals is relatively new, however. According to Scudder and Colson, in the not so recent past, funerals required far less in the way of material resources from the hosts and lineages involved. Scudder mentions the more symbolic gifts of hoes, beads, and "the odd goat" as funeral offerings in the 1980s and before (Scudder, personal communication). Perhaps this inflation of funeral contributions reflects notions of "middle-class" aspirations of conspicuous consumption. Perhaps the increased costs reflect a kind of communitywide adaptation to scarcity whereby everyone benefits over time (within a year or two) from the communal redistribution of extant resources. Most definitely elders and children benefit from the protein they eat at funerals—protein that they most likely do not receive regularly in their own homesteads. And certainly the use of cattle as important gifts between clans at funerals demonstrates the central role that cattle have come to play in village life and is one reason why cattle have become so important in intergenerational exchange.

Throughout the funeral activities, men and women have different roles. Elder men might sit close to the home of the deceased where the old women mourn, but they did not join this group's activities. Men's funeral responsibilities centered on management and organization. Decisions about food distribution and slaughtering were made by men, while women cooked. Elder men were always part of the discussion of property inheritance, even if it was a woman who died. And investigations into the cause of death, including consulting diviners and witch finders, were always headed by men, although female elders in the clan often joined. Elder women, on the other hand, "lived" the funeral; they were always in action, mourning, singing, dancing, and performing the fundamental rituals. Here again in the ritual and spiritual world, we see that men's and women's roles differ in their interaction with resources and emotional facets of life. Men manage events; women create the events and live them.

Manipulation of the Spirit World

Witchcraft and sorcery in African communities receive much attention from both academics and the general public. Popular films and books attempt to bring this mystical world to life, and exaggerate and misrepresent much of what is generally called witchcraft. Many classics in Africanist anthropology (Evans-Pritchard 1937; Turner 1969, 1981) have tried to present and explain the realm of magic and ritual in more realistic terms; these are legitimate belief systems that make sense in people's lives.

When I left for Zambia in the spring of 1994, I did not intend to investigate the supernatural world and people's participation in its manipulation; my research was problem focused. Tonga social organization and household negotiations of support for the elderly were my arena. I naïvely thought that I would be exempt from the dramas of witchcraft and sorcery in village life. Only a week after my arrival in the village, people told me stories of an uncle they avoided for fear of his power as a sorcerer. Also during my first month living in the village I brought home the body of a young girl who had died of malaria at the nearest clinic; she was the only sister in a large family of boys, and her uncle was assumed to have "witched" her in order to control her spirit and thus increase his supernatural powers.

Slowly, and perhaps a bit grudgingly, I realized I would need to include discussions of the supernatural in my interviews.[4] In particular, I became aware of villagers' beliefs and of the differences between men's and women's use and misuse of the spirit world. Older men were assumed to be witches (*bulozi*) who actively engaged in sorcery—learned rituals to manipulate the supernatural world for human goals. Women, however, were not feared as witches but rather for the possibility that they had bad spirits (*zyelo*). These bad spirits were said to "land," apparently randomly, on a host and inadvertently cause harm to others in specific situations. Being the host to zyelo was quite a different matter than controlling spirits and other supernatural powers to effect personal goals. Men actively manipulated spirits and extracted power from both the living and the dead, whereas women were more benign participants in the world of mystical powers.

Old Women and Zyelo: The Benefit of Bad Spirits

Over time and with much effort I gathered information on the details of the bad spirits (*zyelo*). I tried to understand where they came from, how they attached themselves to a particular person, and whether they were subject to the desires of their host. Belief systems exist in the mental processes of individuals, not in the visible world, which makes understanding those systems complicated. People's different explanations for how things work further confuse an outsider's perspective. In my discussions with both men and women, young and old, only a few criteria were consistent. Zyelo are bad spirits that sit with their host and usually cause them no harm. When displeased or angry, the bad spirits spit blood in the cooking pot or urinate in the grain bin of the person who caused their anger.[5] Zyelo fall upon women almost exclusively; a few friends told me that it is possible for a man to have a *chelo* (singular), but in fact no one remembered any such man. Typically, zyelo fall on old women, not the young or middle-aged. People explained to me that zyelo come from a clan and can only land with a person of that clan. Although the host of the zyelo must be of the same clan as the spirit, the damage that zyelo cause primarily affects nonclan members.

Examples of zyelo activity were described to me:

> All old women are suspected of having zyelo. If a person asks for help and she is not given, then she begins complaining that she has been denied. . . . The evil spirits [zyelo] hear these complaints and can hurt the one who denies help. (Chabella, August 1995)

> Complaints about having zyelo come from [other] people. We just sometimes see blood smeared on pots, in a doorway, or on pounding mortars. This is when one can say he has been visited by zyelo. (MukaJosef, August 1995)

In all discussions of zyelo, my informants emphasized that the relationship between these bad spirits and an old woman centers on the woman's pleading activities. An old woman's zyelo are not an issue when she sits at home chatting with friends or sings mourning songs at a relative's funeral. Zyelo become active, and a problem, when an old woman requests assistance; at that moment those in the position to provide assistance become vulnerable to the power of these bad spirits. If they deny an old woman's request, the zyelo may hear the refusal and become indignant, spitting blood into the pot or on the homestead. A child who then eats from the blood-splattered pot will become sick and most likely die.

Viewed from another angle, zyelo benefit an old hungry woman. If her neighbors fear she has zyelo, then they will be more amenable to giving her assistance when she asks. Of course, this interpretation was my own logical conclusion and needed to be checked out with my elderly friends. The popular consensus on zyelo deemed them bad and dangerous. Young people all agreed they were undesirable: people should avoid having any zyelo "land" on them and should avoid contact with them. At this stage in their life, young people would be unlikely to have zyelo and would only be victims of their actions, and their fear is predictable. A number of middle-aged and elderly women chose not to speak of zyelo or sorcery at all, saying that they knew nothing about those topics. My assistant suggested that those who did not want to talk about the subject actually knew quite a bit but did not want to be seen by others as having the knowledge. However, a few spicy old women, known in the community for their outspoken and feisty personalities, told me that "zyelo are good for an old woman so she can get things that she asks for"; "whatever she [a woman suspected of having zyelo] asks for, she should be given"; and "we old women eat because of zyelo."

In addition to hearing people's thoughts on the subject, I heard many stories of families giving food to an old woman who happened to pass their hearth and request a bit of food. The fear of zyelo is so much a part of daily life that even my assistant chose a safe path of action with an old women while conducting one of the GTRP surveys. Drivas and another member of the GTRP team were in lakeshore fields finding members of our sample for a census update. They were approached by an old woman from a neighboring village who is feared in the area for her zyelo. She asked these young men why our project only "wrote" some people and not others?[6] She then said that she wanted to be "written." Rather than deny her, Drivas and his friend pretended to interview her, thus avoiding the wrath of her zyelo. This exchange was not the typical "food-focused" setting for zyelo activity. In the more common scenario, an old woman goes pleading to a homestead, and a wife gives what she can, hoping that her children will not be made sick.

Old Men and Control of the Supernatural

In contrast to old women, with their less controlling participation in the activities of malevolent spirits, old men are believed to actively manipulate the spirit world to their benefit. However, although all old women have the potential to carry zyelo, only some men, and not just old men generally, are thought to engage in the practice of sorcery. Gwembe people fear particular men who have reputations as sorcerers. These men are believed to use medicines and rituals to cause sickness and death among their relatives. By killing, the sorcerer takes control of the deceased's spirit and uses it to help amass resources and power.

Like the bad spirits old women are thought to house, the spirits a sorcerer controls are called zyelo. However, I was told repeatedly that they are not the same thing. In an attempt to help me better understand women's and men's relationship to zyelo, one informant offered me this explanation: "The zyelo that a sorcerer gets by killing someone stay with him until he dies, then they can just go anywhere within the clan. When they are with old women is when they spit blood. So the clans that have big sorcerers also have old women who might have zyelo" (Milicent, August 1995). Milicent also told me that because sorcerers kill many women, they control many women's spirits. Thus, when such a man dies, the zyelo go back to women; "that's why it's old women who mostly have zyelo and not men."

When I first arrived in Sinafala, a number of deaths occurred in one section of the village, including the young girl who died of malaria. I was told that the old man who was the cause of all these deaths was "driving a truck at night [to collect his victims], killing people to have the spirits help him work in his fields." This man was said to have a lot of maize, some of which he was selling at the time, and although it was the end of the dry season, he even had green maize.[7] Villagers explained his success in terms of sorcery; after all, it had been a bad drought year and most of the community did not have enough grain to eat, let alone sell or exchange.

This example highlights the role that jealousy plays in sorcery accusations. Scudder (1983, 1984; Scudder and Habarad 1991) discusses the changing social and economic structures in the Gwembe and suggests that increasing poverty, coupled with increasing social differentiation, has led to increasing fears of sorcery. Drunkenness, adultery, and rising divorce rates also accompany the changing social structures. As people experience social change, especially where people live close together and interact on a daily basis, tensions rise. Sorcery accusations, under these circumstances, are a socially acceptable expression of conflict.

In addition to the view of sorcery from the community's perspective, the experience of those thought to be sorcerers is important. The community does not simply "create" a sorcerer through their opinions; some men behave in ways that raise peoples' suspicions. Men might travel in search of special medicine to use in mystical rituals. Some men also participate in community life in ways that promote their reputations as powerful manipulators of the supernatural. There were at least three court cases brought to the headman during 1995 that focused on men thought to be sorcerers. These men had made verbal threats against relatives, with one threat consisting of the man simply telling his niece to "watch out." Because people suspected him of being a sorcerer, the threat carried great meaning for the niece and her family. Of course any member of the community knows that public comments as well as deeds reflect on an individual. Just as some old women told me that they tried not to plead from people in order to avoid accusations of zyelo, men seem to use the same logic, but in reverse, in making public threats or making known their use of special medicines. By making these actions public knowledge, men promote the community's perception that they are powerful figures. With their power, they can influence people near them.

The fact that relatives of a sorcerer are his usual victims is another important facet of sorcery in Gwembe communities. People related by blood and marriage pose the greatest threat of sorcery because these networks of relations contain the greatest points for conflicts and jealousy over wealth and status. Some of the young migrants I worked with told me that they were afraid of their fathers or maternal uncles and offered this as part of their reason for leaving the village. Yet the brothers of some of these migrants told me that although they knew their father was powerful, they were not afraid. One of these men specifically told me that his father loved him very much and that despite the fact the father "is a known witch," the son wanted to stay near him. Perhaps these variations in young men's fear of the same man reflect the old man's use of his power; he is able to gather together a group of dependents who are loyal to him, while at the same time keeping others in fear and thus maintaining his reputation as powerful. In this way, sorcery can be a mystical form of social control within the family.

Witch Hunting and the Demise of Old Men

Sometimes the mystical power of old men can backfire. Over the past decade the frequency of recruiting famous witch finders, *munganga*, to "cleanse" a community has been on the rise, as has the cost for their services. In one recent dramatic case, a witch finder famous throughout Zambia was invited by the community in general to come cleanse a region in which many Gwembe people live. When I visited the region in 2001, I heard numerous stories from different people about how all the old men in the area were singled out by the munganga, accused of using "black magic" to kill various relatives and harness their souls, and subsequently charged exorbitant fees to be "cleansed" of their evil powers. The process of "cleansing" involves performing certain rituals to remove the power from the accused sorcerer. The witch finder requires payment for each step of the identification and cleansing process.

When I visited Thatcher's homestead in 2001, I found his three wives and two of his fourteen children, but I was told that Thatcher was traveling and would be back in a few days. Thatcher, approximately sixty years old, had worked in one of the nation's industrial towns until his retirement in the early 1990s, when he established his farm in a plateau community. As I repeatedly visited the homestead during those fieldwork months, I asked about Thatcher and his whereabouts. He was one of my favorite senior men—thoughtful, soft-spoken—and he seemed to genuinely like his wives and children; I always enjoyed talking with him. But I was told that he was still traveling. Over those repeated visits, I slowly learned about how the most recent witch-finding spree had affected him and his family.

Through Thatcher's formal employment in town, he had managed to educate most of his children, and the oldest four had established extremely good professional careers in Zambia's formal sector. However, all four of his oldest children had died over the past seven years. During one of my visits with the wives, I asked a few questions about the stories I was hearing of the witch finder passing through the region. They told me that in fact their husband had been accused and that he had paid for cleansing with a large sum of cash, two plows, and at least five animals from his herd. The women suggested that he was traveling in order to call in some debts to regain a portion of his resource base. At least in his family, his wives had some of their own wealth and were not dropped into extreme and sudden poverty as a result of the witch-finding episode. Thatcher's nephews expressed their fear of Thatcher's mystical powers and relief that he was now "cured" but also ambivalence about losing access to some of Thatcher's resources.

In the 2001 "witch-hunting" episode, "Sweeper" the munganga recruited to the region for the massive witch hunt, required a payment of 500,000 kwacha (approximately US$165) from the suspect just to begin the process of divining whether or not he was practicing sorcery. With this payment, the suspect also needed to sign a contract stating "I will agree with whatever you find." Upon finding that the suspect was in fact guilty, the accused then paid another fine, usually in the form of property, including multiple head of cattle, grinding mills, carts for hauling produce, and in one case an old vehicle. As part of the "witch trial," the munganga may give a small portion of the payments to the victim, who is believed to be sick as a result of the sorcerer's activity. However, I was told that usually the victim prefers to receive medicine from the munganga to heal from the witchcraft. In addition to buying medicine for victims of witchcraft, these payments also buy the accused medicines and rituals that cleanse them of their magical powers. And of course, these payments are seen as compensation for the munganga's hard work. In this particular episode of witch hunting, the munganga also gave the two different chiefs of the region one head of cattle each, as appreciation for allowing him to work in the area. Sweeper left the region, after approximately one month of witch finding, with at least 115 head of cattle from at least eighteen accused sorcerers— after making payments to the chiefs—and with an unknown amount of cash and other property.

Often when I relate these stories to those unfamiliar with the power of the supernatural in the African context, people will ask me "Why do the old men go along with this? Can't they just refuse?" The answer to that question lies in the power and importance of maintaining functional social relations with one's relatives and community. If someone is believed to be too powerful and too dangerous, and has been openly accused but not yet treated for sorcery, he will eventually be ostracized to an extreme that allows him no power to maneuver in his social world. By agreeing to be cleansed, an old man acknowledges his own power but also assuages the community's fears and reinstates himself as a legitimate community member. The material cost is great, but maintaining the social networks on which daily life depends supersedes the financial considerations.

Of the approximately twenty senior men of Gwembe origins living in the region where this massive witch hunt took place, all but one were accused of practicing sorcery, and all but one paid the fees in order to be cleansed and reincorporated into their communities. The one man who refused cleansing, Samson, actually spoke on a local radio program and dared the witch finder to come to his homestead and make the accusation. Samson was known to own a rifle, and in local gatherings he told people he would meet any one coming to accuse him with his gun. At the end of my fieldwork season that year, Samson still had not been cleansed, but the witch finder had long since left the region to pursue witchcraft cases in other regions of Zambia, and it seemed that the flurry and fear of witchcraft activity had settled back to more normal levels, for the time being.

All of the men who were accused of witchcraft, it must be noted, were fairly wealthy senior men, with large homesteads and many dependent family members. The one man exempted from accusation, I was told by members of the community, did not have much wealth. This information can be read from a few different angles. Gwembe people will tell you that if an old man is rich, it is because he uses magic to gain wealth. My outsider, Western rationality tells me that the witch finder is a good businessman who knows how to get rich at the cost of the consumer—similar to big business practices in the Western world. At least one local person who commented on the increasing presence of witch finders in village life confirms my outsider perspective; in offering his opinion on the issue, he says that with the high cost for witch finding, all these munganga are just out to make money, and these days they demand more and more for their services. A good businessman, in this situation, identifies a need in the community and finds a way to fill it. Although munganga are good businessmen, local worldviews make their business possible, and with the shifting socioeconomic terrain in Zambia, local people look for some kind of explanation for the changes and upheavals they experience.

There are two end results of a massive cleansing of "sorcerers" in any community. The first is relief among family members, the community, and probably the accused (although this is a topic I have not raised with men who have been cleansed) that the social and mystical worlds have been healed and, at least for the moment, that people are not at great risk of witchcraft and sorcery. The second is that, as the witch finder leaves the region, so does the majority of senior men's wealth, and by association, family wealth. To me this is one of the greatest tragedies of the witch-finding epidemics: men who have worked hard throughout their lives to build their resource base, provide for their families, and make a place of respect for themselves as they age can have everything taken away not just from themselves but from the extended family, in a matter of days.

The witch-finding phenomenon has the potential to completely undermine men's primary strategy for security as they age—amassing enough resources to live on until they die. In earlier witch-finding episodes in the Gwembe Valley, particularly in the early 1980s, some senior men were able to recover from the costs of being accused and cleansed, whereas others died as poor men. These days, with the higher costs of cleansing, the potential for impoverishment is even greater.

Most recently, in my 2004 field season in the migrant region, I heard for the first time people expressing the idea that, with the new inheritance laws enacted and increasingly enforced by the Zambian government, in which wives and children inherit most of a man's property, wives will now begin to "witch" their husbands in order to gain their wealth. When I probed further, no one knew of an actual case of a woman engaging in witchcraft in this way, but a few people vaguely mentioned a news story from another region in which this was supposed to have occurred. And in one Gwembe village in 1999 two women had indeed been accused of witchcraft, although not cleansed. Not surprisingly, one had cattle and the other had just opened a shop. Although the reality of men's sorcery, accusations, and cleansing are clearly documented, the conversations about increasing suspicions of women's malevolent activities indicate that yet again social dynamics are in flux.

As mentioned in earlier chapters, women have been gaining some access to cattle through bride-wealth payments, and possibly increasing their resource base. If women do indeed make more use of the new inheritance laws to access valuable property upon their husband's death, along with accessing bride-wealth payments and gaining wealth through small businesses, they may indeed become targets of the jealousy and suspicion that has made wealthy senior men vulnerable to witchcraft accusations and ultimately to loss of their resource base. One scholar currently examining the relationships between new inheritance laws and increased mortality tied to HIV/AIDS has indeed been finding that women in the region are increasingly becoming targets of social alienation and also targets for extreme power plays by kin trying to control resources and women's independence (Frank 2004).

Engendering the Supernatural

The differences between women's and men's participation in the spirit world are important elements in old people's current survival strategies. As we saw in chapters 4 and 5, men gain access to property, and consequently ensure their own material well-being, through manipulation and control of dependents. Currently, women rely on seemingly more passive tactics to mobilize support, such as calling on kinship affiliation and mother–child bonds. In the realm of the supernatural, men are again manipulating and actively engaging in control of a resource, resulting in an image of power and strength. Women, on the other hand, promote themselves as inadvertently endowed with spiritual power. No woman admitted wanting to host zyelo or attempting to have them "land" on her. Yet the fact that any old woman might have zyelo is common knowledge, and old women are free to use this knowledge tactically in their requests for assistance.

With witch hunting on the rise, the position of senior men may be shifting. In the 2001 episode of witchcraft accusations, old men were forced to relinquish much of the material base they had worked for through their more productive years, placing themselves in a much more vulnerable position than they would have been otherwise. Some men, such as Thatcher, with broad social networks and a range of favors owed to him, managed to weather the storm. But others not as broadly connected as Thatcher became impoverished. Those men, rather than sponsoring dependents, may be forced into positions of dependency to their own children—much like old women, but without the social and cultural background that facilitates women's dependent positions. As the tide of witch hunting ebbs and flows, senior men will surely adapt to the new pressures, just as Gwembe people have adapted to hardships over the decades.

It is clear that senior men's control of resources has already made them targets for people hoping to even out inequalities of wealth. We don't know yet whether the witch-hunting epidemics will impact elderly men's ability to secure support as they age, but the warning signs are dark. And further in the shadows are the growing suspicions that women are gaining supernatural powers on par with those of men, and that they might in the future hold more substantial material resources than they currently do. If that occurs, we can wonder about how such resources will influence women's choices for mobilizing support as they age, and also how they will withstand the costs of being seen with such wealth.

We wonder, then, if the resource power bases (particularly cattle, which itself was a new resource after relocation in 1958) that have sustained men's position over the past forty years dissolve and women gain more substantial wealth, what kind of larger-scale change will occur? The answer is not yet apparent, although we venture a prediction that gender dynamics will shift and women may indeed gain ground in their ability to negotiate relationships through more equal access to resources, but they may also increasingly fall victim to the social forces that minimize extreme wealth differentials among Gwembe Tonga people.

The preceding chapters on economy, residence, and spiritual beliefs illustrated the variety of strategies that the elderly use for survival during daily life in the village and some of the ways that the social landscape that fosters those strategies is shifting. In the village setting, people manage social ties through face-to-face interactions. However, many young people migrate in search of wage employment or better farming opportunities. When children leave the village, elderly parents must develop alternative techniques for managing relationships between the village and migrant destinations. In the next chapter I discuss how elderly parents and their migrant children maintain social ties over distance and time.

7. Migration and Family Ties over Distance and Time

I came here because it is the nearest town to home [the village]. I made a comparison of the job opportunities.... Jobs in Lusaka, ah, they are bad! You have to be a man [a respectable adult]. If I did security [in Lusaka], all my education would be in the river ... to open and close gates all day, ah, it is not a job! Education pays. If I had no education, I could not imagine my life. Now my life is a dream.

Kleener, June 1995

My son ran away [to Lusaka] because of hunger, so he can work and feed himself. He ran away, but I will die of hunger. He used to fish and sell and give me money to buy food ... now I'll die of hunger. If he's well employed he will send me money, but he has no brain.... He hasn't sent anything since he started working.

BinaMister, March 1995

Sitting in the glaring Zambian sun outside the wattle-and-dab hut in which she lives alone, Simuchale told the story of her migrant son's one gift from Lusaka. Through puffs on the gourd water pipe that all old Tonga women keep close at hand, she explained that Clever had sent, through visitors returning back to the village, a yellow and red multipattern chitenge and a two-kilo packet of sugar. This was the only gift Siamuchale had received in the two years since the twenty-five-year-old young man left the village to search for work in town. Nor had she received any money or food to help her struggle through these years of hunger (1994–95). Clever had also not yet visited the home village, where the majority of his matrilineal relatives live.

Clever's employment as a security guard in Lusaka paid approximately thirty U.S. dollars a month, and the room he rented for himself and his wife, Ireni, in a shanty compound cost the equivalent of fifteen dollars a month. From the remaining fifteen dollars of Clever's salary, Ireni bought the month's food and charcoal for cooking their two daily meals, paid the water fees at the bore hole, which was a twenty-minute walk from their room, occasionally bought clothes when one of the few items they owned became too threadbare to wear with any pride, and paid for medicines and doctors' visits that were becoming more frequent now that Ireni was worried about not yet becoming pregnant—a problem not just for Ireni but also for her matrilineage, which expects her to continue the family line, as well as for her husband and his family, who had paid bride wealth in order to claim partial rights to Clever and Ireni's children.

Of course Clever also kept a little cash for himself for drinking *chibuku* at the local beer hall with his friends on weekend evenings. Clever told me that they frequently ran of out money at the end of the month. At those times he would borrow money from a friend, or from a money lender (at interest rates as high as 40 percent), so that they could pay rent and avoid eviction.

Despite barely making it from month to month on Clever's salary, Clever and Ireni frequently hosted visitors from the village, fed those visitors, often contributed toward their transportation costs for the eight-hour journey back to the village, and even sent them back with a bit of used clothing, and in that one instance, a gift for Clever's mother.

Aside from the loud orange and yellow of an old wall calendar and the greenery of a house plant set in an old oil can, Fillip and Florence's living room was drab white—the color that urban houses become as the dust and dirt of city life helps to fade what was once bright and vibrant. Clearly, the house had last seen new paint long before the already ten-year-old calendar graced its walls. Fillip and Florence had moved into their two-room, one-bath Copperbelt town home, issued by Fillip's employers at the regional technical college, in 1990 when he transferred to his new job as clerical officer. Now, five years later, the house still had minimal furniture and no decorations other than the calendar and a few framed photos from their marriage. Their firstborn son, Samuel, aged four, attended a preschool now, and they planned that their two-and-a-half-year-old daughter would join the same school next year. Through Florence's efforts, and despite a group of neighboring children who were playing in the communal room of the house, it was immaculate. Yet the house felt stark and empty compared to the small and cluttered clay-brick houses of their relatives in their Southern Province home village.

Public transport from the Copperbelt town back to Florence and Fillip's village takes almost sixteen hours and costs the equivalent of twelve U.S. dollars, about one-quarter of Fillip's monthly salary. Despite the exorbitant cost of a round-trip journey to the village, Florence had visited her ailing mother for a few weeks the previous year. Five years earlier, in 1990, just before Fillip transferred to his new post, Florence had returned to the village to give birth to their first child. Although Florence remained "at home" for almost a year, Fillip stayed only a few days before leaving for the Copperbelt. Although Fillip had not returned to his home village since that trip, he had news of the village, passed through various town dwellers and visitors. Their most recent visitor, a "classificatory brother" from a farming area six hours from the home village, just spent the night with them a few days before I arrived for the interview. The brother came to the Copperbelt on business to sell animals, and although he did not ask for assistance, Fillip and Florence gave a few gifts of clothing and some cash for "town food" like Coca-Cola. The year before they had another visitor, a relative of Florence's who now lived in a rural farming area near the Copperbelt. She came to their home asking for food and transport money back to her farm, to which they agreed. Although Fillip and Florence received a fairly regular flow of visitors from other towns, and very occasionally from their home villages, Fillip confided to me that "living so far from the village, where there is always hunger, is a blessing in disguise. If people come to us, we must give assistance. But because we are so far from home, those visitors don't come. We are saved by distance."

Although aware that having visitors drained their meager financial base, Fillip and Florence, like Clever and Ireni, in fact did give assistance to relatives and friends who passed through their home, and Florence, in the last year, had undertaken the costly trip home to see her sick mother. The contradictions between their actions and their words suggest that bonds of migrants and their social networks are a complex social arena in which economic, social, and cultural logic all come into play.

In the previous chapters I described the rural life of Gwembe residents. Given the current economic conditions in Zambia, and the increasingly frequent droughts in southern Africa, survival is difficult and opportunities to improve living conditions are few. The variety of coping mechanisms allows residents to maintain daily life, however marginal. Social support networks are fundamental to Gwembe people's survival, whether old or young, but when difficult living conditions prompt some people to choose migration as a strategy, these networks take new shapes as they move across the Zambian landscape.

This chapter focuses on children's relationships with their elderly parents over distance and time, as a way of understanding how migration impacts elderly people's lives. Children leave their home villages for many reasons. In the 1960s and 1970s, those who managed to finish secondary school usually found jobs in town, as this was where the demand for more highly educated people was found. Once employed in town, these educated people often wanted to settle more permanently, because life in town at that time was much easier than in the village, and they had a community of others who had shared similar experiences of school and professional life.

Since the 1980s, life in town has not offered as much opportunity as it used to, nor does it offer the same benefits and comforts as it did when Zambia's national economy was more vibrant. Although the educated still try to find jobs in town, it is just as likely that they will find a decent living farming in a rural community. In the summer of 2004, I met for the first time the son of one of the families I have been visiting since 1994. This son, Raymond, had been going to school in town, sponsored by his older siblings, ever since I had met his parents. Having completed grade twelve and graduated from one of the best secondary schools in Zambia in 2002, he has now settled on his father's farm in one of the plateau migrant destinations, ambitiously farming his own fields of maize for sale and consumption, and cotton. Raymond told me that when he had graduated from secondary school he had ambitions of becoming a medical doctor. But with the deaths of seven of his well-educated siblings, all of whom lived and worked in town, and seeing many of his friends unemployed in Zambia's cities, he has now accepted a future of farming with his parents and making a village-based living.

Although the educated certainly have better chances of finding good employment in towns, other young villagers still have specific goals that a brief period of less-than-ideal employment, such as security guards or "garden boys," can help to meet. Some young men go to town in order to earn the cash to make bride-wealth payments; others go during bad droughts, when there is no hope of a harvest, and town employment offers a chance to feed their family. Other young adults leave the Gwembe villages to open new farms in virgin woodlands on the plateau. And as the story of Turner in chapter 2 suggests, they may also leave because of conflict in the village. And at times, fear of witchcraft can prompt a move. In all cases, women and men leave relatives back in the village when they head to new destinations. When they leave aging parents, they test the bonds of kinship and cultural norms of support.

In addition to describing the migration process and patterns, this chapter raises questions about "remittances" and gift giving as ways of maintaining connection to home communities. Gifts are fundamental to the dynamic social relationships between migrants and their relatives in the village. As scholars of "the gift" have argued, gift exchange establishes a valued form of mutual recognition between donor and recipient that supersedes the material value of the gift itself (Mauss 1990; Derrida 1997; Schrift 1997; Godelier 1999). For Gwembe migrants, giving small gifts (or "gift remitting") to aging relatives and other village-based kin establishes a form of mutual recognition that builds and sustains their social connections (Cliggett 2003a).

A remarkable facet of Gwembe migrants' remitting patterns, and indeed patterns documented for migrants from many regions of Zambia, is that these gifts typically do not involve large cash transfers or expensive material goods, meaning that elders hoping to receive support from migrant children may be disappointed (Moore and Vaughan 1994; Hansen 1996; Crehan 1997; Ferguson 1999). Although the gifts that village relatives may receive offer much appreciated luxury (which can also contribute to village stratification—tied more to the status that such gifts create rather than wealth accumulation), the most startling aspect of remitting in Zambia, as compared to migration elsewhere in Africa and globally, is that rural communities do not live off the remittances that migrants send home. Rather than constitute a basis for improvement of material well-being, the gift remittances that migrants give to relatives at home reinforce social relationships that may create pathways for a migrant to return to the home community sometime in the future, an important consideration as migrants move through their own life cycle and the once young experience the challenges of aging.

Gwembe Tonga Migration and Remitting

Migration is not a new phenomenon in Zambia. Mobile populations shaped Zambia's history both before and during the colonial era (Colson 1958; Barnes 1967; Hannerz 1980; Pottier 1988; Vail 1989; Ferguson 1990a, 1990b; Macmillan 1993; Moore and Vaughan 1994). Zambian domestic migration patterns over the last century followed predominantly rural–urban

TABLE 7.1
Migration destinations for adults above the age of twenty in the GTRP sample

Destinations	No. of Migrants	%
Lusaka (Zambian capital)	209	34.32
Chikanta (Southern Province frontier)	121	19.87
North and/or east of Lusaka	85	13.96
Line of rail towns and farming areas	220	36.12
Other	5	0.82
Total number of GTRP migrants, above age 20	640	30.75
Total GTRP population, above age 20	2,081	

Source: 1994 GTRP census data.

paths (Garbett 1975; Ohadike 1981; Hedlund and Lundahl 1983; van Donge 1984). Colson and Scudder confirm that Southern Province populations historically followed the national pattern of labor migration from rural areas to commercial centers (Colson 1958, 1960, 1971; Colson and Scudder 1975, 1981). In the past two decades, however, Southern Province farmers increasingly have chosen rural migration destinations rather than towns or cities (Scudder and Habarad 1991; Ministry of Agriculture 1995; Cliggett 2000, 2003a).

The Gwembe Tonga Project census (of the four project study villages) from 1994 indicates that 30 percent of all people above age twenty live outside of the valley region. Of these, 34 percent reside in Zambia's capital (Lusaka), 20 percent settled in a frontier farming region to the northwest of the Gwembe Valley (Chikanta), and 10 percent moved to farming regions northeast of the capital. The remainder settled in areas along the line of rail, which include farming communities and small towns (see table 7.1).

The two project villages on the north end of the valley benefit from the opportunity of its inhabitants to earn cash close to home because of an agribusiness located within twenty miles of their communities. About five men from these villages found employment at the farm in the early 1990s. In the past five years, relatives of those first "explorers," including a mother and sisters, found employment at the same company, and the extended families live together in communities surrounding the farm (Bond, Cliggett, and Schumaker 1997).

In all of these contexts, migrants from the Gwembe Valley typically maintain connection to their home villages through a combination of visits from village-based relatives, news shared from other visitors to town, and occasionally, their own visit back home. Although it is common to host a visitor in town and give that visitor a small packet of sugar for a village-based mother, for the most part Gwembe migrants do not give substantial economic support (i.e., remittances) to village-based relatives, which is a topic of much migration literature (e.g., Townsend 1997; Massey and Parrado 1998; Trager 1998; Cohen 2001).

For the Gwembe migrants, regular "remittances," in the economists' terms, do not exist. Sending gifts or cash assistance to family back in the village is almost nonexistent. More commonly, migrants *tola zipego*, take gifts, or *pa zipego*, give gifts, to a visitor in a face-to-face exchange. When a son returns from town to visit the village, everyone expects him *kuleta chintu chibotu*—to "bring something nice."[1] If he does not bring the hoped-for clothing, blankets, or money to purchase food, he should at least bring sugar or vegetable oil. In 1995 Godfrey, who lived and worked in a town along the railway, told me that "we don't go home to see our parents. . . . We must give them something when we go." Gift remitting in Zambia requires the personal contact of giver and recipient, or at least a representative of the recipient; existing in the same location simultaneously is synonymous with exchanging gifts.

Similar to Hansen's (1996) and Ferguson's (1999) descriptions of migrants' links with sending communities, if a migrant wants to maintain his good standing with his family and community in the village, he must somehow maintain his connection to rural origins. A face-to-face exchange accomplishes this demonstration of loyalty—in the form of gift exchange, which reinforces mutual recognition, but also in the form of the gift of physical presence and personal time. In this vein, Godfrey explained to me that he demonstrated his "love" for his mother by giving her a gift from town during his visit home.

The elders in the villages confirmed Godfrey's statement. They unanimously told me that a migrant son "shows his mother he loves her by giving a chitenge, or a dress . . . or other things from town." Munsaka, a particularly candid senior woman in the village, said of her migrant sons, "they should not come to visit without something nice to give. That is how a son tells me he loves me."

Maintaining Links

Migrants from the Gwembe, and probably elsewhere, often change their goals and intentions once they arrive in town. Young men who leave the village during drought years, or primarily for economic reasons, may plan to return to the village. At least they tell others that they will return when they have money to buy a plow or pay bride wealth, or when the rains come again and they can plant.

When they arrive in town, migrants struggle to settle, to find employment and housing, and to establish themselves. Gwembe migrants most commonly find employment with a security guard company, where other workers of Gwembe origin have already established a social network. During the period of transition, migrants rarely give gifts or support to visitors from home because they direct most of their energy and resources to adjusting to town life, a finding that echoes other migration research in southern Africa (Murray 1981; Townsend 1997). After securing employment and finding a home (as opposed to staying with relatives), those who are married often try to accumulate enough cash to bring their wife and children from the village. This move greatly improves a young man's status and quality of life in an urban situation, where he must do household chores on his own if he has no wife, sister, or sister-in-law nearby to work for him. Single men might send a gift, via a visitor, of a bag of sugar, a bar of soap, or a chitenge to their mother as a sign that they are settling and earning a living in town, but also as a sign that they want to maintain contact with the village.

As time goes on, and as a young man becomes accustomed to life in town, his expectations about returning to the village may change. In early 1994, Danny, who had been a town resident for eighteen months and whose mother lived completely alone in the village, said he would return to the village the next year to care for his mother. However, more than a year later, Danny had secured better employment and taken a second wife, who was a long-term town resident from a different ethnic group. Danny made numerous social connections in town, with people outside of his home community of migrants, and was becoming at ease with a variety of urban situations. Additionally, during his first two years in town, Danny and his first wife occasionally hosted visitors from the village, but with the arrival of this second wife, many visitors chose to stay elsewhere rather than "with a stranger." I found that, similar to Ferguson's (1999) discussion about developing "cosmopolitan styles" as opposed to maintaining "localist" self-presentation, the adoption of urban lifestyles and opportunities can interfere with typical modes of contact with the village, like hosting and assisting new arrivals in town.

Although many migrants adjust their goals and intentions upon settling into their new location, the majority still maintain some level of contact

TABLE 7.2
Gwembe migrant visiting, by gender, January 1993–August 1994

Visitors	Total No.	Total No. Visits	%
Migrant children[a]	83	36	43
Male migrants	50	19	38
Female migrants	33	17	51

[a]The category of migrant children refers to those adult children found and interviewed whose parents are members of the population aged 55+ in two Gwembe Valley villages. Also see n. 2.

with their home villages. This contact takes many forms, including hosting a stream of visitors, as Clever and Ireni did, sometimes keeping a young sister or brother for an extended period, and occasionally making costly visits back to the village. Of the 83 migrant children of the 82 elderly people I worked with in 1994–95, 36 (43 percent) visited their home village over a twenty-month period (see table 7.2).[2] Most of these migrants visited only once, with funeral attendance given as the main purpose. Migrants also visited the village because their mother was seriously ill, the migrant needed traditional healing for his or her sickness, or to give birth. Table 7.2 shows that, as a percentage, women visited home villages more often than men did.

One reason women visit more frequently is the system of giving birth in a mother-in-law's homestead. A woman often returns to the village from town two months before she expects to deliver and remains until a month after the birth. Women commonly return for the first birth but may also return for second and third births. In the village, young pregnant women benefit from the assistance of kin and the support available from close relatives nearby, whereas young migrants in town may be forced to give birth in a hospital or clinic, at great expense and without the support networks that ease the process. In addition, giving birth to a child in the village reinforces the link with kin and the connection to home. If a woman gives birth in town, her choice can send a message that she is now a settled urban dweller, echoing Ferguson's (1999) discussion of "localist" versus "cosmopolitan" styles and their associated behaviors.

Women also visit the village because husbands working in town sometimes send wives home to prepare fields for the rains. This pattern of women's return to the village is especially true when a man expects to stay in town temporarily. In the event that the rains fail, the women may return to town, hoping that they will plant the following year. A husband also sends a wife to work in his mother's fields during peak agricultural seasons. Working in another's fields secures rights to part of the harvest. If a woman worked in her mother-in-law's fields, and she and her husband return to the village during the next planting season, they can make claims to be fed. Consequently these visits simultaneously reinforce kinship relationships, provide practical assistance to the family, and ensure access to food for migrants upon return. In this way, examining women's visits home offers a gendered component to the discussion of "remittances."

In addition to the gendered nature of return visits, migration timing also influences migrant–village connections. Migrants who moved to town relatively recently visit home villages more frequently than do migrants who left more than four or five years ago (see also Ferguson 1999, 142). Tonga words for "migrant," *chidakwa* and *muchoni*, colloquially mean "drunkard" and "the one who went to the other place forever." These terms do not suggest warm feelings for those who leave the village.

Elderly parents also express neutral feelings for their migrant children. When asked about benefits of having children in town, many elders responded, "It's good to have a child in town who will bring a blanket sometimes, and it's good to have a child in the village who will give food, help farm, and build houses." Mulonga, another outspoken woman, told me, "ah, my son in town does nothing. He went there for himself. . . . He's just eating *saladi* [cooking oil] and *bredi* [white bread]"—an accusation that implies he is squandering resources. Similar sentiments also appear in Gwembe funeral songs, where death often appears as a metaphor of migration: "my friend has gone to Lusaka and I have remained." Clearly, village-based family members hold ambiguous feelings about those who leave "home."

Blessings in Disguise

The most extreme examples of migrants who abandon their village families are the *chidakwa*—the disappeared ones mentioned above. One such character from the Gwembe, Lambert, moved to Lusaka in 1972. He first owned a small shop, but in the late 1980s he became a bricklayer. Subsequently he built a luxurious house, by migrants' standards, complete with many furnishings, including the coveted "living room set." His wife, a Citonga-speaking woman but from a different region, sells household supplies in a nearby market. According to Lambert's mother, the last time she saw him was in 1992—the worst drought year in the previous fifteen years—when she went to visit him in Lusaka. At that time he gave her money to buy food, but since then she has not seen him, nor has she received any gifts or even information from him. Indeed, he is a man who is difficult to contact; I was never able to track him down throughout my eighteen months of fieldwork, although I met with his wife on two occasions.

Detachment between village and town may include the "disappearance" of a son. In addition to Lambert, I was unable to interview four other young men (of the twenty-six migrant men from one village whom I worked hardest to find) because neither their families nor my research assistants could find them. Hiding in the urban environment effectively avoids pressure from kin for support and the irritations of a foreign researcher asking too many questions about relationships with a distant home.

Physical distance from relatives means that the most direct and effective form of pressure for support, a face-to-face request, is simply not an option. Migrants living in Lusaka have an eight-hour journey costing six U.S. dollars between themselves and a face-to-face request for assistance from their kin. Even with the huge expense of such travel, Lusaka residents can expect visitors from home knocking on their door and peering in their pocket at least a few times a year. But migrants living even farther away, such as Fillip and Florence do, have a buffer from such impositions, thus leading to Fillip's statement that their distance from home is "a blessing in disguise." He suggested that people will not openly admit that they want to live far from home and family but that with great distance it is easier to save what little resources they have for their own needs.

Gifts and Meanings

Despite the existence of these "disappeared" sons and rural people's knowledge of the high cost of urban life, the hope that relatives in town can give assistance often leads villagers to embark on the costly daylong journey to Lusaka. In many cases a younger sibling heads to town to visit, *kuswaya*, with an older brother or sister, but visiting in such circumstances most often masks pleas for assistance. The visitor usually returns home with secondhand clothing from the host, and perhaps return-transport costs, school fees, and supplies. If this visitor has great skill in pleading on

behalf of the village-based family, she might return with money to purchase maize and other food supplies.

The strong adherence to the norm of assistance when requests are
made in person can lead villagers to take loans from wealthy neighbors to
pay transport to town. They assume that once perched on a chair in the
home of a son or brother, the host will meet all needs, including return
fare. One old woman from a Gwembe village claimed she had no proper
family in the village (meaning matrilineal relatives on whom she could depend for assistance) and managed to secure free transport to Lusaka,
where her son and brother lived. Upon arrival in town she learned that her
son recently had lost his job and that the brother was on sick leave. The
weeklong visit she had planned became a three-month sojourn because the
families could not find the cash for her return transport, let alone the funds
she hoped to bring home to purchase maize for the coming year. Mean-
while, back in the village her three younger sons subsisted on foods they
found in the bush and the generosity of their neighbors.

This is an extreme example of how tenuous life in town, and village, can
be. For the most part, when someone makes a request in person, assistance
is given, even if it means that a town family takes a larger loan than usual at
the end of the month so that they can provide gifts to a visitor. The norm
of assistance to extended families underlies the behavior, but the setting
and the personal interaction are key to the outcome. Just as Crehan (1997)
describes rural life in Northwestern Province, rural Gwembe people
weave their relationships with threads of exchange and assistance on a
daily basis; they assume that when a migrant visits, she will participate in
the fabric of village life by offering at least a token gift.

The most common gifts a migrant brings, or gives when a villager ar-
rives in town for a visit, are food and clothing. A son returning to the village for a funeral usually brings some town good such as sugar or a
chitenge to his mother and a shirt or trousers to his father. Occasionally a
visiting migrant will give a relatively large sum of money, perhaps the
equivalent of five dollars or more, so a mother or sister can buy a bucket of
maize. A survey of gifts given to parents found that of 83 migrant children,
65 (78 percent) of them did indeed give gifts to parents in home villages, or
sent them through visitors (see table 7.3). Of the 65 cases of gift giving
from migrant children to their parents, 40 percent involved food, with
clothing accounting for 32 percent of the gifts (see table 7.4).[3] Cash gifts
constituted only 21 percent of the exchanges, were generally small, and
were most often used for purchasing beer or tobacco. Other gifts included

TABLE 7.3
Number of migrant children who gave gifts or remittances, January 1993–August 1994[a]

No. Migrant Children	No. Migrant Children Giving at Least One Gift	%
83	65	78

[a]The category of migrant children refers to those adult children found and interviewed whose parents are members of the population aged 55+ in two Gwembe Valley villages. Also see n. 2.

household amenities such as soap and dishes. Children also assisted their parents with domestic chores when they visited the village. One son helped build a house for his father's new wife. Daughters frequently draw water, collect firewood, and cook while visiting their parents. In this way children periodically add a bit of luxury to their parents' home and participate in basic daily activities.

For the recipients of these gifts, the meaning of the exchange consists of many things, including access to appreciated "town goods" as well as the symbolic experience of personal recognition given by the migrant. For the migrant, "gift remitting" can also mean self-recognition—as a result of gifts being accepted. But gift remitting also means a certain amount of economic expense for the giver. For a man like Clever, mentioned at the beginning of this chapter, embarking on a trip to the village costs at least a third of his monthly salary in transport alone. If he gives a chitenge to his mother and trousers to his mother's brother, he has spent at least another quarter of his salary. These costs, combined with lost pay for missing work days and other expenses that inevitably arise, result in an extremely expensive endeavor. Obviously migrants do not make these trips frequently. But that they visit or give gifts at all gets back to the question of the *meaning* of remittances.

TABLE 7.4
Number and type of gifts received from migrant children, January 1993–August 1994[a]

Type of Gift	No. of Gifts	%
Food	26	40
Clothing	21	32
Money	14	22
Other (plates, soap, etc.)	4	6
Total	65	

[a]The category of migrant children refers to those adult children found and interviewed whose parents are members of the population aged 55+ in two Gwembe Valley villages. Also see n. 2.

In order to understand gift remitting in its broad context, we must look beyond the formal economic views that would see the gifts as having primarily economic value. A more satisfactory understanding incorporates the complexity of gift exchange and thus sees gifting as mutual recognition, as well as exchange of goods, and also a process by which individuals invest in their social relations over time. That gifts most often consist of food or clothing—goods inherently personal—suggests that their value operates at a more complex level than simple economic analyses can capture.

Holding a Place for Old Age

The five old-age homes in Zambia offer a partial answer to why migrants persist in gift remitting when their own financial base may suffer. Approximately 170 elderly people live in these five homes. Each home offers at least one story of a long-term migrant who tried to return to the village upon retirement. Similar to the literature cited above, stories from the old-age homes tell of people in villages chasing the return migrant away or claiming they did not recognize him. Many of the social workers who handled these cases at the old-age homes told me that when a migrant does not maintain contact with his rural relatives, they feel no obligation to welcome him home, so they simply offer "we don't know him" as a polite explanation, meaning "he never maintained contact with us, why should we care for him now?"

These stories from the old-age homes confirm the ideas expressed in the recent Zambian literature and the findings from the Gwembe data. If migrants allow their link with rural relatives to dissolve, they may meet the same fate. Gifts, especially of a personal nature like food or clothing, are one method of nurturing relationships, of confirming to rural "allies" that loyalties remain strong, and ultimately, of maintaining a place in the village.

For young men who leave the village for a few years at a time, maintaining relationships through gift remitting serves to keep lines of assistance open. A maternal uncle who receives a shirt from a migrant nephew knows he was remembered and may be more likely to help the young man with bride wealth, than to help a migrant who never communicated and then appears with expectations of assistance from his kin. This pattern of exchange and investment in social relations with the village resonates with other analyses of resource access in Africa (e.g., Berry 1989; Guyer 1995).

Fig. 7.1. Secondary school students with aspirations for a better future.

In Zambia, a migrant who struggles for security in town benefits from "gift remitting" to his family at home. In effect, he invests in social relations that may offer security in the future when he may decide to return to the village—a kind of "retirement portfolio" in an African context. The behavior simultaneously adheres to a cultural norm of "supporting one's elders," which can strengthen migrants' social connections.

Gifts, once in two years, of a dress, a plate, or a bag of sugar are tokens of affection that tell an old mother she is remembered, although not a remittance on which families can depend for survival in a region where shortages of food are more regular than the rains. Rather than offerings of support for daily life, gift remittances represent a gesture of recognition that will keep pathways for return to the village open and allow a returned migrant to take up residence and farming alongside his kin. Without maintaining even this symbolic relationship with the village, a migrant risks losing his option to return should life in town become undesirable.

For the rural elderly then, most migrant children are not a reliable source of support. In my discussions with the elderly about young Sinafala migrants, most people expressed ambivalence about young people leaving. "They go to feed and clothe themselves" was a common explanation for a young man's departure. Old women with no sons in the village told me that it is bad to have children in town, while women with a few sons at home and one or two in town were more supportive: "It is good to have a son in town and in the village. The one in town can bring you blankets, and the one in the village will give you food" (BinaPatterson, November 1994).

During periods of economic hardship, however, children struggle to support themselves whether living in the village or in migrant destinations; supporting an aging mother can become an extreme burden. Young people living out of immediate contact with their relatives are more able to manage their resources independently; they can choose when and how they will give assistance to aging parents, despite the normative pressures that encourage children to support their elders.

8. Getting By "Just Like That"

"How do you manage with no children living near by?"
"I am seated here, gwaya gwaya (getting by), just like that."

Siafugo, July 1996

Responding to perceived needs of the growing elderly population, private and church organizations in Zambia attempted to introduce old-age homes during the 1970s. In opposition, the Zambian government launched a campaign promoting the African extended family as the proper caretaker of the aged and banned institutionalized care for the elderly (Macwan'gi 1991). These events precipitated former president Kaunda's claim that caring for the elderly is "a sacred and noble duty" (Kaunda 1976, 32). Kaunda's statement expresses the nonnegotiability of this duty; it is assumed that family will care for their aging relatives. Nevertheless, in 1991, when former president Kaunda stepped down, and newly elected president Frederick Chiluba took office, the Ministry of Social Welfare and Development revived the old-age homes and found that they filled to capacity almost immediately, while many more needy elderly continued living as they had on the streets in urban areas or marginally cared for in rural ones. Clearly, despite the assumption that family would care for the old, not all old people had care.

Through the stories in this book, I have tried to dispel assumptions about the inevitability of family providing support to the elderly in rural Africa. Support and assistance are channeled through continually negotiated social networks. Each participant in the network plays a role in how, when, and if support is provided. As the stories suggest, the elderly themselves play central roles in mobilizing their support; the extended family does not simply step in with unconditional assistance. In this context then, we need to recognize that some people may not have the same resources as others on which to negotiate their relationships.

The stories narrated here point out that different groups of people, even in what we might think of as a homogenous rural African village, experience different degrees of vulnerability to food and resource scarcity, social alienation, and general poverty. Although Gwembe people on the whole experience continual risk to their well-being, some Gwembe people experience more vulnerability than others. Factors that may impinge on people's coping capacities include historical circumstances that influence access to resources, kinship systems that define who is and who isn't a "proper relative," belief systems that impact men and women differently, and gendered styles of social interaction. The elderly, as an age group, live on a daily basis with greater risk to their well-being than do other age groups. But because men and women as a group experience different types and degrees of risk as they age, and employ very different strategies for coping with those risks, we must consider poverty, food scarcity, support networks, and vulnerability with a much more nuanced vision.

With these stories laid out in front of us, what do we learn about these people's lives? And about other people's lives who may exist in similar circumstances? Given the Western tendency to romanticize distant and exotic places and imbue them with values we see missing in our own culture (such as altruistic support for the elderly), these stories can help us understand a reality we had no idea existed. These stories also help us to challenge, and complicate, the alternative popular view—of starvation and misery, living on the edge, and general upheaval—in a way that illuminates the impressive creativity that people living in such circumstances must use in assembling a repertoire of survival strategies. Both visions—the romanticized one and the one of stereotyped misery—are different sides of the same coin: generalized understandings and impressions that leave out the variability of human capacity to cope, or at least get by, in the face of adverse circumstances.

As different colleagues read and commented on portions of this book, I discovered that some read the stories with a sense of great sadness, sympathy, and pain for the Gwembe people, who have to endure such harsh living conditions. Others found the stories fascinating and were almost inspired by the vast array of creative strategies people use to survive in the face of very difficult circumstances. Although I experience deep emotions about the fate of Gwembe Tonga people, and poor people around the world generally (including those in our own U.S. cities and rural communities), I am in awe of Gwembe people's ability to manage their circumstances. The creativity with which they go about "getting by just like that" (*gwaya gwaya bubwena obo*) makes me see these people as active and intelligent participants in a landscape of many ruts, potholes, and thorny thickets, not as passive victims awaiting rescue from northern philanthropists. Recognizing the agency of people, especially poor people, forces us to see deeper than stereotypes or romantic visions allow.

The Gendered Division of Vulnerability

The personal agency of elderly people plays one of the most crucial roles in the extended family support systems for the Gwembe Tonga. As the previous chapters illustrate, men and women have differing styles of interacting with their children and relatives. In the present generations, men rely heavily on their ability to control resources, both material and social, to secure their position as they age. Men with agricultural implements that sons hope to use in farming their own fields can extract sons' labor for domestic and agricultural work in exchange for use of the equipment. Older men try to maintain these positions of authority and control indefinitely, for once they lose the ability to control their social world, they lose their security in old age. Women, on the other hand, currently use a strategy that places them in a seemingly more dependent position, through which they manipulate social interactions to their benefit. An old woman emphasizes her frailty, her lack of strength, and her need for assistance, and then she reminds her children that she suffered for them when they were young. These gendered styles of interaction permeate all aspects of the elderly's lives.

Older men's support systems demonstrate the importance of material resources for establishing security in old age. Agricultural change during resettlement in 1958 and afterward resulted in increased access to wealth and cash for men over their lifetime and caused a decrease in women's access to the same resources. The loss of intensive alluvial soil cultivation in exchange for extensive wet-season plow agriculture took valuable resources out of women's hands and placed it directly under the control of men. Compounding the problem was the increasing importance of cattle for both agriculture and wealth. Currently, men accumulate cattle more easily than women because they have more options for cash earnings and receive the bride-wealth payments, in livestock, of their daughters. Under these conditions women, over the past four decades have had limited options for building their own material base and consequently lived with increased material vulnerability. Women have relied first on their fathers and brothers, and once married, on their husbands, for their material well-being.

As people age, becoming less productive household members and requiring more assistance in daily chores, resources can become a basis for encouraging support from children and other relatives. Men are in a particularly good position as they move through the later life stages. Men in their late fifties usually experience the peak in their wealth and power within the family and community. They usually have a substantial herd of cattle, valuable farming implements, at least one wife of childbearing age, and a group of children, hopefully daughters who will continue to bring him cattle through bride-wealth payments. As middle-aged men grow older, becoming less able to work in the fields and more reliant on other people's energy, they carry with them their wealth in things and people. These resources will usually see men through the remainder of their lives.

Women, most of whom do not accumulate wealth in material possessions through their life course, must rely on other resources when they become less productive and more dependent on others. People, social networks, and the social constructs of obligation and entitlement are women's primary source of old-age security. When women do not have material wealth with which to entice supporters and harness resources, they employ other tactics for encouraging support. Old women's emphasis on their own suffering on behalf of their young children reinforces young adults' notions of obligation. A mother's cries of "I carried you on my back and fed you from my breast" reminds her children that they too must sacrifice for their old mother.

Residence patterns reveal the importance of access to people, as a resource, for old-age security. Women, once they are widowed or divorced, most often attach themselves to a married son's homestead. In this setting old women live within reach of both male labor and female labor from a son's wife, allowing an elderly woman to live with a bit more ease than when she had a husband and children to manage. The most important aspect of the domestic setting is the redistribution of resources, especially daily food. By presenting herself as an old woman in need of assistance and reminding children of the sacrifices she has made for them, she places herself in a dependent role. When she shares a homestead with a child, she is usually rewarded for her strategic efforts with fulfillment of her basic needs.

Men are better able to secure their needs through controlling resources and people and do not present themselves as needy. Their goal of influencing and controlling people around them, especially children and wives, is best accomplished by heading their own homestead. In his own homestead an old man can encourage sons to plow his fields in exchange for the use of the oxen or plow. When a son begins accumulating his own wealth, a father's desires have less influence over him, and the old man begins to lose his base of security. An older man who married wives younger than himself, and who still has adolescent children under his roof, lives a fairly secure life.

The role of supernatural power adds another level of creativity in influencing social relationships. These powers are not seen, but people can employ them to affect real outcomes. An old woman will often receive a plate of food eagerly given by a young mother who fears the sickness that the older woman's bad spirits can bring to the homestead. People believe that these bad spirits, which land on old women randomly, cause damage, but at the same time they believe old women simply carry the spirits, not cause the spirits' action. In contrast, men take steps to procure knowledge of sorcery, including learning rituals and traveling in search of special medicines. With this knowledge a man actually controls the spirit world to his benefit.

The difference between men and women in these examples of supernatural power is control; men actively influence the spirit world, while women receive it. Although an old woman does not control the spirits she houses, she can choose to manipulate her social relationships in relation to the fear the spirits inspire. However, she does not manipulate the actions of those spirits, only her relationships to people through their fear of the spirits. In elderly people's interaction with the supernatural world, we see an extreme example of the differing strategies that men and women employ to harness resources. As in their relationships to children and other relatives, people believe men aggressively seek control over spirits in an effort to amass more wealth and control over people. Like reminding children of their obligations to support elderly mothers, old women use their link with bad spirits to encourage assistance from the community. In both cases, elderly people use personal strategies in mobilizing their support. However, the variation of those strategies emphasizes gender differences in people's ability to secure support in their old age.

Of course, with the ways that women access wealth beginning to change and their possibilities for gaining more control of resources increasing, ideas about women's ability to manipulate supernatural powers appear to be changing and could spell a very different scenario for future generations of senior women trying to gain support from their children and relatives.

Losing access to family members, as occurs when people migrate out of the village, tests the strength of cultural norms of support for the elderly. How does an old person manage social relationships, obligations, and entitlements over distance and time? When relatives are no longer available for face-to-face interactions, their behavior reveals more personal attitudes about obligations and norms. Migration of young adults to town or other farming areas removes them from easy grasp of elderly parents. In the stories from chapter 7, many elderly people from the Gwembe Valley accept that once a child has left the village, their assistance has also departed. Young adults also admit that distance allows them more freedom to use their resources as they wish.

For parents of migrant children, face-to-face contact offers the only reliable opportunity to receive support in the form of cash, food, or gifts. Elderly parents in need will venture to town to plead their case with relatives in person, and migrants know that when visiting home they must bring at least token gifts as a sign of their attachment to relatives and the village. The example of migrants choosing when and how to visit, and with what gifts, demonstrates their participation in the negotiation process; they too are players in their parents' support systems, and they anticipate their own aging process and the need to maintain networks for their old age.

The elderly's skills for encouraging support form the crucial component in all of these social relations, whether near or far. How old men and women present themselves to their children, relatives, and community becomes a key aspect of what kind of support they mobilize and when. Women's self-presentation as old, frail, and needy can secure them a place in a son's or brother's homestead. Their developed ability to "plead" for assistance is also a recognized and humorously appreciated skill among Gwembe Tonga people. Along with excellence in pleading, the ability to broaden flexible kinship links to include particularly useful people, especially wealthy people, in the category of "proper family," benefits an old woman with such skills. "Proper family" becomes a social category to which an old woman can make some of her most strong claims for support.

Men, for the most part, do not use these kinds of social resources. A father typically prefers to coax a son into giving him a share of his harvest by lending him planting implements. By heading a homestead, managing resources, and playing a leading role in decision making, men perpetuate the idea that they still provide for their dependents, and thus they justify a share of the produce and profits. However, in the infrequent cases when men lose control of people and resources, they take on more dependent roles within their social spheres. The example of the divorced leper living in his sister's homestead demonstrates how quickly a man can become truly dependent on others when he lacks resources, both in people and in material things.

Men and women in the Gwembe Valley do not have the same bargaining power in their social relationships as they age. Men are often seen as overbearing, domineering, and harsh to children; they do not cultivate sympathies the way that women do. Women develop their relationships with children by calling on clan identity and by nurturing and raising children. When a woman is old she can make the claim "I did everything for you, I carried you on my back, I fed you from my breast . . . so now you can sacrifice for me." Men will more likely say, "Because I am strong, I can extract your labor, your resources and your loyalty, . . . and as long as I can do that, you will help me." Men's bargaining power relies primarily on their control of wealth, including people, while women's power relies on more emotional and maternal ties.

Interim Reports and Longitudinal Research: Further Questions

The descriptions and analyses I present in this book are heavily influenced by the difficult economic situation and the increasing environmental problems of drought and degradation that have taken place in southern Zambia over the past fifteen years. I started working in Zambia when drought years began recurring more frequently and with more devastation. In this context, my research since the early 1990s suggests that in the face of this socioeconomic and ecological hardship, people negotiate social relationships based on a tendency to maximize personal security, but family and community notions of obligation can temper this self-interest. If conditions in the broader society improve, people's strategies will likely shift and reformulate to accommodate the change, possibly to the benefit of vulnerable groups within society.

In describing the lives of the elderly, I dance between two interpretive frames. The one I emphasize the most documents particular styles, strategies, and bases for negotiation and shows how some of those features have changed over the past fifty years. The other interpretive frame appears in reference to how we see large-scale change through time, particularly gender dynamics of power, negotiation, and resource access. My ability to speak about that larger change has everything to do with participating in longitudinal research.

Long-term research offers one of the best opportunities to explore the human experience precisely because change comes in many forms, and from many directions, and our predictive capacities cannot always account for the many pathways of change. As Elizabeth Colson has said, in long-term research, "each publication is an interim report" (1999). Indeed, this is true. The generation of elderly people reaching their senior years during the 1990s has experienced a particular history of political economy, which impacted women and men in specific ways and led to particular differences in their access and control of resources. Those differences in material wealth meant that women and men must use different resources in securing support as they age.

In recent years, women have increasingly been receiving a share of the bride-wealth payments for their daughters' marriages, a change from the pattern that has predominated over the past forty years in which fathers received the majority of the payment. This shift alone may signal new developments in the way women negotiate their social world. Additionally, with the new inheritance laws, women stand to gain in substantial material ways upon the deaths of their husbands. With increased access to important sources of wealth, women will surely be better able to secure their material well-being, even if they use the wealth within their current social networks of support. They will also likely become more vulnerable to the social dynamics of a society with a long history of egalitarian ideals, as men's current position in such a system indicates.

The increasing frequency of accusations of witchcraft and subsequent cleansings may also significantly affect the material base of some Gwembe people (and Zambians more broadly). In less than a month, the massive costs of witchcraft cases, including the expensive services of the witch finder, can sabotage a senior man's long-developed plan for material security in old age. Given that most wealth in Gwembe communities resides in men's hands, that the majority of witchcraft accusations target senior men, and that the costs of these cases are skyrocketing rapidly, senior men may soon become yet another specific group living with increased vulnerability, as they watch their resources leave not just their own hands but leave the extended family all together. But given the dynamics of changing wealth, women may not be far behind in experiencing this phenomenon.

These kinds of shifts in the socioeconomic landscape mean that one-time studies can reveal only a partial story of people's lives. To capture a more realistic vision of people's experiences, we need a longer-term perspective. And in reporting on that long-term perspective, we need to acknowledge the interpretive frames we use to make sense of what we see. Without a long-term vision, we will not know the next chapter as the story continues to unfold, whether it be in documenting the changes we see or in explaining the broader trajectories of those changes.

My commitment to longitudinal research has emerged over time, much like the development of my ideas for making sense of Gwembe lives over the past decade. Early on, my interest in long-term research had more to do with an empirical issue—a perspective that "more data is better." The realization that forty years of field research, data, and writings preceded my fieldwork inspired me to join Elizabeth Colson and Thayer Scudder in seeing the Gwembe Tonga Research Project into the future. I believed that my own work would have an even more empirical base and would be contributing to a kind of ethnographic database of value to academics, policymakers, and Gwembe people (who do indeed look to our "village checklists" to read their family histories).

Over time, that initial concern for empiricism has developed into a concern for practical applications of the knowledge we have accumulated through long-term study. Through repeated visits to field sites, we develop a much deeper understanding of the people and places where we conduct research, which allows us to unravel misrepresentations that come about through snapshot vision. Without seeing, hearing, smelling, and tasting the differences that each new field trip allows, we risk cementing in our minds the one experience we had and claiming it as the true and only reality for that place, rather than recognizing that one experience is a truth based in a moment in time and a specific location in space. Long-term research provides the only way to remotely capture, and then explain, an approximation of another way of life beyond a particular moment in time.

My concern for long-term research also entails a personal aspect, tied to my hopes for the future. Over the past decade, I have never visited the Gwembe during a truly good year, when people harvested a surplus of grain and cash crops and when they had enough material resources to purchase more than a small bag of sugar as a luxury, let alone new shoes for the whole family. I hope that with my continued concern for unraveling the complexity of Gwembe lives, I will one day see a time when Gwembe people get to think beyond issues of basic survival. Obviously, simply having a good rainy season will not bring about the kinds of fundamental changes that will facilitate a long-term improvement in people's lives; those kinds of changes will require multilevel reshaping of government and economic systems, along with local-level action.

However, Gwembe people's energy and determination to get by, despite the challenges they face, become even more evident with each return visit I make. During my 1998 field trip, I found a concentrated community of retirees from professional careers, who were helping to establish a small but vibrant "village" in one region of Gwembe South. In this community a retired doctor opened a nongovernment medical clinic (stocked with medicines donated by an international church organization), and two retired businessmen had established a small irrigation scheme to grow fruit for sale in town, in which they employed a few local residents. The community also had an active church outreach program for women's cottage industries and a workshop for training young men in carpentry skills. These developments at least gave the impression that people in this community had more options for improving their living standards. Discovering pockets of diversification such as this one in a rural area makes me hopeful that at other moments in the future, and in other locations throughout the region, I will find more examples of people's creative energy being used to get more than "just enough."

Making the Local Matter

In addition to believing that long-term research provides a more thorough understanding of people's lives and ultimately better explanations about societal-level change, I believe that a grounding in the local context and a commitment to local people's actions and words offer a perspective not found in most discussions of poverty, vulnerability, and political economy. So often when scholars aim at unraveling the complexity of systems of inequality, they focus their exploration on the multilayers of hierarchy and often aim at explaining the macrosystems that have impacts at the local level but do not explore the many facets of those impacts in the local setting.

By focusing on the local, we can explore the multilevel systems from the ground up, and we can unravel our assumptions about what goes on in families and communities. We develop a much more sensitive vision of what constitutes people's lives and livelihoods, and can better understand how, exactly, higher-level systems, such as national political agendas and global economic forces, impact different groups of people in different local contexts.

The stories presented in this book place local people at center stage and focus on their actions, words, and thoughts. An alternate analysis could have focused on the broader political-economic systems that continue to force Gwembe people to develop these kinds of survival strategies. But precisely because I gave Gwembe people center stage, we come away from the story with an ability to break down stereotypes and generalizations of "poor people in rural areas" who have been acted on by larger systems. Those systems surely exist and surely impact poor people's lives everywhere.

Yet our attention to difference, even at that most-acted-upon (by macrosystems) level—the local—opens our vision of what it means to be poor, old, and vulnerable. If nothing else, I hope this book helps the reader to hesitate when on the verge of speaking of "Africans," "poor people," or "the elderly." In that moment of hesitation, I hope the speaker will consider which people in Africa he or she means to speak of, what aspect of being poor deserves comment, and what being elderly entails.

Notes

1. Aging in the Non-Western World

1. The quarterly newsletter for the Association of Anthropology and Gerontology offers a variety of information about the intersection of anthropology and aging. An increasing number of journals focus on aging and culture: *Aging and Society, International Journal of Aging and Human Development, Journal of Aging and Identity, Journal of Cross-Cultural Gerontology, Journal of Gerontology and Social Science*, and the *Southern African Journal of Gerontology*.

2. The ways that Gwembe Tonga women and men live separate but intersecting lives echoes Poewe's sexual parallelism, that is, the way that men and women must be considered as separate groups, although they interact at certain points of interest, behavior, and ideology. From my readings, however, I suspect that the Tonga do not live with the same kind of extreme separation that Poewe and others describe in northern Zambia. In large part these differences between northern and southern Zambia are the result of the very different history of political economy in the regions.

2. Getting Down in the Valley

1. For a discussion of research site selection criteria in 1956 and 1962, see Colson 1960, 1964b, and 1971, and Scudder 1962, 1985. The technical procedure for determining membership in the sample has been an ongoing discussion for the Gwembe Tonga Research Project (GTRP) team. In 1994 we settled on a formal protocol that clarifies the guidelines (GTRP 1995).

2. From the village census data provided by Colson and Scudder, I was able to determine who fit this age group. In the first GTRP field season during 1956–57, Colson and Scudder used event-based calendars to estimate the year of birth for those individ-

uals who did not know their birth date. Colson and Scudder believe this data to be reliable plus or minus five years.

3. In describing my incorporation into Kaciente's family, I do not mean to imply that I was treated as simply another Tonga relative. Being a foreigner, white, and perceived to have vast resources clearly influenced the way that Kaciente, his family, and the villagers in general interacted with me. In fact, I believe that it is due, at least in part, to my "otherness" and perceived wealth and status that people were so eager to establish a kinship relationship with me. By creating a formal "alliance" with me, they had better access to my resources. The power dynamics of being "white," "foreign," and "rich" cannot be overlooked in the research experience. Nevertheless, the point I make here is that through local systems of incorporation, I was brought into Kaciente's family, and consequently I was expected to fulfill responsibilities and obligations inherent in the role of any family member.

3. The Space and Time of Vulnerability

1. Understanding the history of southern Africa demands far more discussion than this book can undertake. However, it is important to recognize that African societies had been in contact with each other long before non-Africans arrived and Europeans established a presence on the continent. Consequently, these African societies influenced each other in meaningful ways, as the spread of different technologies such as iron forging and hoe and plow agriculture demonstrates. In Zambia, ethnic groups had been in contact for centuries before European exploration, through various forms of exchange and trade (Clark 1950, 1962). There was also contact, trade, and many layers of exchange beyond the continent itself before the European encounter. The east coast of Africa had long-standing trade relations with the Middle East and Asia, which shaped life in that region and further inland (Middleton 1992; Oliver et al. 1963–76; Oliver 1965). Certainly the European encounter and colonialism specifically, although relatively brief in terms of the whole history of Africa, impacted African systems in deep and long-echoing ways. A starting point for exploring the impact of colonialism on Africa includes, among many possibilities, Asad 1973; Curtin 1975; Feierman 1990; Karp and Bird 1980; Mamdani 1996; Murray 1981; Vail 1983, 1989; and Vansina 1990. These sources delve into not just historical events but the cultural processes that made the events so significant. More specific discussions of Zambia's and the surrounding region's history, and the sociocultural change that occurred through the European encounter, can be found in Birmingham and Martin 1983; Chipungu 1992a, 1992b; Clark 1962; Ferguson 1990a, 1990b; Hannerz 1980; Hansen 1989; Macmillan 1993; Moore and Vaughan 1994; Roberts 1976; Seleti 1992; and Vaughan 1987.

2. In the international development "business," agencies such as the World Bank and the International Monetary Fund put demands for improved economic efficiency on the country to which they make loans; the programs under which the country implements the demands are often called structural adjustment programs (SAPs). These demands, or conditions for securing a loan, include privatizing government-run businesses and services either by making departments fiscally accountable or by turning actual companies over to the private business sector; companies include operations such as the copper mines in Zambia, and services include public transportation, health care, and police. Other conditions include government restructuring to reduce waste and improve efficiency by reducing the number of employees, reducing or eliminating work

benefits such as housing subsidies, and generally streamlining government offices and responsibilities.

3. Although AIDS is a huge influence on household structure and resource decisions, I do not go into the details of the AIDS epidemic in Zambia but rather address it as one factor influencing family negotiations. For detailed discussions and insight into the AIDS problem in the Zambezi Valley, see the work of Virginia Bond (Bond 1997; Bond and Dover 1997; Bond and Ndubani 1997, 2000; and Bond, Cliggett, and Schumaker 1997).

4. The history and the variety of effects of relocation for the Gwembe Tonga are examined in detail in two of Elizabeth Colson's books, *Social Organization of the Gwembe Tonga* (1960) and *Social Consequences of Resettlement* (1971). I refer readers seeking more information about that period and the details of those events to these two works, as my own focus is on the current conditions in the Gwembe and how people are responding to these conditions.

4. Making a Village-Style Living

1. For a discussion of migration from Gwembe communities to a rural agribusiness in marigolds, see Bond, Cliggett, and Schumaker 1996.

2. The history of beer brewing in the Gwembe Valley is revealed in Colson and Scudder's book *For Prayer and Profit: The Ritual, Economic, and Social Importance of Beer in Gwembe District, Zambia, 1950–1982*. Gwembe communities first brewed beer for ritual purposes, but over time the social nature of beer drinking gained importance. Colson and Scudder outline the changing economy that promoted secular beer production and drinking, and also discuss the effects on the community of increased beer consumption.

3. During the British colonial era, administrators established the "first-class trading zone" as the location where Europeans did their shopping, while the "second-class trading zone" offered stores, run predominantly by Indian and "mixed race" traders, to serve the African population.

5. Mother's Keepers, Father's Wives, and Residential Arrangements of the Old

1. In Gwembe Central people identify twelve matrilineal clans (*mukowa*). However, in Gwembe South people identify sixteen clans. Although the populations in both areas are Tonga, the differences in kinship, among other things, point to the great variability between regions within the Gwembe, and Zambia more broadly.

2. A homestead head sometimes has a fire, *igobelo*, which he sits around with family, including wives, and visitors on cold winter evenings. At these local gathering points, people discuss daily events, sing songs, tell stories, and laugh but never cook. A man with an *igobelo* in his own *munzi*, usually a middle-aged man with many dependents, is respected by his neighbors, who are drawn to his fire rather than create an *igobelo* of their own.

3. There is a distinction between field rats and house rats in Zambia (see Musambachine 1994). There are three types of field rats that are considered good to eat. As "field" animals, they are considered wild, like any other wild game that people hunt. House or village rats, however, are considered dirty because they rely on human settlements for their survival—eating from pots and grain bins; they are considered something like a parasite and are not edible by Zambian standards.

4. For a discussion of cattle ownership and the increasingly frequent conflicts over cattle, see Cliggett 2003b and Colson 2000.

5. Children living in a homestead call all of their father's wives "mother."

6. Tonga kinship systems are highly complex. For more detail about men's *lutundu*, see Colson 1960, 72–77.

7. I use the term *classificatory father* to mean the man who inherited the spirit of the father of an individual. When a person dies, kin inherit their property as well as their spirit, or as Colson and Scudder call it, the shade. Upon inheriting the spirit of the deceased, the inheritor takes on responsibility for "pouring beer" annually in honor of (or to feed) the spirit and the responsibility for the children of the deceased. Thus a child can go to a father or classificatory father for assistance in times of need. For more discussion of these spirits (shades) and spirit (shade) inheritance, see Colson 1960, 1971, and Scudder 1962.

8. Inheritance of property has traditionally followed the Tonga matrilineal lines. However, there have been increasing numbers of cases in which children try to claim their father's property rather than let it go to his siblings. In the case of Lutinda, she inherited her brother's cattle upon his death, but his children voiced their disapproval at the time, although they never took their complaints to court. The theft of this cattle took place approximately six years after the death of Lutinda's brother, and village rumors suggested it was her nephews finally acting on their words.

9. The term *pleading* captures the nature of "arguing your case," which Tonga people are famous for. Their highly developed skills in presenting their case and pleading on their own behalf for assistance of all kinds have been noticed and remarked on since the first explorers encountered Gwembe residents in the nineteenth century.

10. One womb, *mwida l'omwe*, literally refers to siblings from one mother, as opposed to "siblings" from a mother's sister, whom Western society would call maternal cousins.

11. Tonga kinship system considers the children of sisters to be one's own children, and the children of a sister's daughters to be one's own grandchildren. Thus, Sala's "grandson" was the son of Sala's sister's daughter.

6. Ancestors, Rituals, and Manipulating the Spirit World

1. See Colson and Scudder's (1988) book on the role of beer in the Gwembe for a more detailed discussion of ritual beer brewing and the relationship to spirit inheritance.

2. See Colson (1960, 180–85) for examples of conflict at funerals in the past and mechanisms for dispute settlement.

3. To "eat wealth," or bride price, or anything else of value is a common phrase among the Tonga people with whom I worked. One young man spoke of wanting to "eat his daughter's cattle" (the bride price he would get) when she marries. The implication is that "eating" is a form of wasting. "My father's brother just 'ate' my father's wealth when he inherited the *muzimu*"; the inheritor in this case was known as a drunkard who squandered the cattle and property of his deceased brother. Throughout my fieldwork the phrase "to eat something" reminded me that food and nourishment were not taken for granted in the Gwembe Valley.

4. My hesitancy to focus on witchcraft and sorcery stems initially from my previous work in Haiti during 1988 and 1991. The fame of Haitian Vodun (voodoo) supersedes all other aspects of the public's knowledge of the country. In the popular press, and many

academic works, all aspects of the Haitian social world, including politics past and present are framed by the belief system comprised of syncretized Christianity and West African beliefs. Non-Haitians' preoccupation with this exotic and mystical spiritual world cured me of my own interest in the subject, driving me more surely toward investigations of daily life and practical matters such as simple survival. When I changed regions of study for my doctoral research, I took with me my focus on pragmatic issues of daily life and my dislike of preoccupation with exotic belief systems. However, I quickly realized that to understand village life for Tonga people, I would need to accept the role of their belief systems. Nevertheless, my views of Tonga witchcraft and sorcery are still influenced by my focus on practical issues of survival. In this way I may echo my functionalist anthropological ancestors more than those of the symbolic tradition.

5. In a discussion with Elizabeth Colson about *zyelo* as I was writing this book, she expressed interest in what people had told me about *zyelo* spitting blood into cooking pots. During her periods of fieldwork, people told her that *zyelo* urinated on the grain in grain bins, which turned the food red. She pointed out that the word spitting is *ku-swida*, while the word for urinating is *ku-suba*. We have not been back to the villages to check this variation as of the completion of this book. It is possible that the activities of *zyelo* have expanded or changed over time. It is also possible that both activities have been present all along but that we simply did not hear of the range.

6. During the forty years of the GTRP, people in our sample villages have become accustomed to our regular updating of the data on their families, which we perform to keep track of demographics and family events. We use a checklist printed out and bound into a book, and people often like to look at their page and see their name and names of their relatives. Members of the sample seem to like the visits and look forward to a team member coming to their home "to write" them. Whenever I arrived in a village, people would ask me when I was coming "to write" them. With population growth in the sample villages and intermarriage with residents of neighboring villages, there are more people around who are not part of the sample but who see our presence. These people have begun to hope we will add them to our "lists" and also "write them."

7. Green maize is the early maize harvested and eaten as we in the United States eat corn on the cob. In Sinafala this is a luxury food eaten early in the rainy season or when a lakeshore garden is particularly successful during the dry season.

7. Migration and Family Ties over Distance and Time

1. When I speak of a migrant in general I use the pronoun *he* because most Gwembe migrants are male and because men more typically have wage employment, and thus purchasing power for "town gifts." Women migrants from the Gwembe usually follow husbands or male matrilineal kin and do not find formal employment, although many become market sellers if they remain in town beyond a few years (Cliggett 2000).

2. My primary data on migration patterns from the Gwembe come from my 1994–95 fieldwork. During this period I attempted to track down all of the migrant children from both of my study villages. Ultimately, I found and interviewed 83 now-adult migrant children (who were living in towns or rural frontiers) of the 82 elderly people in my sample. This group constitutes approximately 85 percent of the migrant children of the 82 elderly people living in the two Gwembe villages.

3. One portion of my 1995 survey of migrants' links to home used parents' ability to

remember gifts received from migrant children. This provided information on frequency and types of gifts children brought their parents. Before conducting the survey I hesitated to ask about details of gift giving, thinking it rude and also difficult to recall details. However, I was quickly impressed with people's detailed accounting of gift giving and material possessions. It became clear that acquisition of new things is so unique that people remember the events in great detail. During one interview, a man in his sixties told me of a visit from his daughter in 1992. "She brought me a shirt, trousers, and a sweater, and for the mother a dress, a basin for washing, 2.5 kilograms of salt, and a water bucket."

References

Adger, W. Neil. 2000. Social and ecological resilience: Are they related? *Progress in Human Geography* 24 (3): 347–64.

Agot, Evelynes Kawango. 2001. Widow inheritance and HIV/AIDS interventions in sub-Saharan Africa: Contrasting conceptions of risk and spaces of vulnerability. PhD diss., University of Washington.

Agrawal, Arun. 1995. Population pressure = Forest degradation: An oversimplistic equation? *Unasylva* 181 (46): 50–58.

Albert, Steven, and Maria Cattell. 1994. *Old age in global perspective: Cross cultural and cross national views.* New York: Maxwell Macmillan International.

Anyamba, Assaf, Compton J. Tucker, and Robert Mahoney. 2002. From El Niño to La Niña: Vegetation response patterns over East and southern Africa during the 1997–2000 period. *Journal of Climate* 15 (21): 3096–3103.

Apt, Nana Araba. 1996. *Coping with old age in a changing Africa.* Aldershot, UK: Avebury.

———. 1997. *Ageing in Africa.* Geneva: World Health Organization.

Asad, Talal, ed. 1973. *Anthropology and the colonial encounter.* New York: Humanities Press.

Aytac, Isak A. 1998. Intergenerational living arrangements in Turkey. *Journal of Cross-Cultural Gerontology* 13 (3): 241–64.

Barnes, J. A. 1967. *Politics in a changing society.* Manchester, UK: Manchester University Press.

Berry, Sara. 1989a. Control and use of resources in African agriculture: An introduction. *Africa* 59 (1): 1–5.

———. 1989b. Social institutions and access to resources. *Africa* 59 (1): 41–55.

Birmingham, David, and Phyllis M. Martin, eds. 1983. *History of Central Africa.* 2 vols. London: Longman.

Blaikie, P., and H. Brookfield, eds. 1987. *Society and land degradation.* London: Tavistock.

Blaikie, P., T. Cannon, I. Davis, and B. Wisher. 1994. *At risk: Natural hazards, people's vulnerability, and disasters.* London: Routledge.

Bledsoe, Caroline. 1990. Transformations in sub-Saharan African marriage and fertility. *Annals of the American Academy* 510: 115–25.

Bond, Virginia. 1997. Between a rock and a hard place: Applied anthropology and AIDs research on a commercial farm in Zambia. *Health Transition Review* 7 (supplement): 69–83.

Bond, Virginia and Paul Dover. 1997. Men, women and the trouble with condoms: Problems associated with condom use by migrant workers in rural Zambia. *Health Transition Review* 7 (supplement): 377–91.

Bond, Virginia and Philoman Ndubani. 1997. The difficulties of compiling a glossary of diseases associated with sexual intercourse in Chiawa, rural Zambia. *Social Science and Medicine* 44 (8): 1211–20.

Bond, Virginia, Lisa Cliggett, and Lyn Schumaker. 1997. *STDs and intrarural migration in Zambia: Interpreting life histories of Tonga migrants in relation to the transmission of STDs and HIV.* Bloomington, IN: Population Institute for Research and Training.

Bond, Virginia and Philoman Ndubani. 2000. *Formative research on mother to child transmission of HIV/AIDs in Zambia: A working report of focus group discussions held in Keemba, Monze, November 1999.* Washington, DC: International Center for Research on Women.

Bourdieu, Pierre. 1977. *Outline of a theory of practice.* Cambridge: Cambridge University Press.

Burawoy, Michael, Joshua Gamson, and Alice Burton, eds. 1991. *Ethnography unbound: Power and resistance in the modern metropolis.* Berkeley: University of California Press.

Caldwell, John C. 1982. *Theory of fertility decline.* New York: Academic Press.

Campbell White, O., and A. Bhatia. 1998. *Privatization in Africa.* Washington, DC: World Bank.

Carmody, Brendon. 1999. *Education in Zambia: Catholic perspectives.* Lusaka: Bookward Publishers.

Cattell, Maria. 2002. Holding up the sky: Gender, age, and work among the Abaluyia of Kenya. In *Ageing in Africa: Sociolinguistic and anthropological approaches,* ed. S. Makoni and K. Stroeken. Hampshire, UK: Ashgate.

Chambers, R. 1983. Vulnerability, coping, and policy. *IDS Bulletin* 20: 1–7.

Chipungu, Samuel. 1992a. African leadership under indirect rule in colonial Zambia. In *Guardians in their time: Experiences of Zambians under colonial rule,* ed. S. Chipungu, 50–73. London: Macmillan.

——, ed. 1992b. *Guardians in their time: Experiences of Zambians under colonial rule, 1890–1964.* London: Macmillan.

Clark, Gracia. 1994. *Onions are my husband: Survival and accumulation by West African market women.* Chicago: University of Chicago Press.

——. 1999. Mothering, work, and gender in urban Asante ideology and practice. *American Anthropologist* 101 (4): 717–30.

Clark, J. Desmond. 1950. *The Stone Age cultures of Northern Rhodesia.* Cape Town: South African Archaeological Society.

———. 1962. The spread of food production in sub-Saharan Africa. *Journal of African History* 3 (2): 211–28.

Cliggett, Lisa. 2000. Social components of migration: Experiences from Southern Province, Zambia. *Human Organization* 59 (1): 125–35.

———. 2001. Carrying capacity's new guise: Folk models for public debate and longitudinal study of environmental change. *Africa Today* 48 (1): 3–20.

———. 2003a. Gift-remitting and alliance building in Zambian modernity: Old answers to modern problems. *American Anthropologist* 105 (3): 543–52.

———. 2003b. Male wealth and claims to motherhood: Gendered resource access and intergenerational relations in the Gwembe Valley, Zambia. In *Gender at work in economic life*, ed. G. Clark, 207–23. Society for Economic Anthropology Monographs, vol. 20. Walnut Creek, CA: Alta Mira Press.

Cohen, Jeffrey. 2001. Transnational migration in rural Oaxaca, Mexico: Dependency, development, and the household. *American Anthropologist* 103 (4): 954–68.

Colson, Elizabeth. 1951. The plateau Tonga of Northern Rhodesia. In *Seven tribes of British Central Africa*, ed. E. Colson and M. Gluckman, 94–162. London: Oxford University Press.

———. 1958. *Marriage and family among the plateau Tonga*. Manchester, UK: Manchester University Press.

———. 1960. *Social organization of the Gwembe Tonga*. Manchester, UK: Manchester University Press.

———. 1963. Land rights and land use among valley Tonga of the Rhodesian Federation: The background to the Kariba resettlement programme. In *African agrarian systems*, ed. D. Biebuyck, 137–54. London: Oxford University Press.

———. 1964a. Land law and land holdings among the valley Tonga of Zambia. *Southwestern Journal of Anthropology* 22: 1–8.

———. 1964b. Social change and the Gwembe Tonga. *Human Problems in British Central Africa/Rhodes Livingstone Journal* 35: 1–13.

———. 1966. The alien diviner and local politics among the Tonga of Zambia. In *Political Anthropology*, ed. M. Swartz, V. Turner, and A. Tuden, 221–28. Chicago: Aldine.

———. 1971. *Social consequences of resettlement*. Manchester, UK: Manchester University Press.

———. 1973. Tranquility for the decision maker. In *Cultural illness and health*, ed. L. Nader and T. Maretzki, 89–96. Washington, DC: American Anthropological Association.

———. 1979. In good years and bad: Food strategies in self-reliant societies. *Journal of Anthropological Research* 35 (1): 18–29.

———. 1995. The contentiousness of disputes. In *Understanding disputes*, ed. P. Caplan, 65–82. Oxford: Berg.

———. 1996. Field notes. May 30. Musulumba.

———. 1999a. Gendering those uprooted by development. In *Engendering forced migration: Theory and practice*, ed. N. Indra, 23–39. New York and Oxford: Berghahn Books.

———. 1999b. "Passing the mantel": A discussion on long-term research projects. Annual Meetings of the American Anthropological Association, Chicago.

———. 2000. The father as witch. *Africa* 70 (3): 333–58.

Colson, Elizabeth, and Thayer Scudder. 1975. New economic relationships between the

Gwembe Valley and the line of rail. In *Town and country in central and eastern Africa*, ed. D. Parkin, 190–210. London: Oxford University Press.

——. 1981. Old age in Gwembe District, Zambia. In *Other ways of growing old*, ed. P. Amoss and S. Harrell, 125–53. Palo Alto, CA: Stanford University Press.

——. 1988. *For prayer and profit: The ritual, economic, and social importance of beer in Gwembe District, Zambia, 1950–1982.* Stanford, CA: Stanford University Press.

Coutsoudis, Anna, Eleni Maunder, Fiona Ross, Sarah Ntuli, Myra Taylor, Tessa Marcus, Ann Dladla, and Hoosen Coovadia. 2000. *WHO multicountry study on improving household food and nutrition security for the vulnerable: A qualitative study on food security and caring patterns of vulnerable young children in South Africa.* Geneva: World Health Organization.

Craig, John. 2000. Evaluating privatization in Zambia: A tale of two processes. *Review of African Political Economy* 27 (85): 357–67.

Crehan, Kate. 1997. *The fractured community: Landscapes of power and gender in rural Zambia.* Berkeley: University of California Press.

Curtin, Philip D. 1975. *Economic change in precolonial Africa: Senegambia in the era of the slave trade.* Madison: University of Wisconsin Press.

Derrida, Jacques. 1997. The time of the king. In *The logic of the gift*, ed. A. D. Schrift, 121–47. New York: Routledge.

De Vos, Susan. 1998. Regional differences in living arrangements among the elderly in Ecuador. *Journal of Cross-Cultural Gerontology* 13 (1): 1–20.

di-Leonardo, Micaela. 1991. Introduction: Gender, culture, and political economy: Feminist anthropology in historical perspective. In *Gender at the crossroads of knowledge*, ed. M. di-Leonardo. Berkeley: University of California Press.

Dilley, Maxx. 2000. Reducing vulnerability to climate variability in southern Africa: The growing role of climate information. *Climatic Change* 45 (1): 63–74.

Domingo, Lita J., Maruja Asis, Ma Jose, and Maria Kabamalan. 1995. Living arrangements of the elderly in the Philippines: Qualitative evidence. *Journal of Cross-Cultural Gerontology* 10 (1–2): 21–51.

Draper, Patricia, and Jennie Keith. 1992. Cultural contexts of care: Family caregiving for elderly in America and Africa. *Journal of Aging Studies* 6 (2): 113–34.

Dwyer, Daisy, and Judith Bruce, eds. 1988. *A home divided: Women and income in the Third World.* Stanford, CA: Stanford University Press.

Economist. 2002. Forty million orphans. *Economist* 365: 41–41.

Engels, Friedrich. 1972. *The origin of the family, private property, and the state, in the light of the researches of Lewis H. Morgan.* New York: International Publishers.

Epstein, A. L. 1958. *Politics in an urban African community.* Manchester, UK: Manchester University Press.

Evans-Pritchard, E. E. 1937. *Witchcraft, oracles and magic among the Azande.* London: Oxford University Press.

——. 1940. *The Nuer.* Oxford: Clarendon Press.

Feierman, Steven. 1990. *Peasant intellectuals: Anthropology and history in Tanzania.* Madison: University of Wisconsin Press.

Ferguson, James. 1990a. Mobile workers, modernist narratives: A critique of the historiography, of transition on the Zambian Copperbelt. Pt. 1. *Journal of Southern African Studies* 16 (3): 385–413.

——. 1990b. Mobile workers, modernist narratives: A critique of the historiography, of transition on the Zambian Copperbelt. Pt. 2. *Journal of Southern African Studies* 16 (4): 603–21.

——. 1999. *Expectations of modernity: Myths and meanings of urban life on the Zambian Copperbelt.* Berkeley: University of California Press.

Ferraro, Gary. 1992. *Cultural anthropology: An applied perspective.* New York: West Publishing.

Ferreira, Monica. 2000. Growing old in the new South Africa. *Ageing International* 25 (4): 32–46.

Fortes, Myer, and E. Evans-Pritchard, eds. 1964. *African political systems.* London: Oxford University Press.

Foster, George. 1965. Peasant society and the image of the limited good. *American Anthropologist* 67 (2): 293–315.

Frank, Emily J. 2004. Every day reversals of fortune: Role of AIDS in preserving customary inheritance systems among the Tonga of southern Zambia. African Studies Association Annual Meetings, New Orleans.

Gantenbein, Douglass. 1995. El Niño the weathermaker. *Popular Science* 246 (May): 76–81.

Garbett, Kingsley. 1975. Circulatory migration in Rhodesia. In *Town and country in central and eastern Africa*, ed. D. Parkin, 113–25. London: Oxford University Press.

Gibson, Clark, Margaret McKean, and Elinore Ostrom. 1996. Explaining deforestation: The role of local institutions. Annual Conference of the International Studies Association, San Diego, CA.

Giddens, Anthony. 1976. *New rules of sociological method.* New York: Basic Books.

Glascock, Anthony P. 1986. Resource control among older males in southern Somalia. *Journal of Cross-Cultural Gerontology* 1: 51–72.

Gluckman, H. M. 1942. Some processes of social change, illustrated with Zululand data. *African Studies* 1 (4): 243–60.

——. 1955. *Custom and conflict in Africa.* Glencoe, IL: Free Press.

——. 1958. *Analysis of a social situation in modern Zululand.* Manchester, UK: University of Manchester.

——. 1962. *Order and rebellion in tribal Africa.* London: Cohen and West.

——. 1965. *Politics, law, and ritual in tribal society.* Chicago: Aldine.

Godelier, Maurice. 1999. *The enigma of the gift.* Chicago: University of Chicago Press.

Goody, Jack. 1976. *Production and reproduction: A comparative study of the domestic domain.* Cambridge: Cambridge University Press.

Greene, Melissa Fay. 2002. What will become of Africa's AIDS orphans? *New York Times Magazine* 152 (Dec. 12, 2002): 48–56.

Greenough, Karen. 2003. Development agents and nomadic agency in the Damergou, Niger: Four perspectives in the development market. MA thesis, University of Kentucky.

GTRP (Gwembe Tonga Research Project). 1995. Instruction Manual for GTRP Questionnaires. Unpublished manual. Pasedena, CA: GTRP, Department of Humanities and Social Science, California Institute for Technology (Caltech).

Guyer, Jane. 1986. Intra-household processes and farming systems research: Perspectives from anthropology. In *Understanding Africa's rural households and farming systems*, ed. J. L. Moock. Boulder, CO: Westview.

———, ed. 1995. *Money matters: Instability, values, and social payments in the modern history of West African communities*. Portsmouth, NH: Heinemann.

Guyer, Jane and Pauline Peters. 1987. Conceptualizing the household: Issues of theory and policy in Africa. Special Issue. *Development and Change* 18 (2): 193–326.

Hakansson, N. Thomas, and Robert LeVine. 1997. Gender and life-course strategies among the Gusii. In *African families and the crisis of social change*, ed. T. Weisner, C. Bradley, and P. Kilbride, 253–67. Westport, CT: Bergin and Garvey.

Hannerz, Ulf. 1980. *Exploring the city: Inquiries toward an urban anthropology*. New York: Columbia University Press.

Hansen, Karen. 1989. *Distant companions: Servants and employers in Zambia, 1900–1985*. Ithaca: Cornell University Press.

———. 1996. *Keeping house in Lusaka*. New York: Columbia University Press.

Hedlund, Hans, and Mats Lundahl. 1983. *Migration and change in rural Zambia*. Uppsala, Sweden: Scandinavian Institute of African Studies.

Heine, Bernd, and Derek Nurse. 2000. *African languages: An introduction*. Cambridge: Cambridge University Press.

Holy, Ladislav. 1986. *Strategies and norms in a changing matrilineal society: Descent, succession, and inheritance among the Toka of Zambia*. Cambridge: Cambridge University Press.

James, Deborah. 1999. *Bagagesu* (those of my home): Women migrants, ethnicity, and performance in South Africa. *American Ethnologist* 26 (1): 69–89.

Kamwengo, Martin M. 2002. *Elderly women in South Africa: Issues, challenges, and future prospects*. New Delhi: Sterling International.

———. 2004. *Growing old in Zambia: Old and new perspectives*. New Delhi: Sterling International.

Karp, Ivan, and Charles S. Bird, eds. 1980. *Explorations in African systems of thought*. Bloomington: Indiana University Press.

Kaunda, Kenneth D. 1976. *A humanist handbook*. Lusaka: Freedom House Government Printer.

Kilbride, Philip, and Janet Kilbride. 1997. Stigma, role overload, and delocalization among contemporary Kenyan women. In *African families and the crisis of social change*, ed. T. Weisner, C. Bradley, and P. Kilbride, 208–23. Westport, CT: Bergin and Garvey.

Knodel, John, and Chanpen Saengtienchai. 1999. Studying living arrangements of the elderly: Lessons from a quasi-qualitative case study approach in Thailand. *Journal of Cross-Cultural Gerontology* 14 (3): 197–220.

Kopytoff, Igor, and Suzanne Miers. 1977. African "slavery" as an institution of marginality. In *Slavery in Africa*, ed. S. Miers and I. Kopytoff. Madison: University of Wisconsin Press.

Lam, Tai-Pong, Iris Chi, Leon Piterman, Cindy Lam, and Ian Lauder. 1998. Community attitudes toward living arrangements between the elderly and their adult children in Hong Kong. *Journal of Cross-Cultural Gerontology* 13 (3): 215–28.

Lee, Mei-Lin, Hui-Sheng Lin, and Ming-Cheng Chang. 1995. Living arrangements of the elderly in Taiwan: Qualitative evidence. *Journal of Cross-Cultural Gerontology* 10 (1–2): 53–78.

Lévi-Strauss, Claude. 1969. *The elementary structures of kinship*. Boston: Beacon Press.

Macmillan, Hugh. 1993. The historiography of transition on the Zambian Copper-belt—Another view. *Journal of Southern African Studies* 19 (4): 681–712.

Makoni, Sinfree, and Koen Stroeken, eds. 2002. *Ageing in Africa: Sociolinguistic and anthropological approaches*. Hampshire, UK: Ashgate.

Malinowski, Bronislaw. 1961. *Argonauts of the western Pacific*. New York: E. P. Dutton.

Mamdani, Mahmood. 1996. *Citizen and subject: Contemporary Africa and the legacy of late colonialism*. Princeton, NJ: Princeton University Press.

Massey, Douglas, and Emilio Parrado. 1998. International migration and business formation in Mexico. *Social Science Quarterly* 79 (1): 1–34.

Mauss, Marcel. 1990. *The gift: The form and reason for exchange in archaic societies*. Trans. W. Halls. New York: W. W. Norton.

McCarthy, James J. 2001. *Climate change 2001: Impacts, adaptation, and vulnerability: Contribution of Working Group II to the third assessment report of the Intergovernmental Panel on Climate Change*. Cambridge: Cambridge University Press.

Mehta, Kalyani, Alexander E. Y. Lee, and Mohammed M. B. Osman. 1995. Living arrangements of the elderly in Singapore: Cultural norms in transition. *Journal of Cross-Cultural Gerontology* 10 (1–2): 113–43.

Meillassoux, Claude. 1981. *Maidens, meal, and money*. Cambridge: Cambridge University Press.

Middleton, John. 1992. *The world of the Swahili: An African mercantile civilization*. New Haven: Yale University Press.

Mikell, Gwendolyn, ed. 1997. *African feminism: The politics of survival in sub-Saharan Africa*. Philadelphia: University of Pennsylvania Press.

Ministry of Agriculture, Food and Fisheries (MAFF)S, Zambia. 1995. Sustainable options for increased food production in Zambia. Lusaka, Zambia.

Mitchell, J. Clyde. 1956. *The Kalela dance: Aspects of social relationships among urban Africans in Northern Rhodesia*. Manchester/Livingstone: Rhodes-Livingstone Institute.

———, ed. 1969. *Social networks in urban situations: Analyses of personal relationships in central African towns*. Manchester, UK: Manchester University Press.

Moore, Henrietta, and Megan Vaughan. 1994. *Cutting down trees: Gender, nutrition, and agricultural change in the Northern Province of Zambia, 1890–1990*. Portsmouth, NH: Heinemann.

Murdock, George P. 1949. *Social structure*. New York: Macmillan.

———. 1959. *Africa: Its peoples and their culture history*. New York: McGraw Hill.

Murray, Colin. 1981. *Families divided: The impact of migrant labour in Lesotho*. Cambridge: Cambridge University Press.

Musambachine, Mwelwa. 1994. Eastern Province ecology and the history of "mbeba" (rats) in domestic life. Paper presentation. History Seminar Series, University of Zambia. April 12, 1994.

Myerhoff, Barbara, and Andrei Simic, eds. 1978. *Life's career—Aging*. Newbury Park, CA: Sage.

Netting, Robert. 1981. *Balancing on an Alp: Ecological change and continuity in a Swiss mountain community*. Cambridge: Cambridge University Press.

———. 1993. *Smallholders, householders: Farm families and the ecology of intensive, sustainable agriculture*. Stanford, CA: Stanford University Press.

Netting, Robert, Richard Wilk, and Eric Arnould. 1984. *Households*. Berkeley: University of California Press.

Nomdo, Christina, and Erika Coetzee, eds. 2002. *Urban vulnerability: Perspectives from southern Africa*. Oxford: Oxfam GB; Periperi Publications.

Nrindu, Partson. 2003. E-mail communication to L. Cliggett. Choma, Zambia.

Nyambedhaa, Erick Otieno, Simiyu Wandibbaa, and Jens Aagaard-Hansenb. 2003. Changing patterns of orphan care due to the HIV epidemic in western Kenya. *Social Science and Medicine* 57 (2): 301–11.

Oba, Gufu, Eric Post, and Nils C. Stenseth. 2001. Sub-Saharan desertification and productivity are linked to hemispheric climate variability. *Global Change Biology* 7 (3): 241–47.

Ogunseitan, Oladele A. 2000. *Framing vulnerability: Global environmental assessments and the African burden of disease*. Cambridge, MA: Kennedy School of Government, Harvard University.

Ohadike, Patrick. 1981. *Demographic perspectives in Zambia*. Lusaka: Institute of African Studies, University of Zambia.

Oliver, Roland. 1965. *The missionary factor in East Africa*. London: Longmans.

Oliver, Roland, G. Mathew, V. Harlow, E. M. Chilver, A. Smith, and D. A. Low, eds. 1963–76. *History of East Africa*. 3 vols. Oxford: Clarendon Press.

Peachey, Karen. 1999. Ageism: A factor in the nutritional vulnerability of older people? *Disasters* 23 (4): 350–58.

Petit, Carine, Thayer Scudder, and Eric Lambin. 2001. Quantifying processes of land-cover change by remote sensing: Resettlement and rapid land-cover changes in south-eastern Zambia. *International Journal of Remote Sensing* 22 (17): 3435–56.

Poewe, Karla O. 1981. *Matrilineal ideology: Male–female dynamics in Luapula, Zambia*. New York: Academic Press.

Population Services International. 2003. Abstinence, condoms help cut HIV. Africa News All Africa Services Inc. Press release. Sept. 4, 2003.

Post. 2002. SAP has left many people out of employment—Kavindele. *Post* (Lusaka, Zambia). Feb. 28, 2002.

——. 2003a. Reliance on IMF, the World Bank. *Post* (Lusaka, Zambia). Feb. 20, 2003.

——. 2003b. SAP crisis. *Post* (Lusaka, Zambia). Feb. 13, 2003.

Pottier, Johan. 1988. *Migrants no more: Settlement and survival in Mambwe villages, Zambia*. Bloomington: Indiana University Press.

Pritchett, James A. 2001. *The Lunda-Ndembu: Style, change, and social transformation in south central Africa*. Madison: University of Wisconsin Press.

Reuters. 2003. World briefing Africa: Zambia: Rains destroy homes and crops. *New York Times*, March 27, 2003, p. 6.

Reynolds, Pamela. 1991. *Dance civet cat: Child labor in the Zambezi Valley*. London: Zed Books.

Roberts, Andrew. 1976. *A history of Zambia*. New York: Africana Publishing.

Robinson, William. 1998. (Mal)development in Central America: Globalization and social change. *Development and Change* 29 (3): 467–98.

Saluseki, Bivan. 2003. Poverty, aids would continue to undermine development. *Post* (Lusaka, Zambia). Sept. 6, 2003.

Scheper-Hughes, Nancy. 1992. *Death without weeping: The violence of everyday life in Brazil*. Berkeley: University of California Press.

Schneider, David, and Kathleen Gough, eds. 1961. *Matrilineal kinship*. Berkeley: University of California Press.

Schneider, Harold K. 1979. *Livestock and equality in East Africa*. Bloomington: Indiana University Press.

Schrift, Alan, ed. 1997. *The logic of the gift: Toward an ethic of generosity*. New York: Routledge.

Schuster, Ilse. 1987. Kinship, life cycle and education in Lusaka. *Journal of Comparative Family Studies* 18 (3): 363–87.

Scoones, Ian, ed. 1994. *Living with uncertainty: New directions in pastoral development in Africa*. London: Intermediate Technology Publications.

Scott, Guy. 2002. Zambia: Structural adjustment, rural livelihoods, and sustainable development. *Development Southern Africa* 19 (3): 405–18.

Scudder, Thayer. 1962. *The ecology of the Gwembe Tonga*. Manchester, UK: Manchester University Press.

——. 1966. Man-made lakes and population resettlement in Africa. In *Man-made Lakes*, ed. R. Lowe-McConnell. New York: Academic Press.

——. 1969. Relocation, agricultural intensification, and anthropological research. In *The anthropology of development in sub-Saharan Africa*, ed. D. Brokensha and M. Pearsall, 206–35. Society for Applied Anthropology, Monograph No. 10. Lexington: University Press of Kentucky.

——. 1976. Social impacts of river basin development on local populations. In *United Nations' Interregional Seminar on River Basin and Inter Basin Development, Budapest*, 45–52. Budapest: Institute for Hydraulic Documentation and Education.

——. 1980. River-basin development and local initiative in African savanna environments. In *Human ecology in savanna environments*, ed. D. R. Harris. London: Academic Press.

——. 1983. Economic downturn and community unraveling. *Culture and Agriculture* 18: 16–19.

——. 1984. Economic downturn and community unraveling, revisited. *Culture and Agriculture* 23: 6–10.

——. 1985. *A history of development in the Zambian portion of the middle Zambezi Valley and Lake Kariba basin*. Binghamton, NY: Institute for Development Anthropology.

——. 1993. Development-induced relocation and refugee studies: Thirty-seven years of change and continuity among Zambia's Gwembe Tonga. *Journal of Refugee Studies* 6 (2): 123–52.

Scudder, Thayer, and Elizabeth Colson. 1981. *Secondary education and the formation of an elite: The impact of education on Gwembe District, Zambia*. London: Academic Press.

——. 1982. From welfare to development: A conceptual framework for the analysis of dislocated people. In *Involuntary migration and resettlement: The problems and responses of dislocated people*, ed. A. Hansen and A. Oliver-Smith. Boulder, CO: Westview Press.

Scudder, Thayer, and Jonathan Habarad. 1991. Local responses to involuntary relocation and development in the Zambian portion of the Middle Zambezi Valley. In *Migrants in agricultural development*, ed. J. A. Mollett, 178–205. London: Macmillan.

Seleti, Yona Ngalaba. 1992. Entrepreneurship in colonial Zambia. In *Guardians in their times: Experiences of Zambians under colonial rule*, ed. S. Chipungu, 147–79. London: Macmillan.

Sen, Amartya. 1981. *Poverty and famine: An essay on entitlement and deprivation.* Oxford: Clarendon Press.

Shostak, Marjorie. 1983. *Nisa: The life and words of a Kung woman.* New York: Vintage Books.

Siamwiza, Bennett Siamwiinde. 1993. Hunger in the Gwembe Valley: A case study of Mweemba chieftaincy, 1905–1987. MA thesis, University of Zambia.

Smith, Joan, Immanuel Wallerstein, and Hans-Dieter Evers, eds. 1984. *Households and the world economy.* Beverly Hills, CA: Sage.

Smith, Kevin. 1998. Farming, marketing, and changes in the authority of elders among pastoral Rendille and Ariaal. *Journal of Cross-Cultural Gerontology* 13 (4): 309–32.

Sokolovsky, Jay, ed. 1990. *The cultural context of aging.* New York: Bergin and Garvey.

Spring, Anita, ed. 2000. *Women farmers and commercial ventures: Increasing food security in developing countries.* London: Lynne Rienner.

Stone, M. Pricilla, and Glenn Davis Stone. 2000. Kofyar women who get ahead: Incentives for agricultural commercialization in Nigeria. In *Women farmers and commercial ventures: Increasing food security in developing countries*, ed. A. Spring, 153–70. London: Lynne Rienner.

Stucki, Barbara. 1995. Managing the social clock: The negotiation of elderhood among rural Asante of Ghana. PhD diss., Northwestern University.

Swift, J. 1989. Why are rural people vulnerable to famine? *IDS Bulletin* 20: 8–15.

Tengan, Alexis. 2002. Social categories and seniority in a house-based society. In *Ageing in Africa: Sociolinguistics and anthropological approaches*, ed. S. Makoni and K. Stroeken. Hampshire, UK: Ashgate.

Townsend, Nicholas. 1997. Men, migration, and households in Botswana: An exploration of connections over time and space. *Journal of Southern African Studies* 23 (3): 405–20.

Trager, Lillian. 1998. Home-town linkages and local development in south-western Nigeria: Whose agenda? What impact? *Africa* 68 (3): 360–82.

Traore, G. 1985. A profile of the elderly in Mali. *Africa Gerontology* 3: 11–23.

Turner, Paul. 1995. *Explaining deforestation: A preliminary review of the literature.* Bloomington: Workshop in Political Theory and Policy Analysis.

Turner, Victor. 1957. *Schism and continuity in an African society.* Manchester, UK: Manchester University Press.

———. 1969. *The ritual process.* Chicago: Aldine.

———. 1981. *The drums of affliction: The study of religious processes among the Ndembu of Zambia.* Ithaca: Cornell University Press.

Udvardy, Monica, and Maria Cattell. 1992. Gender, aging, and power in sub-Saharan Africa: Challenges and puzzles. *Journal of Cross-Cultural Gerontology* 7 (4): 275–88.

UNDP [United Nations Development Program]. 2001. *Zambia human development report, 1999/2000.* Lusaka, Zambia: UNDP.

Vail, Leroy. 1983. The political economy of east-central Africa. In *History of Central Africa*, ed. D. Birmingham and P. Martin, 200–250. London: Longman.

——, ed. 1989. *The creation of tribalism in southern Africa.* Berkeley and Los Angeles: University of California Press.

Van Der Geest, Siaak, Mubiana Maewangi, Jolly Kamwanga, Dennis Mulikelela, Arthur Mazimba, and Mudina Mwangelwa. 2000. User fees and drugs: What did the health reforms in Zambia achieve? *Health Policy and Planning* 15 (1): 59–65.

van Donge, Jan Kees. 1984. Rural urban migration and the rural alternative in Mwase Lundazi, Eastern Province, Zambia. *African Studies Review* 27 (March): 83–96.

Vansina, Jan. 1990. *Paths in the rainforests: Toward a history of political tradition in equato rial Africa.* Madison: University of Wisconsin Press.

Van-Velsen, J. 1964. *The politics of kinship: A study in social manipulation among the lakeside Tonga of Nyasaland.* Manchester, UK: Manchester University Press.

Vaughan, Megan. 1987. *The story of an African famine: Gender and famine in twentieth-century Malawi.* Cambridge: Cambridge University Press.

Wallman, Sandra, and Grace Bantebya-Kyomuhendo, eds. 1996. *Kampala women getting by: Well-being in the time of AIDS.* Athens, OH: Ohio University Press; Kampala: James Currey.

Watts, Michael J. 1983. *Silent violence: Food, famine, and peasantry in northern Nigeria.* Berkeley: University of California Press.

Watts, Michael J., and Hans G. Bohle. 1993. The space of vulnerability: The causal structure of hunger and famine. *Progress in Human Geography* 17 (1): 43–67.

Weismantel, Mary. 1988. *Food, gender, and poverty in the Ecuadorian Andes.* Philadelphia: University of Pennsylvania Press.

Wilk, Richard, ed. 1989. *The household economy.* Boulder, CO: Westview Press.

——. 1991. *Household ecology. Economic change and domestic life among the Kekchi Maya in Belize.* Tucson: University of Arizona Press.

Wolf, Eric. 1982. *Europe and the people without history.* Berkeley: University of California.

World Bank. 1996. *Privatization in Africa: The Zambian example.* Washington, DC.

——. 2002. *Reducing vulnerability and increasing opportunity: Social protection in the Middle East and North Africa.* Washington, DC.

Index